Praise for *PERSUADE*

Persuade is masterfully written, a must read for anyone wanting to expand their influence and income by serving others in the sales profession.

Mark Cole,
CEO, The John Maxwell Company

Finally, a book that teaches how to connect with people, not just sell.

Amy Oakes Dunn,
Product Marketing Manager, Facebook

This book is a critical tool for people who are serious about the art of selling. Scott Hogle's book *Persuade* clearly lays out the steps important to producing 6-digit earners.

Bob Pittman,
Chairman & CEO, iHeart Media

Persuade's pages are filled with practical ways to build your sales skills.

Emi Hart Sorenson,
Senior Community Director, Yelp

Scott speaks profoundly to the new emerging generation of sellers. If you plan to make more income this year, buy this book and put it into practice.

Tom Ziglar,
CEO, Ziglar Inc.

Love the sales ideas in *Persuade* on how to grow sales and influence.

Natalie Phanphengdy,
Sales & Onboarding Specialist, Google

Persuade is the best-written relationship selling book in years.

Heidi Dickert,
Fortune 500 Consultant to Visa, Del Monte,
Microsoft, Facebook, LinkedIn, & Clorox

Persuade is a must read for sales professionals who have discovered that their purpose is serving others.

Kevin Hall,
International Bestselling author of
Aspire: Discovering Your Purpose through the Power of Words

What you'll find between the covers of this book is a wealth of sales knowledge you can use to gain confidence, serve your clients well, and earn a well-deserved high income. Read it. You'll see what I mean.

Tom Hopkins,
author of *How to Master the Art of Selling*
and co-author of *When Buyers Say No*

Persuade is a playbook for decoding a customer's needs, then using that information to sell them.

Axel Dahl,
Data Engineer, Cisco Systems

PERSUADE!

THE 7 EMPOWERING LAWS OF THE SALESMAKER

FOLLOW THEM AND DOLLARS WILL FOLLOW YOU!

SCOTT HOGLE

Foreword By

TOM HOPKINS

Made for Success Publishing
P.O. Box 1775
Issaquah, WA 98027

If you are seeking to purchase this book in quantity for sales
promotion or corporate use, please contact Made for Success at 425-
657-0300 or email Sales@MadeforSuccess.net. Your local bookstore
can also help you with discounted bulk purchase options.

ISBN 978-161-339171-8
LCCN: 2017905986

Library of Congress Cataloging-in-Publication data

Hogle, Scott
Persuade: The 7 Empowering Laws of the SalesMaker
pages. Cm
1. Sales/Selling. 2. Business Development. 3. Management

Printed in the United States of America

Contents

"Selling is the *highest paid hard work and the lowest paid easy work you'll ever find."* Those words were spoken to me by my mentor, the late, great J. Douglas Edwards, who was known as *The Father of American Selling.* I took them to heart and worked hard at mastering my craft. I attended every sales and personal development seminar around. I analyzed literally every move I made and every word I uttered with my clients. I tested and tried thousands of variations of the many nuances of selling. And, through proper and effective service to others with those strategies, I became a millionaire at the age of 27. Great effort = great reward! And the "hard work" Doug talked about became fun! Not bad for someone who seven years earlier owned nothing but a motorcycle and had only $150 in the bank. I had failed miserably my first six months in sales—only making one single sale. I was depressed but determined because I saw others winning contests, affording homes, driving new cars, and taking their families on great vacations. If they could do it, why couldn't I? What I began to see was that the only reason I wasn't successful early on was that I didn't really understand sales. I thought if you just showed a great product and explained the features, people would surely buy. I couldn't have been more mistaken.

Selling is both an art and a science. That's because to sell something, you must connect and communicate with *people.* It's not about the product. You have to learn how to understand *them.* You must become a master at asking questions—what I call being a "Master Asker"—and a great listener. Selling requires an incredible amount of patience and the ability to read body language. That sounds like a lot, doesn't it? In truth, it barely scratches the surface if you've chosen to sell as a career that will generate the revenue you need to support the lifestyle of your dreams. Yes, there are a million things to learn about the profession of selling. However, fortunately for you and others like you, those who have gone before are leaving clues. Actually, they're leaving more than clues; they're moving into positions of becoming teachers of the craft they love so well. Scott Hogle is one of them. Scott became a student of mine fairly early in his career. And, he was a good one. He not only took notes, but took the training to heart. He didn't just want to learn strategies to close sales. He wanted to understand why the strategies worked so he could develop even more of them—ones that suited *his* personality. And, he succeeded tremendously.

This book is a culmination of Scott's years in sales, years of analyzing sales situations, years of watching and listening to how others reacted to what was said, actions that were taken, and how clients were served. Scott has recognized that there are certain laws that apply when communicating with others when your purpose is to discover their needs and persuade them to your solutions. These laws will open your mind to what you've been missing in your selling career. They may even startle you into recognizing things you're doing wrong when interacting with buyers. Just remember that with those realizations will come an awareness and a growing desire to improve your skills. There's no going back once we learn something new!

When we serve others how they want to be served, we generate more closed sales, more referrals, and more re-purchases. That's because our clients like us and are willing to trust us. Those buyers come to understand that we value *them*—not just their money—through the way we treat them.

In a time when we are all highly focused on the latest technology, *it's a welcome relief to read a sales book that focuses instead on the interpersonal relationships that are the foundation of every sale.*

Scott's *Persuade* will change the way you look at every client interaction. You will gain a deeper understanding of the psychology of selling with specific suggestions for practical application of the Laws. Scott believes that knowing and using multiple ways of connecting with buyers is the key to great success in sales. I have to agree. What you'll find between the covers of this book is a wealth of sales knowledge you can use to gain confidence, serve your clients well, and earn a well-deserved high income. Read it. You'll see what I mean.

Tom Hopkins, author of *How to Master the Art of Selling* and co-author of *When Buyers Say No*

ACKNOWLEDGEMENTS

I would like to thank Bryan Heathman from Made for Success Publishing, my editor Judy Slack, and Mark Cole and John Maxwell from The John Maxwell Company who inspired me to write *Persuade*. Without amazing mentors to inspire, coach, and invest in me along the way, this book would not have been written. For the many sellers I have had the privilege to work with and the friends who have graced my path over the years, I am grateful for your influence and investment in me. Lastly, a heart-felt thanks to Gregg Mueller from iHeart Media who processed with me in thinking through, talking through, and working through each chapter.

DEDICATION

I would like to dedicate *Persuade, The 7 Empowering Laws of the SalesMaker* to my two sons, Bailey and Casey Hogle, the finest young men that I know. As you grow into adulthood and enter the workforce, much of your success will be dependent on how well you influence and persuade others, make connections and form relationships, and how well you lead yourselves and others through challenges and into good decisions. Whether you go into the sales profession or not, the ideas, skills, and strategies in *Persuade* will help you do more and achieve more with them than without them. As you advance through the seasons of life, the timeless truths found in *Persuade* will help you to become better connectors, communicators, and closers. My hope is that you don't just leverage the powerful principles found in *Persuade* to create success for yourself, but that you are empowered to wield them in the service of others. My hope is that you don't just become better professionally, but better men personally as you grow into maturity and follow the laws found in *Persuade*.

Following The Laws Will Make You Money—Ignoring Them Will Cost You Money.

In any government, society, or industry, there are invisible laws reflecting customs and cultural nuances that govern successful dealings between people and businesses. Knowing these laws, how to leverage them with integrity, and exercising them intentionally, can mean the difference between success and failure.

In the sales profession, following The 7 Empowering Laws of the SalesMaker will create for you greater levels of income, influence, impact, stronger relationships, and success. A SalesMaker's skill level in how they connect, communicate, and close plays a significant role in determining who they get access to and who they do not. The SalesMaker who lives The 7 Laws will do more, earn more, and achieve more than those who live without them. Ignoring or violating The 7 Laws creates the opposite effect and causes the SalesMaker loss in influence, income, and relationship equity.

The Laws of the SalesMaker are in operation whether a seller is aware of them or not. Not knowing the speed limit is not a defense when getting pulled for over speeding. It is not uncommon to unintentionally violate a law, yet nonetheless suffer the consequences of doing so. In the sales profession, ignorance can cost the SalesMaker commissions and the company they represent revenue. Learning and living The 7 Laws will ensure the SalesMaker reaps the rewards while avoiding unintended consequences.

Each sales principle within The 7 Laws has actionable strategies you can use to immediately impact the trajectory of your income and influence. As you grow in following The 7 Empowering Laws of the SalesMaker, you will grow in income. This book is not an exhaustive work on every aspect of sales. Instead, it focuses on helping a SalesMaker increase their ability to persuade and move others to decision. By mastering core competencies within The 7 Laws, you will be equipped to elevate your career to a new level. Core competencies of a SalesMaker include:

- Prospecting for new customers,

- Connecting to form relationships,

- Probing to uncover needs and solve problems,

- Listening and learning the customer's likes and dislikes,

- Presenting product strengths in a meaningful way,

- Positioning customer concerns in ways that advance the sale,

- Negotiating with customers past the point of resistance and into agreement,

- Closing the sale and then servicing the customer in a way that creates return and referral business.

Adapt or become extinct

The 7 Laws are not theoretical. They come from decades of my own personal experience and application in selling, leading sales organizations, and interacting with customers. Sales organizations and their sellers must adapt constantly if they are to remain relevant in today's shifting marketplace. The 7 Empowering Laws of the SalesMaker include both timeless sales principles and today's new sales skill technologies.

The definition of a SalesMaker has evolved over the years. No longer is it only a traditional sales person in a one-to-one relationship with a customer. Today's SalesMakers work at, for, or in social media and search engine companies, online retail stores, marketing departments, inside sales organizations, and the list goes on. Whether you are a seasoned seller or just starting off in a career that requires you to persuade others in order to succeed, the Laws of the SalesMaker will equip you with communication strategies that will empower you to successfully sell yourself, your company, and the product you represent in today's marketplace. As a SalesMaker the only guarantee you have is that if you do not change, nothing will change for you. If you want to achieve more and earn more, you must become more. It's time to level up!

You and you alone can choose to engage The 7 Laws and put them to work in your sales life. You and you alone can choose to grow your skill set or fall behind. You and you alone must take responsibility for your personal and professional growth. It is no one else's responsibility, and no one will do it for you. You must choose to grow and continually stretch yourself if you are to thrive in an industry that redefines itself daily.

As you grow in The 7 Laws, you will discover that growth will spill over from one law to the next. As you apply The 7 Laws, growth will compound beyond the pages of this book and your career into every area of life where communicating, connecting, and relationship-building skills are essential to succeed. Once you begin living The 7 Empowering Laws of the SalesMaker, you will experience an increase in your level of influence, income, and the impact you make in the marketplace.

> "Live the 7 Empowering Laws of the SalesMaker and experience an increase in your level of influence, income, and impact you make in the marketplace."

How to Get the Most out of this Book:
How do SalesMakers convert sales
intelligence into sales commissions?

How you enter a book determines what you will receive from the book. Enter a sales book looking for new closing techniques and your mind will find those techniques. Enter a book for relationship advice and your heart will resonate with tips and tools that help you connect better with others. Enter *Persuade* wishing to grow your sales, and you will uncover insights with every turn of the page. Most importantly, entering *Persuade* with the intent of putting into practice that which you learn will guarantee progress in your sales career. If you don't exercise the insights you gather, you will lose the inspiration that grabbed your heart as you first read it.

Developing your Sales Intelligence Requires C.I.A.

How can you get the most from this book? You can grow in your sales intelligence by connecting the desire within you to the nuggets available within this book. Depending on your level of sales competence, some of the content you encounter may seem informational while other content is inspirational.

There is a simple formula you can employ for maximizing the time investment you are making in this book. The formula is called C.I.A., and here is how to utilize it:

C = Connection: As you read, document the content that connected with you. Underline or highlight that which informed or inspired you. When something resonates with you, it's worth a return visit. So, capture the precepts and principles that speak to you by writing them into a journal.

I = Insight: When inspiration hits, it is usually accompanied by insight. You should be willing to linger and internalize each insight. Consider asking yourself the following questions as a way of uncovering an **insight:**

- What was it about the content that connected with me?

- Why might this information be resonating with me right now?

- Who can I unpack this insight with so I may expand on my experience?

A = Action: Education without implementation is a waste of time. When you grasp the significant content that connected with you, it will change what you see, how you sell, and the influence and income level you can achieve. For transformation to take place, it is essential to incorporate the insights into your daily sales situations as quickly as possible. The forces that lift you to high ground in your career may start with information that inspires, but must end with action if you are to ascend.

C.I.A. CONTRIBUTORS
(Connection, Insights, Actions)

At the conclusion of each chapter, you will be encouraged to follow the C.I.A. format for creating transformative change in your life. In this section, you will also have the opportunity to hear from other professionals about what they learned from a chapter, how they were inspired, their insights and how they are living the laws to increase their influence, impact, and contribution. You will be hearing from sales professionals, service industry experts, marketing moguls, blue chip corporate executive, expert communicators, technology leaders, and social media executives. What all of these SalesMakers have in common is the desire to continually grow, increase their communication and persuasion skills, and their level of contribution to the company and customer groups they serve. I would like to take a moment and thank all the C.I.A. contributors who participated in *Persuade, The 7 Empowering Laws of the SalesMaker*. Your insights have not only served me, but also all those who will read Persuade. Thank you for helping us all level up through your experience.

Special Thanks to the following contributors of *Persuade, The 7 Empowering Laws of the SalesMaker:*

THE LAW OF CONNECTION	Amy Oakes, Product Marketing Manager, Facebook Heidi Dickert, Fortune 500 Consultant to Visa, Del Monte, Microsoft, Facebook, LinkedIn, Clorox, and others Lori Webster, Realtor, HomeSmart Premier
THE LAW OF THE LISTENER	Joe Parker, Technical Program Manager, Amazon Rachel Nagata, Senior Account Executive, iHeart Media Mark Hovland, Founder & Director New Hope Counseling Center

THE LAW OF RELATIONSHIP	Emi Hart Sorenson, Senior Community Director, Yelp Kevin Yim, Senior Director of Global Marketing Communications, Hawaiian Airlines Dana Young, Senior Manager Presales Systems Engineering, Dell EMC
THE LAW OF DISCOVERY	Natalie Phanphengdy, Sales & Onboarding Specialist, Google Carl Ishikawa, Financial Service Professional, New York Life
THE LAW OF THE SIXTH SENSE	Gaylord Escalona, Microsoft, Senior Category MGR, Xbox Bryan Heathman, CEO, Made for Success Publishing
THE LAW OF THE CLOSE	Brian Slepetz, Sr. Regional Marketing Consultant, Clear Channel Airports Nick Malievsky, Sr. Team Lead Business Consultant, Zillow Chris Mills, Sales Manager, iHeart Media
THE LAW OF THE PROSPECTOR	Steve K. Sombrero, Broker/President, NAI Chaney Brooks Realty Gary Goslin, Network Marketing Expert, Karat Bars Gold International

CHAPTER 1

THE LAW OF CONNECTION

**The SalesMaker Connects
Emotionally Before
Communicating Financially.**

My wife, Kate, may appear to be a quiet type of person at first, but she lights up when someone engages her in conversation. Great communicators who know how to connect with others are often like this. They have an on-and-off switch. Great sales people, too, have on-and-off switches that allow them to connect and be charming or disarming at a moment's notice. Kate is very smart and quite good at connecting with others. When I asked her how she developed this ability to connect with others, she proceeded to show me instead of telling me. She did this by turning the focus of our conversation away from her, and toward me. She then demonstrated that I, too, am a good connector and gave me an example out of my life as proof. While she spoke about me, I felt valued and strengthened. Then, after demonstrating how she connects by focusing on the other person, she answered my question on how to connect by saying, "It's easy to connect. Just ask the other person something about themselves. As you get interested in what they are interested in, you connect with them."

In sales, we have a tendency to work at impressing customers so they will buy. Sales people are taught to do three things: 1) Present their product with strong benefits; 2) Position their company above the competition; and 3) Sell themselves in a way that impresses the customer. The talk-track of many sales strategies is made up of these three sales pillars. Utilizing this strategy may help close sales, but it has less impact and may backfire if it is employed before an emotional connection is established. Sales people may impress others with their product knowledge, but SalesMakers connect with others and build their influence by focusing on the other person.

When sales people want to impress you, they talk about themselves. When a SalesMaker wants to connect with you, they will ask about you. It may seem counter-intuitive, but the best way to impress others is to communicate in a way that makes them feel elevated. Talking about yourself or your company may get you in the door, but connecting keeps you in position to build the influence that makes the sale. When a customer feels a connection with you, they will give weight to your words and follow where you lead.

Connecting for the first time with someone can be uncomfortable for both parties. Why is that? Everyone has a degree of insecurity about themselves. Insecurities can include feelings of not being smart-enough, thin-enough, fast-enough, likable-enough, and so on. Most people believe that there is something they lack. This is where our insecurities originate from. This list of "not-enoughs" can create emotional deficits that make us fearful to reach out for fear of being found out. Whether real or imagined, we carry these insecurities around hoping that no one will discover them.

> "When sales people want to impress you, they talk about themselves. When a SalesMaker wants to connect with you, they will ask about you."

Insecurities can become barriers to connecting. This is because insecurity directs our attention inward instead of outward. When attention is directed inward, we become self-focused whereas connecting requires an "other-focused" approach. Meeting someone for the first time requires us to reach out, be vulnerable, and even risk rejection, regardless of the insecurities we may feel. Sales people are no different than others in that they do not like to feel uncomfortable. However, the very nature of their profession requires that they embrace emotional risk and become exceptional at connecting if they are to be successful. The willingness to reach out, embrace risk, and resist the fear of uncomfortable feelings is not enough. A SalesMaker must be equipped with numerous, proven ways to connect with others. In the Law of Connection, I will share with you ten strategies for how you can confidently and comfortably connect with others.

Networking meetings are a perfect example of how sales people seek out their comfort zones. We attend networking meetings for just one reason: To make new contacts that could turn into new customers. Yet, within seconds of entering a room full of strangers, the first thing a typical sales person does is look for someone they know. Why do they do that? Because of a natural tendency to gravitate toward what is comfortable rather than risk rejection by someone new. Often it is a combination of insecurity and connecting incompetency that keeps us from forging new relationships. I will share with you a number of ways in which you can conquer your insecurities and improve your connecting abilities.

Do you connect easily with others? For me, I must work at it, consistently. After a lifetime in sales, I've met very few people who have a natural ability to connect with everyone, everywhere, all the time. The ability to connect with customers and forge relationships has to be developed.

Who do you know that is good at connecting with others? If you had to paint a picture of what a good connector looks like, how would you illustrate their personality? Outgoing? Likable? Sincere? Easy to get along with? The list of attributes of a great connector can be long, but a SalesMaker doesn't have to have them all to connect successfully with their customers.

Whether you see yourself as a natural at connecting or someone who needs to work at connecting and building relationships, the good news is that connecting is a skill that can be learned. Whether you are new to the sales profession or consider yourself a senior seller, the Law of Connection will provide you with tried and true connecting techniques for converting conversations into dollars.

I struggled to connect early in my sales career. If you ask me today if I consider myself a good connector, my answer is yes. Today I am comfortable and confident in my ability to meet total strangers, connect emotionally, and get them to follow me financially all in the first meeting! I am highly competent in my connecting skills, but I still do not consider myself a natural connector. In fact, it took me years to develop the skills to connect quickly on a cold call or first meeting with someone.

I am not unlike many SalesMakers I have met over the years who consider themselves more introverted than extroverted. An introvert is someone who may be a private person, who processes inwardly more than outwardly. In contrast, an extrovert is very outgoing, sociable, and often considered the "life of the party."

Many of the best SalesMakers I have known are more reserved, quiet types who are solid from the inside out. They defy the misconception that all great connectors are outgoing extroverts who easily make friends and were born that way. On the contrary, great SalesMakers know how to turn their "connector switch" to the "on" position when a social situation arises or a sales connection needs to be made.

What are some of the qualities within SalesMakers that make them great connectors? Great connectors are comfortable with themselves, comfortable with others, and can leverage that comfort in ways that help them to increase their influence. In the Law of Connection, you will meet different types of connectors, learn how to level up, and then leverage your connecting ability using actionable strategies. You will learn to connect quicker with customers, close more sales, and create more meaningful, lasting relationships that are beneficial to your financial future.

Five Positive Outcomes of Creating Connection with the Customer

What does it mean to have a connection with someone? The dictionary definition of "connection" is "a binding or joining together; to fasten or tie together." This definition makes perfect sense if we are talking about nuts and bolts in a mechanic's repair shop, but people and their emotions are much more complex than nuts and bolts. They don't always fasten together just because they are placed together. If you've ever struggled to connect with another person, you will identify with this.

In every walk of life, connecting with others and forming relationships are paramount to success. Ironically, connecting classes are not taught in formal education, yet it is the most important skill in all professions where success is dependent on one's ability to move people to action. Most of us learn it through trial and error.

The SalesMaker who learns to create connections with customers early in the sales process can accomplish five successful sales outcomes:

1. **Financial Influence:** Creating connection increases financial influence with the customer. Customers are more likely to follow a SalesMaker's financial recommendations and advice when emotional connection exists.

2. **Emotional Warmth:** Creating connection generates warmth with customers. When a warm environment exists, a customer will remain

engaged longer, both intellectually and emotionally. The tune-out factor decreases significantly during periods of shared emotional experience.

3. **Magnetic Attraction:** Connection increases a SalesMaker's likability factor. Unless a customer likes the SalesMaker, it is unlikely they will buy. On the other hand, where connection exists, magnetism is created that emotionally draws the customer toward the SalesMaker.

4. **Diminish Doubts:** Creating connection can remove resistance early in the sales process. SalesMakers who can connect with their customers will increase confidence while pulling down the barriers of fear, doubt, and insecurity often associated with making a purchase. Doubts diminish where trust exists and the "benefit of the doubt" is more freely given. Connection can bring to an end the inward tug of war that exists between doubt and decision. SalesMakers use connection to bring relief and comfort to tense circumstances in order to reduce inner conflict or doubt surrounding a purchase. Connection neutralizes the "No" during the sales process.

> "Connection neutralizes the 'no' in the sales process."

5. **Motivation to Close:** Creating connection enhances the buying experience for the customer. A customer who has connection with a SalesMaker will be inspired, not just informed. Inspiration is a powerful impetus that will move a customer to action. When the heart feels good, the money flows more easily.

Connecting is the Responsibility of the SalesMaker

My teenage son recently said to me while we were connecting, "Dad, everyone seems to be doing their own thing in the house lately. We are all home but it's like we are not!"

To give you a little context, my son had just finished his sports season and his girlfriend was spending the weekend prepping for the SAT. So, he was spending more time at home and noticing for the first time in a long

> "It is the SalesMaker's responsibility to cross the chasm that exists between the customer and the close by building a bridge of trust that forges connection."

time that even though all four of our family members were home, we were all engrossed individually in our own activities. What my son was implying was that he was feeling disconnected even though we were all present.

This is not an uncommon dynamic in a world where technology intended to create connection has actually created a disconnection. If you have more than one person living in your household, you've no doubt experienced this dynamic yourself. You know that it is possible for everyone to be in the same place yet disconnected.

Another example of this is being in a room with everyone on their mobile phones playing games, responding to the latest Facebook posts, or finding it easier to text a family member than walk in the other room to talk with them. What my son realized is that if he wants to connect with others, he has to make the effort. He must initiate action, come out of his room, and come to where we are in order to connect.

The reverse is also true. If I want to connect with someone, I must join them in their world. Getting connected can be hard work. Staying connected can be even harder. I have discovered to quickly connect with others is to serve them in a way that provides value to them or to come along side of them and join in with what they are doing. The rules for connecting in sales are no different than in other relationships. Connecting requires effort, intentionality, and a sincere desire to reach out to another person. Sometimes it can be scary not knowing what you will find when reaching out. Yet it is necessary in order for there to be a successful connection that leads to any type of agreement. In sales, connecting rarely happens accidentally, although it does happen superficially at times.

For a SalesMaker to connect with a customer there are three rules they must follow.

1. SalesMakers must courageously leave their comfort zones and confidently enter into the customers' comfort zones in a way that is welcoming.

2. SalesMakers must expend the physical effort and emotional energy to capture the customers' attention.

> "Connecting and the building of relationships isn't accidental in sales. SalesMakers must be intentional and strategic in how they approach each new customer."

3. SalesMakers must develop a series of strategies for connecting and never go into a meeting without a plan to connect with the customer. Seasoned SalesMakers know that one size doesn't fit all when it comes to developing connecting strategies that work. Each strategy must be customized to fit the customer you are calling on.

Connecting is the Most Important Sales Skill

Why is connecting the most important skill in the sales profession? Because it is connecting that makes closing possible! Without a developed ability to connect, a SalesMaker cannot set appointments, build trust, strengthen relationships, or close the sale. Connection is the invisible currency that makes closing the sale possible! A healthy customer connection is an aura of invisible energy between two or more people working in harmony to create a rapport. Connection is an emotional energy that may not always be seen, but is always felt. Being able to successfully connect with a customer can mean the difference between success and failure, closing the sale or the sale imploding. Here are a few examples that depict how connecting is critical to closing the sale:

1. **Buy-In makes buying possible.** The first thing a customer must buy is you! Until a customer buys into you, they won't buy into your presentation or product. When the customer buys into you they will buy into what you are saying because you have established trust. Establishing trust in consumer or corporate sales becomes the revenue maker or sales breaker. Trust always precedes the transaction. The sale of the person will always precede the sale of the product.

   "The customer buys into the SalesMaker before they buy what the SalesMaker is selling."

2. **Connecting comes before Closing.** Until a customer connects emotionally with the SalesMaker, they won't commit financially to the sale. With almost three decades in business-to-business sales, I have had the privilege of working with dozens of industries from insurance, to home

   "Trust always precedes the transaction. The sale of the person will always precede the sale of the product."

sales, to automotive, to financial, to home improvement. I have worked with companies that have thousands of employees and small businesses with few employees, to the mom-and-pop retail stores that make up the heart and soul of a local marketplace. One truism for decision makers of every type is consistent, if they don't connect with you, they won't buy from you. There is simply too much choice and competition in the marketplace for a customer to hassle with a seller with whom they can't make a connection. Whether a SalesMaker is selling personal products or business products, creating rapport, connection, and a relationship is crucial to closing the sale. It doesn't matter if the decision maker is a husband making a decision for his wife's birthday at a jewelry store or a national buyer making a decision for a chain of grocery stores, the first connection should be between the SalesMaker and the customer, not between the cost, features, or value proposition of the product and the customer.

3. **Relationships lead to Revenue.** Relationship precedes revenue and connecting emotionally comes before closing financially. A SalesMaker will struggle to move a customer financially until they are able to move them emotionally. If the SalesMaker tries to close a customer financially before connecting emotionally, they will encounter resistance and may not make the sale. But if they connect with the customer emotionally first, getting the customer to follow in order to advance the sales becomes much easier. If you have ever felt a customer resisting you early on in a sales call, it may have been because you were trying to close financially before you connected emotionally.

4. **Relationship Breaks the Tie.** When all things are equal between two competitors, having a strong connection and relationship with a customer can break the tie. When all things are NOT equal, relationship still breaks the tie. In today's hyper-competitive environment where pricing can be identical between competitors and the choices are endless, often the only competitive advantage a SalesMaker will have is their level of connection with their customer. Having a strong connection with the customer is the one differentiating factor that will always weigh in the SalesMakers favor even when all other factors are equal.

> "Without connection, a SalesMaker's ability to influence the direction of a sale is moot."

When Crossing the Chasm of Connection to Form Relationships, the SalesMaker Will Face Headwinds

No matter where you are starting from, you can increase your connecting and relationship- building skills. When I started in the sales profession, I had to learn by trial and error how to connect and forge relationships with customers with whom I had little in common. If you are new to sales, this can be both intimidating and overwhelming. Every SalesMaker will face headwinds when attempting to connect with customers. For me, I had to face a number of headwinds. At the start, I was in my early twenties and new to sales, while my customers were forty-something business owners. My customers needed expert industry advice but I was still learning. My customers had years of life experience and I was inexperienced. The difference between their life experience and mine was enormous.

How did I overcome these headwinds and cross the chasm of years, experience, and age to connect with my customers? The answers to these questions may surprise you! Reaching common ground with a customer is not an issue of years, experience, or age, but an issue of heart.

There are *common threads of emotional connection* and shared interest that bind people together. A SalesMaker who can tap into these will discover a series of strategies that can help them fast track the connecting process. These connecting strategies can help the SalesMaker collapse the distance that exists between them and the customer and replace it with a bridge that points the path to not just closing another sale, but building a new relationship. When you learn to forge new and deeper connections with your customers, you will be well on your way to greater sales and more meaningful relationships.

Headwinds Created by the SalesMaker

What are some of the headwinds you face in connecting with others in relationships? Maybe you face an insecurity, a fear of rejection, a nervousness, or call reluctance. Regardless of the headwinds you face as a SalesMaker, you can overcome them one customer, one challenge at a time. It is possible for SalesMakers to sometimes unknowingly create headwinds for themselves. These headwinds can show up on a sales call and cause the SalesMaker to break connection with the customer unintentionally. Forging connection with a customer takes time and it can be lost in an instant. There are moments of "behavior" in the customer-SalesMaker connecting process that can cause a customer to retreat and disconnect from the SalesMaker. These disconnect moments are created by the seller and can include one or more of the following behaviors:

1. **Not Listening:** A seller who does not hear what the customer is saying can create a disconnect very quickly. When customers feel listened to, they feel comfortable. When they don't they disconnect.

2. **Not Acting:** A seller who is not heeding what the customer has requested can create trust issues. The SalesMaker shows a customer that they listened by the actions they take based on what they heard.

3. **Not Being Prepared:** A seller who is unprepared or appears to be incompetent creates frustration and fear for the customer. Customers will not risk their dollars if a seller does not understand their business.

4. **Not Leaning In:** A seller who is not making an effort to help their customer may be interpreted as indifferent or uninterested. Just as connecting requires effort, disconnecting can happen quickly when indifference is felt by the customer.

> "When we don't value what the customer values, it is the same as devaluing them. You'll never connect with someone who feels you are devaluing something they value."

5. **Not Valuing:** A seller who does not value what the customer values can create a disconnection in an area important to the customer. Presenting product benefits before probing to uncover needs can create a mismatch instead of aligning a product benefit with a customer's need. This misfire will create a disconnect that could send the customer running from the seller.

The SalesMaker Must Connect First with Themselves

To connect with others, you must first connect with yourself. Being aware of what your connecting strengths are and identifying areas of connecting with which you struggle is the first step to growing your connecting capability and capacity. Identifying your connecting strengths will help you to know your connecting language which is how a SalesMaker relates to others. If you had to provide a list of your "go-to" connecting strengths, what would that list look like?

SalesMakers have a few connecting strengths that are dominant and a few with which they struggle. Like a handicap in golf, your connecting capability today doesn't need to be your connecting capacity in the future. You can increase in your strength in connecting while minimizing areas where you may have weakness. SalesMakers must be adaptable and always growing if they are to succeed. They can't afford to be one dimensional in any sales skill, but must instead possess a combination of strengths they use when they need to turn their connecting switch on.

> "The most important person the SalesMaker must connect with is themselves. Until you can connect with and accept who you are, you will struggle to connect with others."

Building a repertoire of connecting strengths will serve you well not just in sales, but in every area of life where creating and maintaining strong relationships is important.

What are your connecting strengths? To help you identify them, here are a few examples with which you may be familiar. To which of the following connecting strengths can you relate?

Meet Debby Data. Debby Data is like the character Data from the legendary TV series Star Trek. Grasping and retaining numbers and information comes easily to her. Debby considers herself a product knowledge expert and can win her customers over with a wave of facts and figures. Debby Data knows that for a sale to stick, customers need to be convinced logically and methodically. She is a whiz at working and weaving numbers into spreadsheets and graphs that impress even the casual customer. Debby Data's analytical mind naturally connects with customers who want to be convinced with facts, figures, and information they can grasp. Debby's informational strength is a powerful tool for the right customers that already know what they want.

On the other hand, Debby's style can be irritating to customers who don't like to be overwhelmed with too much information (TMI) but instead prefer the bottom line. Debby Data can have a tendency to oversell her customers if she doesn't read their connecting language correctly.

Do you have a Debby Data within you? Where would your Debby Data fall on a scale of 1-10? The SalesMaker who learns how to leverage their Debby Data at the right time can provide a very persuasive argument that can close the sale.

Meet Wayne Woo. Wayne Woo is a people magnet. He naturally connects with customers relationally and in so doing, discovers a clear path to connecting financially. Getting to know someone comes easily to Wayne. In fact, he thrives on the thrill of meeting someone for the first time and then making a personal connection. Winning others over is easy for Wayne, but that doesn't mean he doesn't have to work at it, too. Wayne doesn't think twice about talking to his clients after hours or on weekends. When Wayne is wooing heavily, customers who thrive on being wooed like it, while others who want a SalesMaker and not a best friend can be turned off. Wayne's woo can be a powerful tool but only when used in the right proportion.

Are you a natural Wayne Woo, or are you a SalesMaker who can turn on their Wayne Woo when they need to and throttle it back when necessary? In the right environment with the right connection, every SalesMaker can have a Wayne Woo emerge to charm those around them.

Meet Sally Service. One of the most famous branding statements in advertising is the Allstate Insurance line which says, "You're in good hands with Allstate." Sally Service makes customers feel like they are in good hands. There is no doubt that nurturing customers is Sally's strength. She has the heart of a servant seller. Sally lives to serve and satisfy her customers. To say that Sally is a people pleaser is an understatement. Sally can't rest if she feels she forgot to follow up with a customer or left something undone in the relationship. When her customers hurt, she hurts.

Sally is able to close the sale and generate return sales by leveraging her service strengths. The hunger within her to "people please" is satisfied only when she knows she has met the expectations of her customers. When Sally Service senses her customers value good service, she has instant connection with them because she knows she is in her sweet spot. She is not shy about using her service strength to seal the deal. When Sally talks about warranties and guarantees, it's not just about company policy, it's a personal promise from her. When you are with Sally, you know you are in good hands.

Do you live to take care of your customers or do you prefer to make the sale and move on? Not every SalesMaker can be a "Sally Servicer," but every SalesMaker can provide good service. Acknowledging the level of your service abilities will better help you to manage your weaknesses and leverage your strengths when connecting with your customers.

Meet Larry the Listener. Larry is a natural listener. Everyone who has ever met Larry knows that when they are with Larry, they can feel him listening. Larry connects with his customers because his default position is to identify and connect with customers through empathy. Because Larry is naturally quiet, his energy level may appear low and not get people excited. But the deep connections Larry forms through listening are lasting and meaningful.

When customers are with Larry, their confidence level goes up because they know Larry won't let anything fall through the cracks. Larry shows people he is listening not just with a head bob, but with the way he responds, follows up, and communicates through email, text, and social media. Larry is tough to rattle because he is constantly in receiving mode like a catcher behind the plate in baseball. Larry lives to let others pitch and direct the conversation. From his positon of listening he is able to convert this connecting strength into dollars. Larry believes his strength in connecting comes from how he listens, not from what he says.

Are there situations where you can switch on your Larry Listener? Within every SalesMaker is a quiet place where their attention is arrested, mind is focused, and nobody matters in the moment but the customer. When you discover that place within you, you have met your Larry Listener.

Meet Chris the Consultant. Chris the Consultant closes sales because he asks great questions. Chris never pitches the product before he probes for needs. It's important for Chris the Consultant to thoroughly diagnose his customers need before he presents options or a solution. Chris is naturally curious and doesn't want to know just the "what" of a situation, but the "why" behind it. Discovering important insights and information about his customer is what shows Chris a clear path to closing the sale. If you are like Chris the Consultant, you have a natural tendency to ask questions before arriving at conclusions and prefer leading a customer with questions to close the sale versus pushing them with selling statements. Customers who know what they want and don't want to go through an investigative process may become impatient with Chris' connecting style.

To what degree are you a Chris the Consultant? Do you know how and when to turn it on and off and for whom?

> "After SalesMakers learn to connect with themselves, they are better equipped to connect with others."

Knowing your natural tendency to connect can help you develop an awareness of when to use your Chris the Consultant versus Debby Data, your Wayne Woo versus Sally Service, or your Larry the Listener. In the Law of the Sixth Sense, I will share with you insights that will help you to read the customer and the emotional environment so you will know which connecting style to use and when.

Most SalesMakers don't just have one connecting strength but instead possess a combination that helps close the sale. Your customers are the same way. In a sense, everyone has a type of connecting language that is natural to them. And, we all have a connecting language that resonates within us. Once you can identify the connecting strengths within you, you will be better equipped to identify the connecting language of your customer. SalesMakers are versatile and know that one-size does not fit all. For this reason, the development of multiple connecting strengths over time will lead to more sales.

Connecting in Sales = Building Relationships

Success in sales is all about building relationships." That's the advice I got over and over again my first few years as a young SalesMaker. The seniors on staff would always tell me, "Just build relationships and the money will flow." That advice sounded great but I always wondered, "How do I do that?" I don't recall taking a relationship-building course in school. So where was I supposed to start?

If you've seen the Matrix movie series, you are familiar with the character, Neo. Neo is the "one" who is destined to save the world. Early in Neo's training, observers witness training programs in every type of combat being downloaded into Neo's neuro net so he had instant access to knowledge and training that would normally take a lifetime to acquire. This is analogous to a video game when a player goes from one level to the next and with each level is granted new capabilities and talent sets. In the same way, what if a SalesMaker could receive a downloadable program that equips them to connect and build meaningful relationships, both personally and financially, and convert these skills into higher sales commissions? If a download on "connecting" of this magnitude was available think how valuable that would be!

In the following sections, you will receive connecting strategies to help you attain the next level. What does the next level look like? I will give you a hint. It includes the confidence and capability to create connection with almost any personality type you might meet.

> "Success in sales always involves building relationships. You can't close someone you can't connect with."

Before we get into connecting strategies, there are three important issues of the heart that are involved in the art of connecting.

Connecting is All About Heart

1. **Connecting Heart to Heart with your customer will close more sales.**
   Regardless of your approach to connecting with others, how you bend
   your connecting strengths to blend with the customer in a way that
   closes the sale is as important as the heart posture you bring to the
   process. Connecting is entirely about how you make the other person
   feel while they are with you. How they feel about themselves as well
   as your product and company will determine their level of connection
   with you and your level of influence with them. If connecting is about
   how we make others feel, then connecting is a heart issue.

   My friend Wayne Cordeiro, author and Senior Pastor of New Hope
   Oahu says it this way, "A mind can reach a mind, but only a heart can
   reach a heart." A healthy heart posture for a SalesMaker includes being
   genuinely interested in learning the needs of the customer and having
   the heart to help them.

   One of my early mentors, Jerry Del Core, said, "Some of my best
   clients have become my close friends." Why would he say this? Because
   sales isn't just a financial transaction, it's a heart transaction. The better
   you get at connecting and building relationships with your customers,
   the wealthier you will become not just financially, but relationally as
   well. Jerry understood this and that is why when he was working to
   create a new customer, he was also working to make a new friend.

2. **Loving your customer guarantees you will connect, even when they can't.**
   Love who you sell to, not just what you do! This may sound unrealistic.
   After all, some people are not loveable. In fact, some are not even likable.
   Love them anyway! That is the heart posture of a successful SalesMaker!
   How does a SalesMaker learn to like, and eventually love, those who
   may be unlovable? They identify the qualities that others value in their
   customers and then adjust their perspective so they can see what others
   see. When a SalesMaker is able to perceive what others value in their customers, they will feel what others feel toward them. A lovable perspective
   on people is what makes connecting possible! You can't sell those you do
   not value. If you consciously make a habit to look for the best in others,
   you will always find the best in others. The opposite is also true. If you
   consistently see the worst in others, you are destined to develop a critical
   spirit and will struggle to love the "unlovable." I have discovered that it

is impossible to love my profession and not the people that it serves. Yet, there are days I don't enjoy either. For this reason, if I am going to maintain a heathy heart posture, I must be intentional about shifting my lens to see the good in those I hope to serve and sell.

Another reason for adjusting my perspective so I can always see the best in others is because *people can instinctively tell if you care for them or not.* Difficult customers are hard to connect with, but consider this: If they are having a hard time connecting with you despite your best efforts, it is possible that they struggle to connect with others as well. If you love them in spite of their "unloveableness," you may be one of the few people they interact with who has an opportunity to reach them emotionally and turn them around. Although you may not feel like you are in the relationship rehabilitation business, isn't it true that the most difficult customers, once won over, become the most loyal? After spending enough time in sales, you will find this to be true more often than not. For the customers you discover this not to be true with, love them anyway!

3. **Ongoing connecting requires ongoing maintenance.**
   Connecting is not a one-time event. In many relationships, connecting in *new* and diverse ways becomes part of the fuel that feeds the relationship. For a relationship to remain healthy, I recommend giving your relationships regular check-ups. Like going to a doctor for an evaluation, a Relationship Check-Up is a way for the SalesMaker to take personal inventory of how they and their customers might perceive the health of the relationship. Courageous self-honesty and soliciting customer feedback will allow the SalesMaker to identify the strong and weak points in the relationship. Identifying and addressing relational issues before they become problems allows the SalesMaker to invest more time selling and less time repairing the relationship.

   If you sense discomfort or feel disconnected in a relationship, may I suggest you give yourself a Relationship Check-Up and identify where the misfires may be. Where there is friction or a need not being met, a fire could be brewing. It is always less costly to identify a problem early before it leads to a breakdown in relationship and revenue.

   The Relationship Check-Up starts with the SalesMaker asking the following 12 questions of themselves and in some cases, their customers. The answers a SalesMaker receives can be challenging. In some circumstances where you can't identify the problem, soliciting feedback from your customer by probing in the following twelve areas can be revealing. Advanced planning to strengthen a relationship before the start of a struggle is always better than after the fact. The better you become at knowing where problem areas can develop in relationships, the better you will be at maintaining unbroken connection with your customers.

The Relationship Check-Up Questions   Y/N

R eliability!	Does the customer feel they can count on you?
E ngagement!	Does the customer feel you are engaged in meeting their needs?
L istening!	Does the customer feel you listen to them or just head bob them?
A ction!	Does the customer see you taking steps to fulfill their need?
T rust!	Does the customer feel they can trust you?
I nterest!	Does the customer feel you have their best interests at heart?
O pen!	Does the customer feel you are open to new ideas, input, criticism?
N earness!	Does the customer feel you are available when their need arises?
S ecurity!	Does the customer feel comfortable sharing private "confidences?"
H istorical!	Does the customer feel you have good or bad history together?
I ntegrity!	Does the customer feel you will always protect their interest?
P rincipled!	Does the customer perceive you as being principled?

> "When the customer discovers that the SalesMaker values them and what they care about and not just the sale, trust develops, a connection is made, and a relationship is born."

SalesMaker Strategies for Connecting with the Customer

I started in outside sales selling radio advertising in 1990. I was fortunate early on to learn about what the great motivational speaker Zig Ziglar called "automobile university." It's where you stop listening to the radio, and instead listen to audio recordings of people you can learn from. One of my first teachers in sales was Tom Hopkins. Tom has taught millions of sales people just like me. He is best known for teaching practical, how-to selling strategies. Strangely, I learned what to say so I could close the sale

> "If customers don't bond to you emotionally, it will be difficult to get them to follow you financially."

before I knew how to effectively connect with customers. I learned the words that could close the sale, adapted them to my industry which was radio advertising sales, and had success. However, something was missing. I was in a business that thrived on renewal and return business, not just new business. Renewal selling skills are dependent upon relationship skills and connecting is always the first priority in building relationships.

Connection is the entry point to starting a new relationship and the lynch pin that often closes the sales. Without the ability to connect and build relationships, a career in sales will be short lived. So how does the SalesMaker create connection with their customers either on a first time call or on an ongoing basis? Below there are ten SalesMaker Strategies for Creating Connection. Each of the connecting skills are also necessary relationship-building skills. Some are best in the first meeting, while others are needed in every meeting. If growing your sales business is dependent on cold calling, performing needs analyses, generating referrals or renewal business, you will find the intentional connecting process of the SalesMaker relationally helpful and financially rewarding. Like Lego bricks that connect one to another, use the ten strategies of the SalesMaker to connect with others and watch your relationships deepen while your income skyrockets.

You Need a Plan to Connect with the Customer

Developing a high-level ability to create connection, avoid conflict, and build relationships, is non-negotiable for a SalesMaker if they are to reach their sales and income potential. Everyone has an inherent level of connecting skills. Some are natural connectors while others have to work at it. What makes the SalesMaker's ability different?

1. **SalesMakers Connect on Common Ground.**

   Common ground is one of the easiest ways to identify a connection point with your customer, if you know what you are looking for. There are a number of questions the SalesMaker can ask to facilitate quick connections. Here are seven areas of commonality to help you identify the common ground you and your customer share. Think of these questions every time you meet a new customer and you'll quickly find and establish common ground.

Commonality	Interrogative Question	Keyword
People:	Who do you know that I know?	Relationships
Places:	Where have you been that I've been?	Experience
Passion:	What moves you that moves me?	Emotion
Price:	What do you "go above and beyond" for?	Sacrifice
Pinnacle:	What have been your greatest achievements?	Pride
Pain:	What or Who causes you to hurt?	Avoidance
Plans:	What are you reaching to achieve?	Goals

   There are many other areas of commonality that can create connection, however, these seven will get you started in discovering meaningful connecting points when forming new relationships.

2. **SalesMakers Connect on Higher Ground.**

   Customers don't hang out with sales people because they have nothing better to do. If a customer is shopping, they are trading their time in search of something meaningful to them. What is the customer's ultimate goal? It could be to solve a problem or satisfy a desire. It's your job to discover the reasons and ideas the customer may have as they pursue a purchase. Here are five P-questions the SalesMaker can use to connect with the customer on higher ground:

Driver	Introspective Question	Keyword
Purpose:	What is the reason the customer is shopping?	Motive
Problem:	What problem is the customer trying to solve?	Resolution
Pursuit:	What is driving the decision to buy now?	Motivation
Preferences:	What options does the customer prefer?	Priorities
Pendulum:	What is the determining factor that will swing the decision?	Tipping Point

Once you learn the answers to these questions, you're well along the road to a closed sale. In fact, the answers to these questions will point the way to the sale.

3. **SalesMakers Connect on Credible Ground.**

We've all seen TV reporters who go onsite to report on an epic event and then interview those onsite who are experiencing the event. Why do news organizations bear the expense of sending someone onsite in today's technologically advanced world? Because there is no substitute for sharing up close and personal what you and others are experiencing on the scene. Reporters want you to see what they see and hear what they hear so you can feel what they feel. Being onsite creates credibility in the moment.

In the same way, a SalesMaker who has personally lived, walked through, and experienced the buying decision process and the benefits of using the product has a powerful story to share. When you can articulate what you've been through, what you've experienced, and the conclusions you've come to that led you to do what you've done, your story can lead your customer to feel the same way you felt before saying "yes" to a purchase. SalesMakers who can leverage the power of their stories are able to not just deliver the message, they become the message! There is not a more credible messenger than one who has been there, done that, and lived to tell about it. Customers connect with the credibility that is inherent within a story. When I know you've walked where I am about to walk, gone where I am about to go, or experienced what I am about to experience, we share a connection and your influence with me grows. There is no higher authority than the credibility that comes from a personal story.

4. **SalesMakers Connect on Relevant Ground.**

Relevant ground is determined by what the customer deems relevant. It is easy for a SalesMaker to make product knowledge the dominant part of a conversation. What the customer hears when a sales presentation lacks meaning for them is... blah, blah, blah. The most important frequency a SalesMaker can tune into is "WII-FM," (or What's In It For Me?). Every time a SalesMaker promotes a major benefit for their product, they need to follow it with why it is important or meaningful to the customer. Unless the SalesMaker can make their product relevant to the customer's needs, what is meaningful to the seller will become meaningless to the customer, and irrelevancy severs connection and creates lost sales.

The So-What Exercise: To better illustrate what irrelevant ground sounds and feels like, role play with a coworker and ask them to begin to list a number of major product features and their benefit to the customer. At the end of each benefit statement, say out-loud, "so what?" The SalesMaker makes a feature relevant to the customer by tying it to a benefit that is meaningful to the customer. For example:

• Our Corian counter tops come with a lifetime guarantee from chipping and scratching. What this means for you, Mr. Jones, is that no matter how much your kids climb on, drop on, or crawl on your new Corian counter tops, they will look the same in year five as they did the day you bought them.

• Our new Ford F-150s are the only trucks made out of aluminum. At some point, all metal rusts and rust will reduce resale value. With the aluminum F-150, you are guaranteed never to lose resale value due to rust.

5. **SalesMakers Connect on Emotionally-Charged Ground.**

Have you ever been in a conversation and knew you had just hit a nerve? If you've seen or experienced the reaction from someone after hitting a hot spot in a conversation, you know the emotional impact the right words can create. The most meaningful moment on a sales call is not what the SalesMaker experiences emotionally, but the emotional charge the customer experiences. Like stumbling onto a hot spot in a cold swimming pool, the astute SalesMaker, once discovering a positive reaction from the customer, remains in that area of the conversation. The more the SalesMaker circles around an area of interest to the customer, the more meaning can be extracted from the moment. This meaning can create momentum in the sale process. Here are a few suggestions of what to say in order to remain in an emotionally-charged area:

- I'm listening, please go on.

- That seems important to you, can you explain why?

- Can you elaborate on that?

- That's an interesting perspective, please continue.

- Can you explain that again, but in a different way?

> "The significance of a question is only discovered after it is asked and the emotional response of the customer is observed."

When a SalesMaker can identify, capture, and then convert on the emotionally-charged moments in a sales call, there is quite simply not a better and more meaningful way to connect with a customer.

6. **SalesMakers Connect on Strengthening Ground.**
In his book, "The Bucket Dipper," Tom Rath said that there are two types of people we encounter throughout our day. There are those who dip into our emotional buckets and withdraw from them, and those who contribute to our emotional buckets with deposits. One adds value. The other reduces value. To encourage another is to strengthen them.

> "To affirm someone we have to see value in them before we add value to them."

SalesMakers connect on strengthening ground by acknowledging and affirming something they value in their customers and then expressing it to them.

To affirm someone we must see value in them before we can add value to them. Identifying a strength they possess, observing a uniqueness about them, sharing an insight on something they said, or acknowledging something we admire, can create an emotional deposit that strengthens a person. When we add value and strength to another, we are connecting on strengthening ground. In some cases, a SalesMaker can create strengthening ground where none may exist. When you begin to become a "depositor" of strength into another, you will inadvertently create a magnetic pull between yourself and the other person. That magnetic pull forges a strong connection and that connection equates to relationship influence.

7. **SalesMakers Connect on Comforting Ground.**

To connect on comforting ground, SalesMakers put customers at ease by adapting to them. The ability to adapt to a new environment is paramount to surviving and thriving in the sales profession. Every time a SalesMaker greets a new customer, they are in a new environment that may require adaptation. The greatest connectors in the world are, above all things, great at adapting to others. SalesMakers who adapt to the different types of communication and connection styles of their customers will thrive more than those who do not. Here are two simple examples you can mirror and mimic to create comforting ground for connection:

> "SalesMakers are casual, but strategic in the way they communicate non-verbally."

- Casual mirroring and mimicking of the customer can have the effect of creating comfort and connection during communication. There are many under-the-surface nuances of communication that can determine closeness or distance. These include body language, facial expressions, rhythm and volume of speech, gestures, and many other forms of non-verbal communication. Management consultant, Peter Drucker said, "Over 50% of communication is below the surface." By identifying two ways of communication that the customer uses and then mirroring that behavior, SalesMakers can create an unconscious—or "under the surface" as Peter Drucker would say—sense of similarity and comfort.

> "Everyone's body language emotes. So emote intentionally. Know what signals you are sending off."

- Returning the Volley: The first response in volleyball when you receive the ball is to volley it back. In the same way, returning back to the customer something they said to you in the form of a question has the potential to create connection. When we deliver back to the customer what has been said to us, it indicates we cared enough to confirm that we heard accurately what they said. Acknowledging and confirming what has been said can have the force of creating quick connection. It says, "I want to make sure I heard you right and I don't want to miss anything you said."

8. **SalesMakers Connect on Shared Interests.**

There are many types of commonality that can connect two people in the beginning stages of forming a relationship. One type of common ground is shared interest. For many customer types, connecting on shared interest is how they conduct business. A SalesMaker communicating and connecting on shared interest with their customer can accelerate the effect of creating a quicker and more enjoyable type of connection, especially from the customer's point of view. Connecting in an area of life that is not business related can be appropriate and necessary to forge a connection with customers the SalesMaker may encounter.

By way of example, the business culture where I live in Honolulu, Hawaii demands that people connect personally before connecting professionally. It is not uncommon to spend 30 minutes breaking the ice and connecting and only the last 15 minutes of the meeting talking business. In some company cultures, the transaction is the reason for the relationship but in others the relationship is the reason for the transaction. Connecting on shared interest isn't only a location (geographical) or cultural (behavioral) way of doing business, it also reflects a personality type. This is simply how some customers like to conduct business. Here are some non-business ways to connect with a customer that opens doors to an area of shared interest.

> "If you knew you could make an emotional connection with every customer and form a relationship, is there anything that could stop you from converting connection into closing?"

Shared Interest	Investigative Questions	Keyword
Enjoyment	What do you like to do for fun?	Bliss
Friendships	Who do you enjoy spending time with & why?	Influence
Down Time	What do you enjoy doing during your free time?	R&R
Desire	What do you wish you could do more of?	Pleasure
Avoidance	What do you not like to do?	Resistance
Intentional Time	What do you like to read, watch, or listen to?	Interests

Once you learn the answers to these questions, you are well on your way to connecting with a customer who likes to talk about their interests, and not just their business.

9. **SalesMakers Connect on Spiritual Ground.**
Nearly every person you meet will agree that there are forces within and without, some under their control and some not. Nobody can deny that there are feelings they experience and thoughts they ponder, some of which can be traced and some that cannot. From where do these feelings and thoughts come? Some say God, some say other people, some say the "muse" within, and some say they are simply "spiritual." People don't always agree on the answers but they are aware of the forces and feeling, and the resulting beliefs that are formed.

A customer's "world experience" greatly influences their belief system and that same belief system dictates their behavior. When you know what a customer believes or what they have experienced, you will have a better understanding of how to develop a strategy that can connect with their mindset. In the Law of Connection, I have focused much of the connecting and relationship language around emotion because connecting is tied to the heart. It is with the heart that we feel and it is there that connections and relationships are formed. Connecting on spiritual ground requires having access to the heart and knowledge of the customer's mindset.

10. **SalesMakers Connect on Sacred Ground.**

A few years back, I had the opportunity to spend a weekend at the Youth with a Mission (YWAM) Base in Kona, Hawaii. Kona is on the Big Island where the renowned Iron Man Triathlon competition takes place every year. It is also known for YWAM, which is the largest missionary training base in the world. Students come to Kona for a short period to attend the University of the Nations to learn new skills, cultural nuances, and often new languages and ways to communicate. Driven by purpose and passion, YWAM Missionaries are based in every country in the world.

While visiting the base, I met Jim Oredd, Leadership Coach & Consultant. Jim was one of the key leaders at the base, and he asked me an intriguing question. He asked, "Scott, if you could spend only one hour with someone you knew you'd never see again, how would you spend it?" This intriguing question caused me to dig deep and ask myself, "How would I go about connecting with someone I had just met and then help them in the one and only meeting I would have with them?" I knew then that I would invest more of the conversation asking questions about them than talking about me, but also that I would focus on three key areas in order to connect: 1) their past, 2) their future, and 3) their present.

Connecting on sacred ground is not something you leap into. Until you sense an opening or emotional invitation of sorts to take the relationship to a deeper level, probing a customer's past, present, and future will produce surface answers unless you have already have established a foundation of rapport.

Here is How the SalesMaker Connects on Sacred Ground in the Past, Future, and Present

(Note: Use probing questions when connecting on sacred ground as they are non-restrictive and meant to create an open, inviting atmosphere. The goal is that the person answering the questions feels the freedom to reply in a way that is comfortable for them. Remember, connecting is about making customers feel the comfort and confidence that comes from being with you.)

A. **The Past.** The history question asks, "Where are they coming from?" When you understand what a person's experience has been, you are more able to walk a mile in their shoes and connect with how they think. When you know how someone thinks, you will know why they feel what they feel and that is the key to connecting.

Meaningful Memories:	What past experiences stick out in your mind?
Anchored Beliefs:	What have been some of your greatest life lessons?
Proven Wisdom:	What has worked best for you in the past?
Regret:	What would you do over if you could?
Secret/Protective:	What is sacred to you?

B. **The Future.** The future question asks, "Where are they going?" For many people, asking about the future gives them emotional permission to dream about what might be. Most people feel there is "more" out there and questions about a potentially better future jump start a visionary conversation that can be highly motivating. It can be easier to ask people about the past than about their potential future because personal futuristic conversations open doors that may require encouragement, buy-in, and advice. When a customer feels a SalesMaker speaking belief and encouragement into their future hope or dream, the relationship connection proceeds to a higher level.

Relationships:	Who would you like to meet one day?
Resource:	How can I assist you in helping you reach your dream?
Hidden Dream:	What is the unsung song you'd like to sing one day?
Perfect Picture:	What does the ideal future look like?
Hope:	What would you like to see happen down the road?
Bucket List:	What is still left undone?

C. **The Present.** The present question asks, "Where are they now?" The "now" questions open the door for the SalesMaker to find today's problems, uncover opportunities, and connect immediately. The better the questions the SalesMaker asks about today, the more meaningful the answers.

Worry:	What keeps you up at night?
Motivation:	What gets you up in the morning?
Perspective:	How would you describe your present season of life?
Wish:	If you had a magic wand, what would you change today?

Friction:	Are there any relationships that are challenging right now?
Obstacles:	What is stopping you from pursuing what you want today?
Partnership:	What can I do to help you today that would make a difference?

As a SalesMaker, how would you answer these questions? Knowing your own answers will aid you in connecting with a customer when they share their stories.

In the Law of Connection, you've learned that everyone struggles to connect from time to time yet there are strategies that will help you close the distance that exists between you and the people you serve in sales. Whether you are focused today on creating a new customer relationship or strengthening a relationship you have had for years, employing the strategies in the Law of Connection will help you go deeper, go farther, and go higher—to achieve more in your day to day interactions with people in your life. It's time to level up and take your connecting abilities to higher ground. In the following C.I.A. section, you will have an opportunity to put what you have learned into practice and take your career to the next level.

"Connecting on sacred ground shows us that what connects us is far more important than the things that separate us."

C.I.A. CONTRIBUTORS

The LAW OF CONNECTION

Amy Oakes, Facebook

Heidi Dickert, Fortune 500 Consultant

Lori Webster, Realtor, HomeSmart Premier

My name is **Amy Oakes** and I work at **Facebook**. For over 15 years, I have worked in sales, online search, and now social media. I attribute my success to being resourceful, a problem solver, and being able to help clients reach their goals in the future. Below are some of the key points that I connected with in the Law of Connection:

1. "The key to connecting is to be focused on others." In sales and in business relationships in general, I am focused on what the other person is going through and needing and not on what I am trying to sell. If I impress my customers with tidbits about me, but don't convince them that I've put them first, I have failed. Customer focus first has always been my priority.

2. To be a good connector, I have had to be willing to be vulnerable, risk rejection, risk failure, and embrace the unknown in order to form new relationships.

3. "Connecting is the most important sales skill." I have worked at companies that had great product momentum/demand and the sellers didn't need to make an effort to connect. But those who made an effort

to connect and become good at it always did better than those who relied only on the product alone to carry them through. Creating connection in sales is the first step to building a relationship.

4. Sales people can create a disconnect if they are unaware of what breaks connection. Not making an effort to receive real time feedback from your customer and focusing on your own goals will cause a customer to retreat from the relationship. I will be more intentional in taking real time feedback in every conversation I have.

5. I am the classic sales introvert, but I can flip a switch and go into extrovert mode. I agree that connecting can be learned and the 10 strategies for connecting lay out practical ways to create new relationships and strengthen existing ones.

6. "Connecting is a heart issue." People I work with and do business with can tell if I genuinely care for them. I too can tell also when I am with someone if they are authentic or not. Facebook is an extraordinary company at connecting people, shared interests, and helping people to grow their connection base.

7. "The SalesMaker must first connect with themselves before they can connect with others." Being able to identify a person's connecting strengths will help me to connect quicker with others.

8. "When you look for the best in others, you will find the best in others." This statement resonates because there are always people who are difficult to connect with, yet if I focus on looking for the best in others and avoid a critical eye, it's amazing what I find. I've lived this principle—it's how I met and then married my husband. By looking for the positive in others, I am guaranteed to never miss out on the richness of the relationship that a critical eye can be blind to.

9. The 10 connecting strategies in the Law of Connection are very rich. This section asks a lot of the questions I use when wanting to connect with people and questions I can ask myself. My insight here is that no matter how good of a connector I am, I can always learn more. Connecting on relevant ground has always been a strategy for me. I will also incorporate shared interest strategy into my personal style of connecting.

My name is **Heidi Dickert** and as a Fortune 500 Consultant, I work with a diverse range of Fortune 500 clients such as **Facebook, Del Monte, Visa, Microsoft, LinkedIn, and Clorox**. For over 20 years, I have worked with clients to better assess market needs and strategize on how to optimize opportunities that stem from these needs. Although I am data driven, I attribute my success to my strength in connecting and building relationships with coworkers and clients by being caring and interested in their success. My friends call me "The Connector" but I am always looking for ways to improve. Below are some of the key points that I picked up in the Law of Connection:

1. "Identify your connecting strengths." I am a combination of Debby Data, Sally Service, and Chris the Consultant. Being aware of my connecting strengths will better help me to leverage them, and also help me to better identify the connecting strengths in those around me.

2. "Give Yourself a Relationship Check-Up." Taking inventory on relationships regularly is a good go-to system for evaluating the health of my personal and professional relationships. I will use these questions to evaluate then address any relationship issues I may be facing.

3. The introvert example resonated with me because my circle of friends and coworkers have always labeled me as an extrovert, but I am not. I have learned to be both types depending on what the situation calls for. Being able to adapt makes me a good connector with all personality types.

4. Found in the ten strategies for connecting, the Interrogative and Introspective Questions will give me a resource for having ways to open up conversations with strangers that may lead to unexpected connections. The Sacred Ground Questions will also help me find ways to deepen existing relationships.

5. I always felt like my connection with others was part of my personal "brand." And when my company cannot deliver quality that was to the level I know my client needed/wanted, there is a risk of damaging my connections and ultimately my personal brand. This motivates me to strive all the more to be competent in my deliverables so my relationships with others are not negatively impacted.

My name is **Lori Webster** and I am with **HomeSmart Premier**. For the last 30 years, I have worked in Real Estate lending, Sales & Management. I have always felt that my strengths included Relationship Development and Marketing along with a strong work ethic and a desire to strive for customer loyalty. My love of the Real Estate industry allows me to share Arizona and its beauty with my customers. Below are some of the highlights that connected with me as I read the Law of Connection:

1. Insecurity and fear of rejection IS a barrier to connecting. Be "other-focused" when trying to connect with someone.

2. The ability to connect with others and forge relationships has to be developed. I can use the specific connecting strategies at the end of the chapter to grow my connecting capabilities.

3. Connecting is the most important skill in sales because connecting makes closings possible. Connection neutralizes the "No."

4. Relationships lead to revenue. The better I get at connecting with others, the more referrals and relationships I will be able to convert to sales and commissions.

5. Relationships break the tie when all things are equal. By focusing on creating strong connections, I will have an advantage in my industry in building relationships.

6. Relationship Check-up Questions—this would really help when trying to figure out why you can't connect with someone.

7. Connecting Heart to Heart: "A head will reach a head but only a heart will reach a heart." Be genuinely interested in learning the needs of your customer and having the heart to help them will come through and help forge a stronger relationship connection.

8. Ongoing connecting requires ongoing maintenance. Connecting is not a one-time event.

9. Connect on Shared Interests: I will use the Investigative Questions to help with my relationship development.

Put the 7 Empowering Laws of the SalesMaker to Work And Convert your Insights into Income

Now that you've completed the Law of Connection, it is time to convert learning into earning. The first step is to return to the sections of this chapter that you highlighted, underlined, or made notes from. Of the key points that you connected with, pick three that resonate the most with you. Following the simple formula for transformation found in the C.I.A. process in the introduction (Connection, Insight, Action), identify and write down that which resonated with you. Then, identify the insights you gathered, and finally decide how you might put them into action. Reading, doing, believing in, and incorporating three sales insights into your daily routine will create a transformative impact on your sales volume and sales commissions.

Here is how I will convert my insights into income:

C = Connection: As I read, the following content, principle, or idea that connected with me was:

_____

_____

I = Insight: As I reflect, the idea or insight I received is:

_____

_____

A = Action: The action I will take to convert my insight into income will be to:

_____

_____

CHAPTER 2

LAW OF THE LISTENER

Value is exchanged on both sides of a conversation when Focused Listening occurs.

In 1994, I had an opportunity to go to Israel on a business trip with my uncle T.J., who was also my first mentor in broadcasting. This would be my first trip to Israel, and I would get to see the Holy Land with my uncle who was an expert tour guide. It was going to be a great adventure. The plan was to do a couple days of business on the front end of the trip, and then spend a week being a tourist.

T.J. needed to meet with clients while in town consulting Middle East Television. The first meeting was to fix a situation that had gone wrong and resolve an escalating problem. When dealing with difficult circumstances and differing points of view, communication can be strained and the ability to listen becomes very important.

Because we were traveling together, I tagged along to the business meetings. For this one particular meeting, there were four of us in the room: myself, my uncle TJ, the unhappy party who was a client of Middle East Television, and a gentleman named Modi who was our interpreter both for language and culture. After the introductions were made, the client proceeded to talk *to* me (not *with* me) for 45 minutes about his situation. I must have looked like the official listener in the room. He went on and on with his story. I just sat there quietly and attentively. No one else even attempted to engage in conversation with the client.

I was focused so intently on what was being communicated that I was listening with my eyes, my ears, my heart, and every one of my senses. The customer communicated with words, hand gestures, facial expressions, body movements, speed of speech, and voice tone. The meeting seemed to go on forever as I never uttered a word, but rather just listened. I was an engaged listener even though I was a bystander and not a participant in the situation. I guessed the client didn't know that at the time. This would not be the only thing the client didn't know. Yet, there were things they could have discovered if they had taken a moment to pause in the conversation to listen for feedback or ask a question.

As the client spoke, he was passionate and upset. He felt strongly about his viewpoint, but was also concerned and wanted some help. I could tell he felt frustrated and stuck, just as I did. After venting and a very long explanation of the circumstance, he abruptly stopped talking. It seemed like an abrupt end to what he way saying, or at the very least, a long pause. I guessed he felt it was my turn to speak. I could instinctively tell by his pause, body language, and folded arms that he had exhausted his point of view and now wanted to hear my response.

There was a delayed moment of silence as the client waited for my response, but none came. The client gestured to me and everyone else at the table with his arms open because I wasn't responding. It was as if his body language was communicating, "Please, I want to hear what you think." After another delayed moment of silence, Modi turned to the client and spoke the first words I could understand in the conversation, "He's from America. He doesn't speak Hebrew." I was listening even more so now, because the first words I could understand in the last hour had just been spoken. A moment later, the client burst into laughter. In hindsight, I wondered why the interpreter allowed the client to go on and on for so long while I just listened. I guess he felt the client just needed to be heard.

Although I didn't understand the words being spoken, I was able to understand much of what was being communicated. In retrospect, I learned a lot about listening that day. In the undercurrents that exist within communication, value is exchanged on both sides of a conversation when Focused Listening occurs.

SalesMakers are professional listeners. This means that they get paid to listen. In fact, most failed sales with customers who had the money, authority, and need to buy are the result of failed listening. SalesMakers who practice and pursue improved performance in the art of listening are in a position to hear what competitors don't hear, see opportunity competitors don't see, and capitalize on closing moments others might miss.

Listening isn't just an important skill for a SalesMaker; it is non-negotiable for SalesMakers who want to reach their income, influence, and relationship potential in the profession of sales. Regardless of your field or profession, the Law of the Listener will make you better in knowing how to listen, what to listen for, and how to achieve more in your field through the art of listening.

Listening is Not the Same as Hearing

Most of us think that hearing means the same thing as listening. This couldn't be farther from the truth. What is the difference between hearing and listening? Hearing is an automatic activity that one can't turn on or off. But listening is an activity we can intentionally choose to turn on and tune in, or turn off and tune out. The ear hears regardless of what we are focused on, but listening is a choice. Hearing is triggered on the outside, while listening is triggered by flipping a switch of intentionality on the inside. That switch of intentionality for the SalesMaker, once flipped, focuses their attention on all that is being communicated, not just on what is being said.

> "I know you are hearing what I am saying, but that doesn't mean you are listening to me"

On the surface, it may appear that listening is a passive activity, but it is not. Although SalesMakers may be silent when they listen, are very much active on the inside. The act of listening to a casual listener may only be an exterior activity that involves taking in what is being heard through the ears. However, for the SalesMaker, listening engages all aspects of what is being communicated. SalesMakers are listening to what is being communicated with the eyes, the ears, facial expressions, voice tone, speed of speech, volume of voice, arm movements, body posture, a customer's level of excitement or disinterest, and other non-verbal forms of communication, subsequently using that information to inch closer to the close.

Instinctively, people can tell when they are or are not being listened to. Consider the following short letter to a listener that ends abruptly. They are pointing out how they observe others listening to them during a conversation when they realize no one is listening. In that moment, they stop talking. Maybe you've experienced this before.

Letter to the Listener

"I can tell when you are listening and when you are not. I can tell when you are just waiting for your turn, or when you really want to hear what I have to say. I can tell if the lights are on, or if no one is home. I can tell if you value me by how you listen. I can tell what you think is important by how you tune in or tune out. I can tell if you are listening by the questions you ask, and I can tell if were listening by how you follow up after our meeting. I can tell…"

Do you consider yourself a good listener? To become a good listener, SalesMakers train themselves to be focused listeners. Here is a quick listener evaluation you can use to check yourself. It can also be used as a gauge in your future conversations to see who is engaged while listening to you and who is not.

Are You a Good Listener?

Y/N	Do You...
	Sit patiently still & silent while the other person is talking?
	Stay mentally tuned-in to what the other person is saying?
	Communicate physically that you are listening with your body language?
	Take written notes to capture the facts and feelings of what is being said?
	Watch for what is communicated non-verbally, physically & emotionally?
	Interrupt while the other person is talking?
	Get anxious or fidgety when it is your turn to listen?
	Multitask while the other person is talking?
	Allow environmental interruptions to distract you while you listen?

When Giving Feedback, Do You...

	Acknowledge what has been said? "If I'm hearing you right..."
	Ask questions to clarify areas of uncertainty? "Can you explain to me what you meant when you said..."
	Acknowledge how the other person feels? "If I was in your shoes, I would feel..."
	Provide sincere feedback with an empathetic emotional tone? "I understand where you are coming from."

If you are honest with yourself, you scored yourself higher in some listening situations than others. If my boss is talking with me, I may be totally tuned in to what he is saying. If my wife is talking with me, sometimes I let distractions keep me from taking in all that she is communicating. Nobody is perfect at focused listening all the time. Becoming a Master in the art of listening is not a process that we perfect, and then forget. It is a commitment to being a consistent practitioner because it is possible to be a good listener in one conversation, and then not in the next.

You Can Fake Hearing, But Not Listening

There is never a time when a SalesMaker doesn't have to intentionally practice the art of Focused Listening. Listening like a SalesMaker is an art form to be practiced, not a "set it and forget it" sales skill once it is learned. We all have the tendency to hear but not listen from time to time. Habitual hearing is automatic but it takes a tuned-in listener to participate in two-way communication in order to connect with the customer and close the sale.

> "The skill of listening is more important in one-to-one communication than speaking. It's easier to be forgiven for saying the wrong thing, than for refusing to listen."

To set the record straight, I have failed at listening before, and still catch myself forgetting to listen at times. It's easy to assume that listening *automatically* occurs when the other person is talking. Just because one is speaking does not mean that the other is listening during communication.

In one of the most important relationships in my life, I forgot what it means to listen. One of my most memorable moments as a father came during a moment of a failure to listen. It is said that your "money or your mess becomes your message." If you are financially successful, then your financial success can become a platform for your message. It is also true that if you have made a mess of things and have learned from past mistakes, your ability to fail forward can be turned into a message of success—what to do and what not to do. With regards to listening, I have had success during times of Focused Listening, and failure when I failed to listen. A mess I created in the past has shaped my message on listening in the present.

My youngest son Casey was about seven years old, and the two of us had fallen into the habit of arguing when we communicated. Whether you are a parent or remember having this issue with your parents at one point, you can likely relate to this dynamic in communication. Whenever I would ask Casey to do something, he would argue with me or ignore the instruction—not uncommon for a seven-year-old boy. All kids, to some degree, have selective hearing. Arguing with daddy during conversations had become habitual for him, and frustrating for me. Instead of managing the situation as a parent should, I became a participant in the argument. This becomes counter-productive as the parent becomes as repetitious in their responses as the child does. Fortunately, we were able to break the pattern with a simple fix. What caused the pattern to be changed? Listening!

While standing in the doorway of the kitchen I was telling Casey to do his homework and he began to argue with me. Like always, we went back and forth a few times and then I began to raise my voice. I wasn't even realizing in the moment that I was perpetuating the situation with my repetitious response to his rebellion. All of a sudden Casey stopped arguing, dropped his head and began to cry. I turned toward him and asked him, "Why are you crying?" He said, "You never listen to me." Right then, I realized that I wasn't in the moment. I needed to engage Casey emotionally so I could intentionally listen to him and hear what he was feeling, not just saying.

Wanting him to know that I was now listening, I dropped to my knees so I could see him at eye level versus standing over him. I looked into his face, and with tears streaming down, asked with the softest tone I could muster, "What is it that you want daddy to know?" That moment forever changed my relationship with my youngest son for the better. I learned two important lessons that day about listening: 1) I never again treated communication with Casey as a one-way event and 2) I knew I had to manage myself better in the area of listening. That day, I vowed to become a Focused Listener. That day also ended a season of emotional disconnection between Casey and me and birthed a new, more intimate father-son relationship.

That is the power of Focused Listening. It can create connection, intimacy, and strengthen relationships. I also learned that hearing but not listening also carries with it the power to hinder connections or cause a break in relationships as I had experienced.

> "Connection occurs when people feel listened to, not talked to."

It is easy for us to become unintentionally tuned out or repetitious during communication and miss important signals during conversations. For the SalesMaker, this can lead quickly to lost dollars resulting from missed buying signals and lost sales. Listening is taken for granted too often when communication takes place, and it is assumed that listening is occurring when the opposite is true. Being talked to is not the same as being talked with just as hearing is not the same as listening.

There are a number of assumptions we make when we listen. Some of the following listening assumptions will likely resonate with you. As you read through them, get a picture in your mind of those you communicate with regularly and ask yourself, "Who comes to mind that falls into any of these categories?" If the answer is "you," then asking these questions of yourself may help you become more aware of your own listening behaviors.

Assumptions of Listening Can Cause Us to Miss the Mark

1. When one is talking, the other is listening. **Are you Tuned-in or Tuned-out?** Edgar Watson said it this way, "No man would listen to you talk if he didn't know it was his turn next."

2. When one is talking, the other is interested in what is being said. **Are you Curious or Disinterested?**

3. When one is talking, the other understands what is being communicated. **Are you Comprehending or Misunderstanding?**

4. When one is talking, the other is focused on listening and not on themself. **Are you Self-Focused or Others Focused?**

> "We can hear and not know. But when we listen, we learn and connect."

5. When one is talking, the other experiences the feeling of the one communicating. **Are you Empathetic or Unaffected?**

SalesMakers Develop a Trained Ear for Listening

SalesMakers develop trained ears in the art of listening. Effectiveness always starts with training and training starts with knowing what to listen for. By way of example, meet Dale Machado, affectionately known as "Megawatt Machado."

Dale has been a chief engineer for iHeart Radio for over three decades. You could say that Dale has a trained ear. When Dale listens, there are certain things he listens for. When Dale hears audio on the radio, he hears things that others may not perceive. That is because Dale has developed what's called an "engineer's ear" over the years. Dale hears differently because he is trained and tuned-in to what to listen for in his field of expertise.

For example, when Dale listens to the radio, he listens for static, interference, crispness of signal, strength of signal, and many other things. Dale is a focused listener and turns on his "engineers ear" when he is working. In the same way, the SalesMaker develops a "SalesMakers Eye & Ear" by learning what to focus on during communication with a customer. If you think listening in sales is only about what you hear, you would be wrong.

SalesMakers Convert Listening into Closing Currency

Regardless of the profession you work in or the industry you are selling for, becoming a student in the art of listening will equip you to discern the many ways in which communication occurs. The more you learn to pick up on all that is being communicated in one-to-one conversation, the more effective you will become at influencing others and moving them to decision.

SalesMakers listen with a bias toward converting conversations into closing moments. In the Law of the Listener, there are four areas in which SalesMakers practice to become highly effective in the art of listening.

1. SalesMakers develop trained eyes and ears to apprehend and comprehend all that is being communicated.

2. SalesMakers learn "what" to listen for by discovering the myriad of things that are being communicated in the C-Suite of Listening. More on this later.

3. SalesMakers learn "how" to listen by intentionally transforming themselves from casual listeners to focused listeners.

4. SalesMakers develop listening strengths so they can identify the ways in which communication occurs.

More Than Words: SalesMakers Develop a Trained Eye for Listening

If you are sensing that I am about to link listening to the eyes and not just the ears, you are correct. You may be wondering what listening has to do with the eyes. Much of communication is experienced through the eyes—not just the ears—and is felt with the heart. Even when words are not spoken, we can listen with our eyes. To listen means to hear, see, and experience more than words. With the ears we hear, but it is with the heart that we experience all the communication that is taking place around us.

A baby at birth can't understand words, yet it experiences life in its early stages through the five senses, which include touch, taste, smell, sight and sound. It can pick up on many forms of communication without the benefit of words, yet it ascertains and understands what is being communicated through a voice tone, a facial expression, gestures of affection, and touch.

> "Listening is more than what the eyes see and the ears hear. Listening is experiencing all that is being communicated in the moment."

To illustrate that "listening" transcends so much more than hearing, I want to share with you a letter written to a parent by a child that was passed onto me by my mother years ago. My mother was a pioneer in the day care business during the 1980's in the suburbs of Chicago where I grew up. When she came across the poem "When You Thought I Wasn't Looking," she shared it with me and taught me that children always see and hear more than we realize. If it is possible for a child to observe so much through the senses, how much more is there for a SalesMaker to learn and discern what the customer is experiencing while they communicate. The following poem is a good example of how some communication takes place without words.

When You Thought I Wasn't Looking

(Written by a child)

When you thought I wasn't looking, I saw you hang my first painting on the refrigerator, and I immediately wanted to paint another one. When you thought I wasn't looking, I saw you feed a stray cat, and I learned that it was good to be kind to animals. When you thought I wasn't looking, I saw you make my favorite cake for me, and I learned that the little things can be the special things in life. When you thought I wasn't looking, I heard you say a prayer and I knew there is a God

I could always talk to and I learned to trust God. When you thought I wasn't looking, I saw you make a meal and take it to a friend who was sick and I learned that we all have to help take care of each other. When you thought I wasn't looking, I saw you give of your time and money to help people who had nothing, and I learned that those who have something should give to those who don't. When you thought I wasn't looking, I saw how you handled your responsibilities, even when you didn't feel good, and I learned that I would have to be responsible when I grow up. When you thought I wasn't looking, I saw tears come from your eyes, and I learned that sometimes it's alright to cry. When you thought I wasn't looking, I saw that you cared, and I wanted to be everything that I could be. When you thought I wasn't looking, I learned most of life's lessons that I need to know to be a good and productive person when I grow up. When you thought I wasn't looking, I looked at you and wanted to say, 'Thanks for all the things I saw when you thought I wasn't looking.'

When we realize how much we are communicating non-verbally, we become much more cognizant of our actions and the ways in which we are impacting others. SalesMakers are always being observed by customers, supervisors, co-workers, and anyone who they influence or whom they have influence with. Actions can often speak louder than words. For this reason, a SalesMaker's lack of focused listening skills can either become a lid on their career potential or a release button that lifts the lid and raises their potential.

> "When we realize how much we are communicating non-verbally, we become much more cognizant of our actions and the ways in which we are impacting others."

SalesMakers Pick Up on Signals Being Broadcast During Communication

Can you hear the music? Your favorite song is playing somewhere on someone's radio. It's everywhere, all around you all the time. Country Music, Adult Contemporary Music, Top 40 Music, Hip Hop and Rap Music is always playing somewhere whether you notice it or not. And it's not just on the radio; it's available on your phone and other devices. Right now, you can tune in to thousands of LIVE radio stations on the iHeart App, personalized custom Artist Radio Stations, top podcasts and on-air personalities. If you are in your

> "The sounds and signals the SalesMaker needs to grow his or her income and influence, while strengthening their customer relationships are all around them, waiting to be received."

car, you can tune in to a local AM or FM station and hear your music or favorite DJ. Consider this: radio waves passing through the air have left an antenna somewhere and have entered a receiver close by. But, unless a receiver is turned on and tuned in to the right channel, the music is mute. In the same way, there are listening channels the SalesMaker tunes into and those channels of listening are found ahead in the SalesMakers C-Suite of Listening.

When the SalesMaker Turns Their Listening Receiver on, What Do They Listen For?

> "Everything has been said before, but since nobody listens we have to keep going back and beginning all over again." Andre Gide, Nobel Prize Winner for Literature

Did you know that it pays to listen? Seriously, there are people paid to just listen. They are professional listeners. As a SalesMaker that shouldn't surprise you. In a fast-paced business environment where the velocity of information exchange and communication is accelerating, the art of listening can often be missed. For this reason, there is a market that is willing to pay for listeners who "just want to be heard."

Mike Bechtle, author of *How to Communicate with Confidence*, related a story of a friend who was carrying out a class assignment when he ran a classified ad once that promised to "listen for one hour without interrupting for $50." Before he knew it, he had made $600. Listening isn't just a business. It's the business of the SalesMaker who wants to reach their relationship and revenue potential in sales. It doesn't just pay to listen. It can cost a seller who doesn't learn how to listen and what to listen for.

> "SalesMakers are paid to listen and penalized with lost business when they don't."

To be able to listen, learn, and discern what a customer is saying is an art form that is developed over time with training and intentional practice. Listening is big business because without it, dissatisfied customers can quickly become your mouthpiece for marketing their experience out in the community. Customers don't just communicate with their words, they communicate with their dollars. If a SalesMaker misses what a customer is saying, the financial consequences can add up quickly.

The SalesMakers C-Suite of Listening

The term "C-Suite" is often used in referring to executives with titles like CEO for Chief Executive Officer, CTO for Chief Technology Officer, or CFO for Chief Financial Officer. Did you know that some companies have a CLO or a Chief Listening Officer? The Chief Listening Officer is often an extension of a customer service department whose job is primarily to listen to what customers are saying about the company and its products on the web. They are paid to listen because what they are trained to hear is so valuable to the business.

> "Customers don't just communicate with their words, they communicate with their dollars. If a SalesMaker misses what a customer is saying, the financial consequences can add up quickly."

With the overload of information that professionals experience in today's hyper-connected business environment, it is too easy to miss important pieces of communication so this position has been added in recent years. With the data-drowning many people experience today, the lost art of listening has now become a newly-founded focus for some individuals and companies.

However, the SalesMaker doesn't have the luxury of delegating the responsibility of listening. SalesMakers are in many ways directly or indirectly in business for themselves and must have their own C-Suite of executive skills that act as agents to run their business. One of those executive skills is listening with a capital L.

There are seven things a SalesMaker listens for within the C-Suite of Listening, and each of them starts with the letter C. Each C in the Suite carries within it its own power to close the sale when it is identified and converted into closing momentum. Each of the C's is like currency that has the potential to be converted into closing momentum when heard. The SalesMakers C-Suite of listening includes the following seven C's. You may not hear all of the

> "I remind myself every morning, nothing I say will teach me anything. If I'm going to learn something, I'll have to do it by listening."
> Larry King

following C's when listening, but that doesn't mean they don't exist at one time or another when communication occurs.

> "SalesMakers listen with a bias toward moving people to decision."

1. SalesMakers listen for **CONTENT** during conversation that will assist them in serving the customer. With the intent of how to best serve their customer, the SalesMaker listens for insights from what is being said above and below the surface of communication. There is an undercurrent of content the SalesMaker must listen for in every exchange. This is the non-verbal part of communication.

2. SalesMakers listen for **CONNECTION** points during conversation that draw them and the customer closer together. Where connection exists, a sale is likely. Without connection, a sale becomes very unlikely. Connection grows into trust. Where there is trust, there is cooperation and a willingness to follow the SalesMaker where they may lead. A SalesMaker who can identify connection and cooperation during communication can discern if enough influence has been earned to advance the sale.

3. SalesMakers listen for **CONTEXT** during conversation, so they can gather historical background for "why" something is being said. If a SalesMaker can discover what a customer has bought before, they will know what they are likely to buy again. To know what a customer avoided in the past will tell the SalesMaker what they will also avoid again. Knowing the "what and why" of the past can provide the SalesMaker valuable insight into a customer's future behavior.

4. SalesMakers listen for an emotional **CHARGE** during conversation to alert them as to what a customer's hot buttons are. Body language and voice tone don't lie. When people communicate, they put emphasis both verbally and non-verbally on areas that are emotionally-charged for them. A SalesMaker trained and tuned-in to look for and listen to these charges gathers great insight into which direction to take a customer and which direction to avoid.

5. SalesMakers listen for the sound of **CONCERN** during conversation to identify a customer's pain points or problems. A concern shared outwardly is an unspoken assignment for the SalesMaker. If the SalesMaker can solve the customer's problem, remove their pain point, or address their concern, the reward is financial. A customer's concern is an open door to a financial opportunity. Unless a SalesMaker identifies a customer concern (objection or problem) and addresses it, a sale is unlikely.

6. SalesMakers listen with **CURIOSITY** so the customer feels that their story is of interest beyond the sale itself. Customers can tell whether a SalesMaker is pretending to listen or listening with curiosity and intent to serve. SalesMakers know that for a customer to get excited about their offering, they must first get excited about what the customer is excited about. They do this by making the customers priorities their priority and this starts with a genuine curiosity.

7. SalesMakers listen with an internal mental **COMPASS** that points the way to the close. A SalesMaker listens very differently than someone might in a casual conversation. A SalesMaker's compass listens for clues that might help them close the sale. Below is an example of how a SalesMaker may converse and listen during conversation vs. someone in an everyday casual conversation.

SALESMAKER CONVERSATION	EVERYDAY CONVERSATION
Ask relevant questions.	Make statements that relate conversationally.
Listen for what is important to the customer.	Listen for what is important to you.
Wait for opportunity to emerge before you act.	Assume and act before you listen.
Look for a closing moment to convert on.	Look and wait for your turn to speak.

Read the emotional mood & adjust accordingly.	Experience the mood of the moment and proceed.
Emotionally engage the customer while you listen.	Remain emotionally neutral while listening.
Act on what they've heard to advance the call.	Finish up the conversation and move on.

> "There is an advantage to listening to the customer. If we listen closely, the customer will always tell us how to sell to them if we know what to look and listen for."

When a SalesMaker Listens, How Do They Listen?

Focused Listening is practicing the art of intentional listening. The job of a SalesMaker is to listen. In fact, SalesMakers are students in the art of listening.

> "Most people think 'selling' is merely 'talking,' but the most effective salespeople know that listening is the most important part of their job." Roy Bartell

Did you ever imagine that your income potential would be equally dependent on how well you listen as how well you present, position, and close? Listening is one way a SalesMaker leads a customer with more than questions. Listening is an important tool in the tool belt of a well-equipped SalesMaker. For a SalesMaker who makes their living on commission, FOCUSED LISTENING is what makes closing possible. In the SalesMakers C-Suite of Listening, you learned "what" the SalesMaker listens for. Focused Listening is about "how" to listen to the customer so a SalesMaker can apprehend all that is being communicated, whether it is being communicated intentionally or not.

What does it mean to be a focused listener? Focus is the ability to ignore everything but the "one thing." Concentration is thinking deeply on one thing. To be a Focused Listener, the SalesMaker is thinking deeply about what they are feeling, hearing, and thinking while the customer communicates. Other forms of listening include tuning out what you are thinking and feeling and only focusing on what the other person is saying. A SalesMaker doesn't have that luxury. They must listen, learn, and leverage what they are hearing in order to create a closing moment.

Focused Listening, like concentration, is like a muscle. The more it is exercised, the stronger it gets. In the same way, the more a SalesMaker practices Focused Listening, the stronger they become at it. Focused Listening may not currently be a developed strength for you yet. However, with a little time and attention, you can add this silent sales skill to your selling tool belt. As your Focused Listening muscle grows, your relationships will deepen, your skill set will widen, and your earnings will expand. You will be able to convert and close more of the opportunities around you.

When new sellers enter the sales profession, they naturally become intent on listening closely in the early stages of their careers. They are eager to learn what to say to a customer. Tom Hopkins, who has trained over five

> "Listening is a silent sales skill of the SalesMaker."

million sales people, said this the best when he told me, "New sales people come into the business with so much enthusiasm, but just don't know what to say." But after learning what to say, it is not uncommon for many sellers to forget how to listen. Value is exchanged on both sides of the table when Focused Listening occurs. If listening is left behind, value is lost when all the emphasis is on what to say and how to present. It is in the "listening" that the SalesMaker learns how to close the sale. SalesMakers focused only on "magic words" to help them close the sale miss the muse that points the way to the sale—if they would only look and listen for her.

Focused Listening Does Not Remove Confusion from the Customers Communication

Focused Listening is a discipline that must be practiced. Without an intentional effort to exercise the listening muscle, it is too easy to fall back into the habit of hearing what is said but not really listening to all that is being communicated. Part of Focused Listening is intentionally tuning into what the customer wants. But there are challenges to discerning what a customer wants. For example,

- Customers do not always know what they want and this can be frustrating for a SalesMaker. Customers who are "just looking" are in discovery mode and may be unsure of what will satisfy their needs or desires. In the Law of Discovery, I will share some strategy for using questions to get to the heart of a customer's needs when they themselves may not even consciously know what they need.

- Customers don't always communicate what they want with clarity. Customers can be confusing and this confusion can sidetrack a sale.

- Customers don't always mean what they say. Customer can misdirect a SalesMaker as a negotiation tactic to see what they can get during a sales cycle. In the Law of the Close, you will learn how to confidently and competently isolate issues and bring negotiations to a positive ending for yourself and the customer.

"I know that you believe you understand what you think I said, but I'm not sure you realize that what you heard is not what I meant." Robert McCloskey

It is the SalesMaker's responsibility to bridge the gap between misunderstanding and understanding so what the customer is communicating is what the SalesMaker understands. Where gaps of understanding exist, communication is strained, connection is delayed, frustration takes place, and the sale can be in jeopardy.

However, practicing Focused Listening can close the gaps in communication.

Focused Listening Isn't Easy

Focused Listening requires a deployment of the SalesMakers emotional and mental energy in the moment. To be a focused listener, there are a few requirements the SalesMaker must adhere to:

1. **Patience:** The beginning and end of a conversation is based on the customer's pacing, not the SalesMaker's. This can be challenging because a SalesMaker is typically exercising conversational control with customers.

2. **Concentration:** The SalesMaker remains present in the moment by eliminating distractions.

3. **Attention:** The SalesMaker's energy is required in order to concentrate, interpret, and respond to what is being communicated by the customer.

4. **Reciprocation:** There is an unspoken expectation for the SalesMaker to speak and respond in a way to the customer that communicates that they were tracking with what was said and that the content was understood.

5. **Conversion:** Before a conversation ends, a SalesMaker has a financial responsibility to their company to convert what they have received during communication and convert it into a closed sale.

Benefits of Focused Listening: Focused Listening Unleashes a Creative Force During Communication

The SalesMaker who develops the skill of Focused Listening has the ability to reveal not-so-easily seen and sometimes hidden elements of communication. Listening is also the creator of many things—some visible, some not. Significant moments on sales calls are realized when we are listening, not when we are speaking. Significant moments in life are also missed when we are speaking and not listening.

> "Focused Listening creates an invisible current whereby emotional intelligence is activated between the SalesMaker and the customer."

Focused Listening has the potential to create a number of positive outcomes for the customer, a company, and a SalesMaker. These outcomes add value to the relationship in ways that transcend the transaction. In a sense, the SalesMaker possesses creational powers of conversation by exercising Focused Listening. Author Brenda Ueland said it this way, "Listening is a magnetic and strange thing, a creative force. When we really listen to people there is an alternating current, and this recharges us so that we never get tired of each other. We are constantly being re-created."

Some of the Creative Elements the Salesmaker Can Bring Forth in Communication Through Focused Listening Include...

1. **A Focused Energy.** Focused Listening creates an invisible current whereby emotion and intelligence are exchanged between the SalesMaker and the customer. This invisible energy can be felt and

witnessed during Focused Listening. The "focus" that exists during Focused Listening directs the energy to explore the depths in communication.

2. **Authority.** When a SalesMaker is focused on a customer and the customer knows that their words are being given weight, the customer in turn gives weight to the words of the SalesMaker. Meaningful moments are created as much in how a SalesMaker listens as in how they speak. These meaningful moments can increase the influence a SalesMaker has with a customer as they listen authentically in transparency with a desire to serve the customers best interests.

3. **Experience.** Think back to the most profound moments of your life. What was happening when you intercepted the "a-ha" that turned in to an "oh-yeah?" You were seeing, hearing, and experiencing something you will never forget. What were you doing that created that memorable experience? You were listening, but not just with your ears. You were listening with your eyes, your heart, your inside voice, and everything that makes you, you. Some of these memorable experiences happen upon us while others are created through Focused Listening. There is a magical sense that comes through our observational powers of listening that transcends what is being said in the moment. Focused Listening can bring this experience to the customer.

4. **Closing Moments.** Because of how the SalesMaker listens, SalesMakers see what others don't see, hear what others don't hear, and perceive what others might miss because they are focused on *all* that is being communicated. As I mentioned in the C-Suite of Listening, listening is a silent sales skill of the SalesMaker.

5. **Connection.** Connection isn't lost when we stop talking, but rather when we stop listening. When people feel they are being heard, that meaningful moment forges connection. Rarely do we experience uninterrupted listening. A patient listener who isn't waiting for their turn to speak—but is only focused on hearing and feeling what is being communicated—is rare to find. A SalesMaker who connects through listening is able to create an "in the moment" connection with the customer. Customers can pick up on when a SalesMaker is completely "present" with them and not mentally elsewhere. It is in these rarest of

moments that the SalesMaker stands out, and with their silence communicates, "I'm listening. Go on." There is another word that the letters from the word L I S T E N spell. Can you rearrange the letters and guess what other word can be made using the same letters? I'll give you a hint. The first letter is S and the last letter is T.

6. **Insight and intelligence on inside information.** When people feel listened to, trust is birthed and they are more willing to open up and express what is going on within them. Without trust, insight and intelligence is difficult to

> "Without trust, insight and intelligence are difficult to uncover but a listening ear is the key that unlocks the door to secret and sacred information."

uncover but a hearing ear is the key that unlocks the door to secret and sacred information. Getting a customer to open up beyond providing surface answers to probing questions is a skillset of a Master SalesMaker. Next to asking great questions, the ability to engage in Focused Listening is what creates the atmosphere where walls come down and transparency points the way to the sale.

7. **The Sale.** Through listening, the SalesMaker can make or lose the sale. Listening is required in every aspect of selling. Whether you are presenting, positioning, closing, trying to get an appointment, or answering an objection, how a SalesMaker listens, what they listen for, and what they hear when they listen can increase or reduce their chances for success.

8. **Attraction.** Some of the most important words a customer can hear include, "I want to hear your story," or, "Tell me why you feel that way." The power in that moment doesn't come from the words, but from the way in which the person who uttered them listens. SalesMakers who focus in the moment create a magnetic pull

> "Deep listening is miraculous for both listener and speaker. When someone receives us with open-hearted, non-judging, intensely interested listening, our spirits expand." Sue Patton Thoele

that draws others in emotionally. This strange magnetic pull isn't mystical at all; it's a natural force or energy that exists in the space between two people having a conversation when Focused Listening is occurring. Author Sue Patton Thoele said it this way, "Deep listening is miraculous for both listener and speaker. When someone receives us with open-hearted, non-judging, intensely interested listening, our spirits expand."

9. **Creates Relationships.** Without Focused Listening, developing long term relationships is impossible. Without intentional listening, a sale meant to be recurring may not happen more than once. A listening ear is like a water well, ready to receive water. However, relationships are not meant to be reservoirs. They are meant to be rivers in which their ebb and flow provides nourishment.

> **We** can all instinctively tell whether we are being listened to or not."

If the giver doesn't feel that their contribution is valued or received, they will not return to contribute to or draw from that well again. Instead, they will seek conversation where what they communicate is valued and returned. At best, a relationship will be on thin ice if one party feels they are going unheard for a long period of time. We see this play out not just in one-to-one personal relationships, but in business relationships and in all forms of communication where feedback is required.

10. **Expectations.** Expectations emerge when people are investing time, emotion, and energy into another. During communication, the customer develops spoken and unspoken expectations that are not unlike the expectations we experience in our everyday walk of life. These expectations are common to professional and personal relationships. Some of these expectations from the customer include:

- Customers want to be heard.

- Customers want to be understood.

- Customers want to feel like you care for them.

- Customers want to be encouraged by a seller's response.

- Customers want a seller to put their agenda aside and put them first.

- Customers want to know that what they are saying is important to the seller.

- Customers want the seller to avoid distraction and interruption when they are talking.

- Customers want to feel confident that the seller will take action on what they've heard.

- Customers want to know a seller will hold in confidence what is being said privately.

- Customers want to know a seller can put themselves in the customer's place and feel what they feel.

If you are starting to get a sense of the powerful influence you can wield through listening, I know you are not just reading this chapter, but listening to what it is communicating. Listening is a foundational skill for the highest performing SalesMakers. It is building upon this foundation that they become highly effective closers, presenters, negotiators, and income-earners. Becoming a Focused Listener will help you turn your influence into income and your customers into friends.

SalesMakers are Strategic in How They Approach Listening

To be a Focused Listener means to concentrate and think deeply on the person you are listening to and on what is being communicated. The **FOCUSED LISTENER** acronym will show you "how" a SalesMaker concentrates and what they concentrate on during Focused Listening. A SalesMaker who knows how to concentrate during Focused Listening will see more than others see, learn while others observe, and earn more than others earn because they

> "When you speak to my focus, you have my attention. When you care about what I care about, I begin to care about you and what you care about. When you speak to my focus, I am all ears."

are concentrating on what is essential with a customer during communication while eliminating distractions.

A SalesMaker is strategic in how they approach listening. They have a plan for how they listen, a process they follow, and a purpose for why they listen the way they do. Consider the following **FOCUSED LISTENER** acronym as a guideline.

Focus on the customer, eliminate distractions, and announce your intention to listen. You can announce your intention to listen with phrases like: I want to hear your story; where are you coming from; can you help me to understand; why you feel that way; tell me about…

Observe the customer's body language and adjust yours to signal you are ready to listen. Leaning forward, taking out a pen and note pad, and sitting quietly while you wait for the customer to begin speaking will signal your intent to pay attention with your pen and pad.

Confirm with the customer that you understand them with statements such as, "What I hear you saying is…," "It sounds like what you mean is…" "This feels to me like…" or "The word picture that came to mind for me while you were talking is…."

Uncover insight with investigative questions like, "What do you mean when you say…." "Why do you feel that way?" "And then what happened? "How would you like me to respond?" "What can I do to help this situation?"

Stop every now and then to summarize what you have heard, offer thoughtful input, and then listen some more. Begin to summarize with statements like, "What I've heard so far is…. Is this correct? Have I left anything out? Is there anything else that is important to you?"

Encourage the customer to continue opening up with statements like, "I'm still listening." "Keep going." "Please continue." "Yes, go on." "I'd like to hear more."

Deep dive into conversational areas the customer has put emphasis on or shown interest in. When an area has been identified that is important to the customer, use probing questions to go deeper and unlock the meaning behind the emotionally-charged area will uncover the significance to the customer.

Listen all the way through without interrupting the customer.

Intentionally tune in to verbal and non-verbal clues in order to pick up on what is being said and what is not being said. The SalesMaker will want to observe the customers' tone of voice, body language, speed of speech, eye contact, ability to concentrate or be distracted by the environment, and their willingness to continue or desire to wrap up the meeting.

Set aside your "inside world" so you can walk through theirs. By asking yourself, "How would I feel if I was in their shoes?" the SalesMaker can better empathize, relate, and connect with the customer.

Thank the customer for their willingness to tell you their story, share their concern, invest their time with you, unpack a delicate situation, and trust you with the problem. Demonstrating gratefulness to someone who has invested their time and emotion with you is always met with appreciation.

Enlarge the customer with your words of recognition or affirmation. Statements like, "You have a way with words," "I can see why you are successful," and "It's obvious why you are a leader in your industry," make others feel big on the inside. SalesMakers who encourage their customers will always connect deeper than sellers who don't.

Note what you have learned and verbalize the follow-up steps you will take to the customer.

Entertain internally gathered information and the emotional exchange you experienced from your time spent in Focused Listening with the customer. Reflecting after a meeting with a customer on what was communicated and how it was communicated can reveal insights.

Remind the customer in your next conversation of something they said previously and why you remembered it. Bringing a salient point to the surface from a former conversation will signal to the customer that you were focused on them during your time together and valued what they said by retaining what you heard.

Listening Strengths—Are You a Natural?

If you had to list your listening strengths right now, what would they be? What adjectives would you use to articulate the way in which you listen? If someone were to film you during communication, what do you think you would observe? How would others describe you as a listener? How you answer these questions can provide

> Everyone listens through the lens of their strength."

insight into what some of your natural gifts are in the area of listening. In *The 15 Invaluable Laws of Growth*, John Maxwell says, "In order to grow yourself, you must know yourself." This is also true for the SalesMaker who desires to grow in the art of Focused Listening.

Just as it is important to develop a trained ear in the art of listening, a SalesMaker also has natural gifts that can be developed over time. These gifts or natural bents can be developed into strengths through awareness and with diligent practice. Regardless of your talent set in the art of listening, you can improve your listening prowess by observing other great listeners, learning how to listen as they do, and by using your observational powers through trial and error to learn what works and what does not. Nobody is great at listening to everyone all the time, but everyone has the capacity to turn on their listening strengths when it becomes necessary to bring their talents to bear in a sales situation and when dollars are on the line.

Earlier in this chapter, you were introduced to Dale Machado, a Chief Engineer who works for iHeart Radio. Although Dale and I both have many years in the radio business, we hear differently because we listen differently. We don't just listen differently by accident, our listening skill sets are different, and our developed gifts in the listening arena have been molded and shaped over the years as a result of our training, background, and natural predispositions.

> Focused Listening will make you ready for the shifts in conversation; it makes you intuitive so you can predict what happens next."

Because my strengths are different than Dale's, I don't hear what Dale hears. In the same way, your listening strengths and natural tendencies will vary also. Up to this point, you have learned how a SalesMaker listens by becoming a Focused Listener and what they listen for in the C-Suite of Listening. Listening is a teachable skill. But there is another, highly effective way to learn the art of listening and that is through experience. By engaging a great listener in conversation, you will be able to experience the emotional and influential atmosphere that a great listener can create. Great listeners are closer than you may think. Ask yourself this question, "Who do I go to when I want to be heard?" By identifying the great listeners in your life, you will identify the atmosphere that listening creates and the conversational control a SalesMaker can create through listening.

Tuning In Transforms the Moment into a Magnetic Pull Between the SalesMaker and the Customer

There are many ways in which people tune into us, and how they tune in determines our experience with them. How a customer is listened to will determine how they are made to feel while with a SalesMaker. The word "feelings" may not be correct corporate speak when talking about a work environment or on a sales call, but they are both all around us all the time and speaking to us. These feelings dictate the emotional environment. A customer's mental process may participate in how they make decisions, but how they feel will ultimately drive the buying decision. For this reason, the SalesMaker is in the business of creating, managing, and directing feelings within a customer. Creating feelings within another isn't easy, but it is possible through questioning, positioning, and listening. Listening is one of the key elements that create the mood of the sale.

> "Listening is that strange magnetic pull that draws a customer toward a SalesMaker and keeps them coming back for more. That magnetic and mysterious pull is not magical at all—it is a trained ear turned on and leaning in to listen whenever the customer is speaking."

Experience the Power of Focused Listening For Yourself

By way of example, consider the emotional transaction that takes place while you are communicating and connecting with those closest to you. Imagine how those in your inner circle listen to you while you are speaking, and how it makes you feel. What is it that draws you toward them to share yourself with them?

Who do you go to when you are in need of a hearing ear? Maybe you go to a friend, a mentor, a pastor, a spouse, favorite customer or a colleague at work. One way we can improve our listening skills is by becoming aware of those around us who model great listening techniques by the feelings they engender within us while they listen to us. A SalesMaker can set out to intentionally improve their listening skills by tapping into the listening strengths within them and around them.

There are many ways in which people experience listening. In what ways do others capture your attention by how they listen? I would like to ask you to identify the best listeners in your life and what qualities make them great listeners. Here are a few people in my life that I consider great listeners. Maybe you know someone like them who will inspire or activate a similar listening strength within you.

Portrait of Effective Listeners
10 People in My Life Who are Great Listeners

The Empathizer: Kate is present with you in the moment and when she listens, she listens with quietness, with openness, and with the look of empathy on her face. When you are with Kate, you can feel her listening to you. I sense that Kate feels like I feel when she is listening to me, and she is the best listener I know—that is why I married her.

The Rememberer: Matt is someone I see every two years, and his SuperPower is listening. Matt is remarkable in the way he remembers what people said in years past, and in the way in which he reintroduces it into the present moment in a relevant way. If you are communicating with someone who reminds you or repeats something to you that you said "way back when," you know that your words were given weight when you said them and you were being listened to by a Matt.

The Deliverer: Marshall is a customer magnet. Customers are drawn to him because of how he makes his clients feel when they are under his care. Customers of Marshall's will never go to a competitor because he always services his customers in a way that makes them feel safe, looked after, and thought of. Marshall is "thinking in the best interests" of his clients even when he is not with them, and he demonstrates that by listening for clues during the conversation on how he can over-deliver, over-service, and surprise them. And then he does it, delivering over and over again.

The Reiterator: Rob likes to reiterate what you said to him by summarizing what he heard while you were speaking. Hearing your words repeated back to you makes you feel like you are being listened to. Listening is a strength of Rob's because he communicates in email and proposals in a way that confirms what you said—and you know that you were heard. When you are in a conversation and are feeling like you have been heard, you are likely being listened to by a Rob. Rob is a model for how customers want to be talked to after being listened to.

The Receiver: Sheila shows excitement when she listens by showing eagerness to hear what you are going to say next. In the way she sits, leans in, and embraces every word, Sheila's body language communicates that she is listening and wants to hear what you have to say. If you have been in a conversation with someone who makes you feel like they "value" what you are saying, you've encountered a Sheila.

"Listening is the chief duty of a friend." Unknown

The Fixer: Chuck listens with a problem solving lens. He is a gifted problem solver. Through his lens, he sits quietly and listens with his heart so you feel heard, but he lives to listen with the intent of helping you solve your dilemma after you've talked through your situation. If you feel empowered to move forward or break free after a conversation, you have likely been heard by a Chuck.

The Meditator: My dad was always a great listener. When he listened to you, he would listen silently and patiently while you processed your thoughts and feelings in his presence. By the way he listened, you felt like he had been there before. This made you want to return whenever you needed to sort something out or think something through with someone. If you experience someone thinking deeply about what you've said, and you are able to think slowly and deeply while they

"Sometimes people just want to be heard." Chuck Cotton, Market President, iHeart Radio

listen patiently, you've been listening to someone who has the heart of a parent.

The Identifier: Stu makes you feel like you are listened to because he says what you are feeling without you having to say it. When he does this, you know he has "walked a mile in your shoes," and you have instant connection because of how easily you relate to him. If you are conversing with someone who easily relates to what you are saying, you know you are talking to a Stu.

The Concentrator: James listens with great concentration and makes you feel like he is totally tuned into what you are communicating. You feel his deep level of interest in what you are saying by how his concentration is locked onto you while he listens. His follow-up questions show that he is not just tuned-in, but is interested in what you are interested in. When you feel a listener's focus locked into you, you are likely being interviewed on a sales call by a James.

The Learner: Jovi is a learner because he is a student when he listens. When he is with you, you can see his internal motor running. He leans in while listening and studies the environment so he can understand what is being communicated. Jovi follows up on the items he wrote down because they were not just heard, but learned. The SalesMaker is a learner and if you are on a sales call with someone who looks like they are learning while they listening, you are with a Jovi.

The Motivator: You can tell he is engaged with you in the moment because he adds value to you in the area of your focus when he listens. If you feel motivated after being listened to, you've been heard by a Scott. Listening for someone's purpose, passion, or pursuit is my natural bent when I am in a conversation. My receiver is tuned in to hear from the other person's perspective and then help them connect the dots from where they are to where they want to be. If you find yourself being taken to higher ground, you are with a motivator.

You may have some of the listening strengths from those listed above, as well as others not listed. You may also know of other listening strengths you've seen modeled in others around you. When you are listened to, you can feel it. When you are with a Focused Listener, there is no mistaking it.

The SalesMaker's C-Suite of Listening has pointed out what to listen for and why a SalesMaker listens differently than others. The FOCUSED LISTENING acronym has shown you how to listen, and going through the exercise for identifying the great listeners in your life has modeled for you what others can experience when you develop your listening strengths. Becoming a great listener can be approached methodically, intellectually, and professionally but it must ultimately be embraced emotionally for a SalesMaker to become effective in utilizing all the listening tools. Master listeners become Master SalesMakers because they are able to convert listening moments into closing opportunities that connect the customer to commitment. The better you become at Focused Listening, the more customers will want to be around you and follow where you lead. What is the relationship requirement for a SalesMaker to reach their potential in communication, connection, and closing? Listening! Value is exchanged on both sides of a conversation when Focused Listening occurs. That's the Law of the Listener.

> "Insights watered turn into wisdom, but insights ignored diminish and disappear."

It's time to turn on the listening learner within you and transform yourself into the Focused Listener you are capable of becoming. In the following C.I.A. section, you will hear other SalesMaker insights from the Law of Listening. Write down your own along with an action plan and remember to return to that which resonated with you as you read The Law of Listening.

C.I.A. CONTRIBUTORS

The LAW OF THE LISTENER

Joe Parker, Amazon

Rachel Nagata, iHeart Media

Mark Hovland, New Hope Counseling Centers

My name is **Joe Parker** with **Amazon** and I have been in information technology and cyber security for 27 years. I attribute my success to a systematic approach, persistence, and a constant love of learning. I love what I do because it challenges both my technical abilities and my interpersonal skills. Here is a summary of my observations, ideas, insights, or sales nuggets that connected with me as I read.

1. Hearing is not the same as listening. This point was made clear to me by watching my wife struggle with hearing loss. She hears but lacks the ability to understand due to a high frequency loss. She overcomes this by using all of her senses to listen, and totally concentrates on the person who is talking. This has made her a great listener even with her hearing loss.

2. I never thought that listening was so closely tied to my income and career potential. As I have advanced in my personal career my technical skills have become less valuable. My ability to listen, persuade, and communicate with others has become one of my most marketable skills.

3. Failing to listen to all that is being communicated can cost me the sale and my credibility. When people notice I'm not fully listening, they can feel like I don't really care about them. On the other hand, intentionally listening to all that the customer is communicating will help me to pick up on clues that may help me close the sale.

4. If I can tell when someone is not listening to what I am saying, then my customer can too. I need to be intentional about staying tuned-in. My wife is amazing at this. She can tell if I'm not totally focused on what she is saying—even if we are on the phone.

5. I found the 15 tools in the Focused Listening Acronym to be thought-provoking and a very systematic way of improving my listening skills.

6. Becoming a Master listener is an ongoing practice, not a one-time skill to perfect and then forget.

7. The SalesMaker's C-Suite of Listening really connected with me. I will write the 7 C's on a 3x5 card and carry it with me during meetings. It will remind me to listen for content, connection, context, the emotional charge in a conversation, and concerns, as well as listen with curiosity and set my mental compass to pick up clues to help me close the sale.

My name is **Rachel Nagata** and I have been in sales with **iHeart Media** for 7 years. I attribute my success to maintaining a spirit of curiosity and my love for connecting with customers. Below you will find a list of great insights I picked up on and actions I have committed to taking in order to become better at what I do.

1. "SalesMakers who practice and pursue improved performance in the art of listening are in a position to hear what competitors don't hear, see opportunity competitors don't see, and capitalize on closing moments others might miss." My goal is to separate myself from the competition; to stand out from the crowd. Going the extra mile by incorporating Focused Listening will help me connect with my customers in an emotional, intellectual and an even more professional manner.

2. "SalesMakers listen to CONTENT during conversations that will assist them in serving the customer. With the intent of how best to serve their customer, the SalesMaker listens for insights from what is being said above and below the surface of communication." Before each meeting with a client, I will set aside my agenda so I can hear all they are communicating about theirs.

3. "There is an advantage to listening to the customer. If we listen closely, the customer will always tell us how to sell them, if we know what to look and listen for." My sales intuition needs to kick in to full gear here but what will fuel it is Focused Listening. I will utilize the strategy to become a Focused Listener.

4. "I know you believe you understand what you think I said, but I'm not sure you realize that what you heard is not what I meant." – Robert McCloskey. Focused listening gives you the full picture of what the customer is communicating. Don't miss what the customer is trying intentionally or unintentionally communicate.

5. "When a SalesMaker is focused on a customer and the customer knows that their words are being given weight, the customer in turn gives weight to the words of the SalesMaker." Validation and affirmation feel good. By listening well to my customers, I am giving weight and affirmation to what they are saying.

6. "A listening ear is like a water well, ready to receive water. However, relationships are not meant to be reservoirs. They are meant to be rivers in which their ebb and flow provides nourishment." Don't allow the relationship with the customer to get stale. With each encounter, we should walk away learning something new about the customer and leaving them with something of value. I will commit to walking away from each meeting with ONE new thing I learned from the customer. I will put that in my mental customer vault, and save it for when I need to advance the sale.

My name is **Mark Hovland** and I have spent a career listening as a Professional Therapist. I am the Founder and Director with **New Hope Counseling Center** where I practice listening for a living and also teach it at the college level. Being an effective listener is critical to success in my profession. There were more than a few similarities between the strengths of a successful SalesMaker and professionals in my line of work that get paid to listen for a living. Below you will find a list of my observations.

1. Your stories through the chapter helped to connect my heart and mind to the material. In the field of psychotherapy, study after study shows the most important part of the change process is the quality of the relationship between the therapist and the client (or counselee). I can see that the relationship a SalesMaker has with a client is what will most impact change in purchasing habits.

2. In the therapy world, the importance of being fully present with your client in the here and now is extremely important in developing a strong therapeutic alliance. This same strategy is found in the Law of Listening. Well done.

3. The explanation of the difference between hearing and listening is very similar to how Norman Wright's book called *Crisis Counseling* explains it. The same listening skills that are used to make a sale are used to help a client that is suicidal or a client who has just gone through a divorce. I am reminded to listen for all that is being communicated, not just what is being said.

4. When I am teaching college courses, I have students take time to review pictures of people that reveal non-verbal communication. We do this exercise so students can learn to pick up on all forms of communication. This can be helpful to grow in awareness.

Put the 7 Empowering Laws of the SalesMaker to Work And Convert your Insights into Income

Now that you've completed the Law of the Listener, it is time to convert learning into earning. The first step is to return to the sections of this chapter that you highlighted, underlined, or made notes from. Of the key points that you connected with, pick three that resonate the most with you. Following the simple formula for transformation found in the C.I.A. process in the introduction (Connection, Insight, Action), identify and write down that which resonated with you. Then, identify the insights you gathered, and finally, decide how you might put them into action. Reading, doing, believing in, and incorporating three sales insights into your daily routine will create a transformative impact on your sales volume and sales commissions.

Here is how I will convert my insights into income:

C = Connection: As I read, the following content, principle, or idea that connected with me was:

_____

_____

I = Insight: As I reflect, the idea or insight I received is:

_____

_____

A = Action: The action I will take to convert my insight into income will be to:

_____

_____

CHAPTER 3

THE LAW OF RELATIONSHIP

The SalesMaker clears the bar of customer expectation with room to spare, setting themselves and the company up for renewal and referral business.

There is something wrong with the disproportionate emphasis put on sales versus service. For example, if you call a cable or car insurance company, the first automated prompt you may receive may say, "For new service press 1, or for service to your existing account press 2." If you press 1, a live person picks up the phone and quickly assists you in taking your new business order. If you press 2 on the telephone menu, you are guaranteed more questions followed by longer waits, sometimes wait times up to an hour. There is something wrong in how a company or SalesMaker might value a new customer acquisition over a current customer's business.

Relationship is a compound word created with the words RELATION and SHIP. In the 14th century, relation meant "connection," as in one who is connected to a relative or close family member. It also meant "correspondence," to tell or communicate something. The word "ship," of course, is a vessel that transports valuable cargo or persons

"Closing skills may determine the first sale, but good service is the currency that secures future sales."

from one port to another. When a SalesMaker embarks on a new relationship, they set sail in order to create a connection with a customer whom they value. That value becomes the currency that forms the relationship.

To be "in relationship" means to be connected to someone by something of value. SalesMakers enter relationships by firmly establishing a mutual understanding of what the customer values, and then delivering value. As a result, the customer feels valued and willingly returns for repeat purchases. They also recommend the SalesMaker and their company to other potential customers by sharing their positive experiences.

An experience expressed to others is considered "word of mouth advertising." It's the best way to grow return sales and referrals. In this way, SalesMakers create reputations for both themselves as people others want to do business with, and their company as a place customers are drawn to. The relationship that exists between a customer, a company, and the SalesMaker is founded on trust that must be stewarded well if it is to continue. The degree to which a customer feels their business is valued will determine whether or not they return with their business and tell others to do the same. The SalesMaker demonstrates a customer's value to them in the way they service the account.

> "Relationship selling is about renewal and referral business. Dollars follow relationship. It's that simple."

Good Service Closes More Sales than Skilled Closers

When I was a young boy, my father would take me down to the car dealership with him on Saturday mornings. It was a thrill to be able to roam a car lot and sit in all the cars. My dad worked in the service department, and they had a saying, "The front end makes the first sale. The back end makes the next sale." This meant that a salesperson might sell a customer the first car, but it would take a series of good service experiences to sell the next car. If the service was good, the relationship would continue and grow into another sale. If the service was poor, the relationship was strained and the chances for a referral or repeat business reduced. In some cases, poor service led to an end to the relationship, permanently. This isn't only true for the auto business, but most businesses. Good service has the potential to close more sales than a skilled closer can. A SalesMaker may make the first sale, but the quality of service will decide future sales.

> "The quality of service from the first sale is what closes or sinks the second sale."

Relationships are Birthed Out of Reputation

Creating customer buying relationships that repeat and generate referrals to other customers has never been more important, both for individual SalesMakers and their companies. Consumers do not just have unlimited options to choose from, they have a plethora of reviews telling them if they should reward a company with business, or reject them because of what others are saying about them. Reputation matters more than ever before. Tales of a customer's service experience can travel at the speed of light and multiply exponentially as it morphs into a reputation that reproduces or eliminates business for a company or its SalesMaker.

The Rules Have Changed

If you touch any aspect of service in your company, you can be classified as a SalesMaker. SalesMakers are no longer just the selling and closing arm of an organization. If you are in touch with customers in any way, shape or form, you are a SalesMaker. How you handle each customer's business will influence whether there is a repeat order, a referral, or a review online that helps or hurts your company's reputation.

SalesMakers today do not have traditional sales titles, or only work in a sales capacity. SalesMakers are entrepreneurs, marketing directors, social media managers, review experts, service specialists, help lines, accounting personnel, receptionists or greeters, and the list goes on. For this reason, while most of this chapter will focus on the role of a SalesMaker in one-on-one relationships with customers, I will also reference how the experience of service can become repeat business, reduces revenues, or eliminates relationships altogether.

Don't Become Extinct

To some degree, it is everyone's responsibility to sell or take care of the customers. The lines between who sells and who services are more blurred than ever before. SalesMakers are required to service and service specialists are required to sell. Out of necessity, your skillset in the sales and service arena must expand if you are to remain competitive and avoid extinction in your career and industry. The world of selling and servicing has changed because the customer, environment, and service expectations have changed! What has not changed is the common link that still binds the customer, a company, and a SalesMaker together. That common link is relationship.

Relationship selling is about earning the right to repeat and referral business. Dollars follow relationships. It's that simple. The Law of Relationship will help you to create repeat and referral business while avoiding losing business. There are service behaviors that close business while others lead to lost business. Missing the bar of customer expectation will drive customers to seek out a competitor to meet their needs.

The Law of Relationship is not a "Pollyanna" approach to providing customer service where SalesMakers only see service in a positive light. Instead, it demonstrates how all service behaviors can be leveraged to grow revenues, commissions, and relationship equity in a SalesMaker's Service Account. In this law you will learn service behaviors that win and lose business. You will hear directly from customers who control millions of dollars a year in business and their very direct statements about what wins and loses business. I will also share a few service experiences that have made me a fan of some companies but leery of others.

A customer's service experience with a SalesMaker is expressed by how a customer "feels" about the SalesMaker, their company, and the product during and after the purchasing experience. The customer's feelings are intrinsically linked with whom they invest their dollars. With every purchase they are voting with their wallets based on how they feel toward their SalesMakers and the service they are experiencing.

Every purchasing decision is either the beginning or the continuation of a relationship with a SalesMaker or company. Having a customer switch vendors can mean the end of a relationship. But it's not all bad news when a relationship ends—if you are the SalesMaker who benefits from a competitor's failure. A service failure by a competitor that is turned into a new piece of business for a SalesMaker is a win.

The number one reason customers leave a SalesMaker is because they become uncomfortable with how their business is being handled or uncomfortable with the person handling their business. For example, a customer who once felt courted may now feel ignored. Or, a customer who has communicated a service problem multiple times *without resolution* is no longer willing to wait for a solution.

In both examples, the customer has become uncomfortable in the relationship. When a SalesMaker is servicing a customer, they are dealing with dollars, and dollars are like live ammo. If you don't handle it correctly, your mistake can lead to significant loss. How a customer is handled directly impacts whether dollars go to a SalesMaker or one of their competitors. Service mistakes cost companies money, and commissions to their sales teams.

While all companies need to provide good customer service to survive and thrive, there is a difference between the types of service a customer expects as a one-time purchaser versus a customer buying from a SalesMaker repeatedly. Where one may expect a short-term relationship to facilitate a transaction, the other may require the development of a long-term partnership for repeat transactions.

The Law of Relationship will help the SalesMaker level up in what I like to call "The Three R's of Servicing Success" that lead to higher sales. These are: Relationships, Renewals, & Referrals. There are five areas that will help the SalesMaker maximize their repeat and referral business from the customer relationships they form. These include:

Relationship Research:	The SalesMaker will learn first-hand what customers say they want in service along with what wins and loses business.
Relationship Expectations:	The SalesMaker will learn what expectations the customer has and the unwritten contract that is entered into once the sale is closed.
Relationship Equity:	The SalesMaker will learn how deposits and withdrawals are made in the SalesMaker's Service Account, and how these lead to more business, less business, or no business at all.
Relationship Branding:	The SalesMaker will learn how their personal brand is created in the marketplace and how their reputation influences a customer's level of trust, behavior, and buying habits.
Relationship Insights:	The SalesMaker will learn how to strengthen customer relationships beyond the sale by discovering what makes a customer draw toward them or retreat from them.

Customers ask themselves three questions when evaluating the likelihood of entering into or returning to a relationship with a SalesMaker. They are…

1. Can the SalesMaker be trusted with my business?

2. Will they be there for me through and after the sale?

3. Do I sense a relational connection or a transactional relationship developing?

These three questions are either consciously or unconsciously asked by customers. They have all answered them yes or no with regards to SalesMakers they have done business with in their past. The Tale of the Lost Customer illustrates a relationship that starts off well with a SalesMaker in pursuit, but finishes poorly due to the decay of the relationship. Taking a customer for granted will drive them away. For this reason, it is important for the SalesMaker to remember that the close isn't the end of the sale, but the beginning of the next step in the service experience.

The Tale of the Lost Customer

I am the customer you are calling on.
I am the customer you called for 8 months before I agreed to see you.
I am the customer you asked for business, and I gave it to you.
I am the customer you recommended what to buy, and I bought it.
I am the customer who was asked how you could improve, and I told you.
I am the customer who when I spoke, you listened intently.

And now…

I am the customer who calls you and it takes two days for you to get back to me.
I am the customer whose order was wrong and you blamed the people in another department.
I am the customer who was waiting to meet with you and you showed up an hour late.
I am the customer you cc'd when you emailed another to complain about my account.

I am the customer who believed you when you said you'd be there to service my account.

I am the customer who gave you another chance when you asked.

And I am the customer who is now shopping for another to handle my account.

I am the customer you are calling on again.

The Tale of the Lost Customer is all too often told by customers who were once pursued, but now feel taken for granted. A SalesMaker with a "sell it and forget it" versus a "sell it and service it" mentality will find themselves facing unnecessary attrition in their book of business. It is not sufficient for a SalesMaker to be great at winning customers over in the beginning stages of a relationship only to lose them in the later stages because they didn't follow through. Great SalesMakers know how to win customers and keep customers.

Customers are Cutting the Cord

Customers are cutting the relationship cord and most companies don't even know why they are leaving. According to the U.S. Office of Consumer Affairs, "For every unsatisfied customer who complains, there are 26 other unhappy customers who say nothing. Of those 26, 24 won't come back." This is the horror story of lost revenue for a company and lost commission for a seller. Consider the following outcomes of this statistic.

1. Companies and commissioned sellers may not be aware they are sending customers away based on the experience the customer is having.

2. Over 90% of unhappy customers won't make the time or put forth the effort to complain, but instead just go in search of a new company or SalesMaker.

3. Insight into a customer's psyche.

Customers would rather begin a new relationship than invest the time and energy to repair an existing relationship. Can you blame them? What customer wants to face confrontation, address conflict, or counsel a company or SalesMaker on how to improve their processes when the quickest fix is simply a phone call or Google search away? Customers don't have to go very far to get their needs met— unless you or your company represents a truly one-of-a-kind product.

Wishing to avoid a confrontation, it is often more desirable for a customer to shop for a new SalesMaker than confront the one with whom they are unhappy. When one SalesMaker drops the ball, another is always within reach ready to pick it up and take over the business. Business Consultant Kate Zabriskie said it this way, "Although your customers won't love you if you give bad service, your competitors will."

Attrition is Enemy #1

Without customers, a company can't survive. If a company loses more customers than it is gaining, it will eventually go out of business. According to New Voice Media, an estimated $41 billion is lost by U.S. companies each year due to poor customer service. For this reason, billions are spent by companies every year in customer acquisition. New business is the life line for growth. Without a robust customer acquisition program, a company in a competitive marketplace will struggle to survive. Companies grow, die, or tread water, but treading water in a competitive market will put them one step away from decline. Many companies are great at teaching sales strategies, and closing skills to win business, but sometimes neglect the skill of keeping and reselling existing clients.

> "Poor service is the #1 reason why American companies lose business. It often costs a company five to ten times more in time and effort to attract new customers as it does to keep the ones they currently have." Voice Magazine

Early in my career, I became aware of the impact attrition can have on a company's growth and momentum. Attrition of tier one employee talent and customers can be a company's biggest threat. While employees are a company's most appreciable asset, a returning customer is a company's most important.

I realized that attrition of current customers was Enemy Number One when managing a sales force dependent on recurring, renewal, and referral business. It occurred to me that if we could just hang on to the customers we had and grow them, we wouldn't need to expend as much time and energy in new customer acquisition mode. Don't misunderstand. There are controllable and uncontrollable factors that determine whether a customer renews and becomes an account that regenerates consistently, or calls it quits and enters the attrition pool.

My focus was to identify the controllable factors so I could minimize the number of unhappy customers who might go away and never tell anyone. More often than not, it is the invisible service mistakes a company or SalesMaker makes that cause a customer to shop elsewhere. These blind spots in service show up in lost income for the SalesMaker, lost revenue for the company, and one more lost customer. The worst part of this scenario is that the customer disappears without telling the company why or gives

> "While employees are a company's most appreciable asset, a returning customer is a company's most important."

them a less than candid answer as to why they are taking their business elsewhere because they want to avoid what they believe would be a confrontation.

Service Gaps can Sink the Sale

In the movie Rocky I, Rocky Balboa turns to his soon to be wife Adrian and says, "You got gaps. I got gaps. We all got gaps." Rocky is referring to qualities a person may lack. These missing qualities show up in the form of gaps. A gap is an empty space or a distance between two points.

In sales, gaps in service by a SalesMaker will soon be filled by the competition, if not addressed. A SalesMaker's ability to develop self-awareness is the first step to closing those gaps. Every SalesMaker has a degree of sales and service deficiencies they need to become aware of if they are to grow in their customer relationships and commissions. A characteristic of these

> "Service isn't sexy like sales, but it's where the big money is."

gaps is that they can also be blind spots. Not addressing these service deficiencies can lead to lost business for the company and lost commissions for the seller.

SalesMakers often want to prioritize the next sale or sales conversation ahead of the current service experience for the sale that has just been made. Why? Because service isn't sexy, but it is where the big money is! Closing skills may determine the first sale, but good service is the currency that secures future sales. The SalesMaker must be aware of the following gaps:

The Service Gap:	The customer's opinion of the service they experience often differs from the seller's perception of the service they render.
The Value Gap:	The customer assigns value to a seller and a company based on the quality of products, and service they receive. Sellers and companies assign value to customer relationships based on the volume of dollars and frequency with which dollars are spent.
The Relationship Gap:	In personal relationships, we are judged by what we say first and what we do later. In business relationships, we are judged by what we deliver based on the spoken and unspoken promises of the product and person who sold the customer.

Closing the Gaps

> 82% of consumers quit doing business with a company because of a bad customer experience." Customer Experience Impact Report 2010

The Law of Connection says that a "SalesMaker connects emotionally before communicating financially." Once a connection is made and a close takes place, the amount and type of service provided will either prevent gaps from appearing, close the gaps that exist or widen them. The quality of service rendered will strengthen or weaken the relationship that is being formed. This happens because service is the great exaggerator in a relationship. The quality of service rendered in the relationship either takes the relationship equity farther in the right direction or faster in the wrong direction. And the service equity a SalesMaker creates, whether positive or negative, compounds over time. Just as consistently meeting and exceeding a customer's expectations eliminates service gaps, consistently missing the bar of expectation will widen the service gaps. The stronger the service rendered, the stronger the relationship. Repeat and referral business flow when the gaps of service are closed.

> Closing skills may close the first sale, but good service is the currency that closes future sales."

A Blind Spot in Service Causes Customers
to Cancel Future Business

A service blind spot can kill off your customers.

For a flight from Honolulu to Phoenix, my plane was set to depart in the early evening on a Friday. Four hours prior to departure, I received a notice from the airline that my flight would be delayed. It was then set to depart no later than 10pm. A couple of hours later, I was told it would now depart at 11pm, and shortly thereafter I was told that there were not enough seats on the 11pm flight. I was given a choice to "take a flight out the next morning or...." That was the end of the sentence. The customer service representative told me over the phone that my options were very limited if I wanted to go to Phoenix. The challenge I faced was that my trip was only a 72-hour trip and the airline debacle I was facing had already cost me one day. I chose to depart the next morning and lose the day. I had to get to Phoenix.

On the return flight, I had to connect through Los Angeles because there were no direct flights available. Faced with sitting in the airport for hours, I visited the airline lounge and asked if I could buy a day pass. I told the person behind the counter how I had been inconvenienced. I was very polite while confident that I was minutes away from relaxing in the comfort of the airline lounge versus waiting for three hours at the gate. I'll never forget the airline representative's response after hearing my story. He said, "We are not a distress lounge." Wow! No empathy. No concern. No care for the disappointing service experience I had, and he appeared to be completely unaware of the compounding impact of his comment. I am also sure he was unaware of the repeat business he just lost for the airline. You could say that in an instant, and with one response, this was the straw that broke the camel's back for me.

The irony in this story is that the airline considered me a tier one customer. I had a higher than average flying status with them. With this status, they regularly sent me comment cards that would allow me to fill in my thoughts of appreciation for an employee so I could hand them to one whose service had impressed me. I was about to become one of the lost customers—the 90% that go away without a trace. Whether the airline employee was indifferent or ignorant didn't matter after such a comment. While the front office was trying to win my business in an "even-steven" priced industry, the back end was about to lose my loyalty. That's called a corporate blind spot, and it can happen to individual SalesMakers too.

If we could see ourselves as SalesMakers through the eyes of our customers, what would we see? What would our customers say about us? If a customer felt comfortable to speak candidly about their experience with us, how would they compare and contrast us with our competition?

If we could know in advance the impact we as SalesMakers have on the customers we aim to please, how valuable would that intelligence be? Service intelligence includes knowing what wins and loses business and then being able to apply that knowledge to keep and grow business. Gathering service intelligence is extremely valuable, but can be a tricky business because people get uncomfortable when you ask them what they don't like about the service provided by you, your team, or your company.

Service Secrets that Close More Sales (As Told by Decision Makers)

The first time I attempted to outline a sales course on what wins and loses business with customer service, I realized that my information would be incomplete if I limited it to only my own experience. If I was going to learn what wins and loses business on a bigger scale, I would have to go to the source—the customers themselves!

> 78% of customers say that competence is what makes for a happy customer experience; 38% say it is from a customized service approach." The Cost of Poor Customer Service by Genesys Global Survey

So, I began to make calls on customers for the express purpose of uncovering why they buy what they buy; why they buy from whom they buy; and what wins and loses business from their perspective. I called this research study on customer service, "Through the Eyes of the Customer." I asked both big and small customers for their candid feedback in a sincere and open-ended way. I listened closely for what they were saying and not saying. Some of the questions I asked included:

- What does it mean to go the extra mile?

- What do the worst service providers do?

- Who do you not like to work with and why?

- What do the best service providers do for you?

- Who do you call first when you have a need, and why?

- What in your opinion is good vs. bad customer service?

- Who are your favorite account representatives and why?

- What are your deal breakers when doing business with a sales representative?

- Without mentioning names, can you give me an example of someone you won't do business with and why?

What surprised me was that when I asked these questions, and many more like them, the customers were more than eager to open up and share their service experiences. Every customer had stories to tell, both good and bad. Some shared a service story that sounded like a love affair, while others had a bone to pick. Each customer had a set of service preferences unique to them.

> "Great service is the secret sauce that closes repeat sales and generates referral business."

I could tell from listening to the customers that if a SalesMaker could identify these service preferences for each one, they would hold the key to higher sales. I also learned that while service preferences of one customer may be different than another, they all shared a commonality. Every customer has a set of service hot buttons that when hit or missed could win or lose business in an instant for a SalesMaker. Knowing a customer's service priorities was the secret to new and repeat sales. These secrets became a service currency that could close the sale.

Here are seven secrets of service that I discovered when asking customers about their service story. It transformed the way I viewed customer service. It may do the same for you after you have similar conversations with your customers.

1. When customers are asked about their service experience, the longer the conversation goes the more open they get about what they hate and love about the service they experience from sellers.

2. The service of the SalesMaker is the driving factor for how a customer feels about a company—not its price, product, or other items. The SalesMaker is the front line that sets the tone for the relationship.

3. There exists a significant gap between what a SalesMaker perceives as good service and what the customer perceives the service experience to be. This gap is the result of a blind spot that can be avoided by asking the customer about their service preferences.

4. SalesMakers may be unaware of the impact their service behavior has on business. In many cases, the SalesMaker is not cognizant of the customer's impression of them or the service behaviors that form the customer's opinion of them.

5. There is a disconnect between the level of service a SalesMaker thinks they are providing and what the customer is actually experiencing. This disconnect is the result of a SalesMaker judging themselves on their intentions, while a customer judges them based on their actions.

6. [80% of companies say they deliver "superior" customer service. 8% of people think these same companies deliver "superior" customer service. Source: "Customer Service Hell" by Brad Tuttle, Time, 2011]

7. Every company and SalesMaker has a reputation based on the service a customer has experienced in the past. This reputation drives a customer to renew their business or retreat.

8. Customers gravitate towards SalesMakers they can count on and avoid those they can't.

After spending countless hours with customers hearing about the good, the bad, and the ugly, I concluded that the difference between the best and worst service providers resided in the SalesMakers ability to uncover a customer's spoken and unspoken needs, identify and meet expectations after the sale, and adapt their sales and service behavior to make and keep the customer consistently happy.

In sales, an unhappy customer can lead to a loss of revenue and lost commissions. But service failure can be redeemed and converted into higher revenues. Bill Gates, Co-founder of Microsoft said it this way, "Your most unhappy customers are your greatest source of learning." Mistakes cost money but they can also make the SalesMaker more money if they know how to convert them.

The best way to avoid trouble and keep a customer happy is to get a clear picture of how a customer wants their business to be handled. Hearing directly from a customer what service behaviors they value, and which behaviors irritate them, will bring clarity to a SalesMaker with respect to what wins and loses business. By becoming aware of a customer's service priorities and your personal blind spots when servicing them, you will be better equipped to shore up weaknesses and leverage strengths.

Sam Walton, Founder of Walmart, understood how important it was to make a customer happy when he said, "There is only one boss: the customer. And he can fire everybody in the company from the chairman on down, simply by spending his money somewhere else."

Identifying Relationship Expectations

If the following customer quotes seem a little sharp, it's because they are. What follows are direct statements from customers speaking about the service priorities they expect their sellers to provide on their accounts. Only the names have been changed.

Twelve Transforming Truths About What Moves Money

1. "My confidence goes up when I know my sales rep is walking my order through at the company level." – Confident Carrie

2. "Business owners are busier than ever doing multiple jobs these days. The biggest time wasted is scheduling an appointment without an agenda." – Prepared Peter

3. "Deliver what you say you're going to deliver. Follow through and don't make us have to chase you." – Follow-through Fred

4. "I like sales reps who ask me about my business. I like sales reps who show me how to get most out of their company, their inventory, and their special packages." – Peter Partner

5. "If you are not a vendor I traditionally buy from, have something beneficial for my business. That's your hook to get in the door." – Oscar Opportunity

6. "Be gracious if you lose out on business. Don't get angry, pout, argue, or bring your sales manager by to hear the rational again. When you lose, lose graciously and learn from your mistakes." – Grow-Up Gary

7. "If you can't learn to follow instructions, please get off my account. Nothing frustrates me more than having to chase a sales rep down to get what I need because they didn't do it right the first time." – Frustrated Phyllis

8. "If you don't call on me consistently, you're losing my attention. I have known some sales reps who have gotten business and then don't communicate with us after the order is placed." – Annoyed Annie

> "The real opportunity for success lies within the person and not the job; you can best get to the top by getting to the bottom of things." Zig Ziglar

9. "When sales reps call and act like they are one of my 'best friends,' they come across as being insincere and unprofessional. I want to work with sales reps who are sincere about helping my business." – Cozy Carrie

> "Smart businesses should come to realize that the customer service bar is lower—and that today, it's easier than ever to differentiate your company from the pack with (crazy as it seems) actual quality customer service." Brad Tuttle, "A Few thoughts on the God-Awful State of Customer Service," Time, 2010

10. "If I leave a voice mail or send you an email and don't hear back the same day, I think you are inaccessible or ignoring me. Both are bad." – Responsive Randy

11. "Our turnaround is very quick. When I can't get in touch with you, the business goes to another sales rep because I have to move on." – Available Adam

12. "Don't change my sales rep when I have a good one because you have an internal change. I don't want to

have to train the new sales rep. Nothing is more frustrating than getting the call 'Hi, I'm your new sales rep,' and they are really new." – Experienced Ernie

All Customer Relationships Come with Expectations

As long as there have been relationships, there have been expectations associated with each relationship. Prior to the moment when a SalesMaker closes the sale, the bar of expectation is low. Once the sale closes, that is when the real work begins and the customer's "expectation meter" is turned on.

Prior to purchase, the customer is buying on the promise of the purchase and the deliverables they believe will be forthcoming. Post purchase, the customer expects delivery on the things, whether real or imagined that caused them to decide in favor of the purchase. When expectations are met, the value of the SalesMaker goes up in the eyes of the customer and the relationship is strengthened.

The Bar of Expectation

The Bar of Expectation is a mental and emotional set of expectations the customer will have of the SalesMaker, the company they represent, and the products they sell. In the Olympic Games, the high jump event requires highly-trained and practiced participants to compete for a bronze, silver, or gold medal. There are three outcomes an Olympian can experience at the high bar jump. The high jumper can hit the bar, miss the bar, or clear the bar with room to spare.

> "No one ever attains very eminent success by simply doing what is required; it is the amount and excellence of what is over and above the required that determines the greatness of ultimate distinction." Charles Francis Adams, Politician and Diplomat

In the same way, a seller will meet the bar of a customer's service expectations, miss it, or clear it with room to spare. In sales there is no bronze, silver, or gold medal. Success and failure in sales is judged by how good a SalesMaker is at getting the business, not losing the business, getting a high share, low share, or no share at all. When the SalesMaker consistently meets or exceeds expectations, their chances of retaining an account and generating renewal and referral business goes up.

An invisible contract exists between the SalesMaker and the customer that infers that the customer's expectations will be met and even exceeded. That invisible contract is an unspoken assumption early in the relationship. While the contract is honored, the customer has no reason to go elsewhere. If the contract is broken, a customer may seek a new solution provider. While it may seem natural to talk about customer care and concern while the money is flowing, not addressing customer care could lead to a broken relationship and develop into revenue loss.

Some SalesMakers make it a practice to identify expectations early in the sales process to ensure a happy customer returns with repeat or referral business. Some companies like Lex Brodie Tire Company in Honolulu exercise the same service principle by setting service expectations high before the first transaction.

Customer Retention Through Service Attention

Lex Brodie Tire Company is a company that publically displays a six-foot Customer Bill of Rights in every store that defines the commitment to service excellence their customers have come to expect. They hold themselves accountable for meeting the customer's expectations, whether spoken or not. They know that if they don't hold themselves accountable to deliver excellence in service, their customers will with their dollars, social media posts, or in other forms of "word of mouth" advertising. They work tirelessly to earn and keep their customers' business.

Founded over 55 years ago, and the winner of the National Top Shop Award, Lex Brodie's is legendary in customer satisfaction and retention of business. They lavish attention on customers by doing business the "Aloha Way." The time and attention provided to customers is what drives their return business. Recognized over the years by many organizations, their commitment to service excellence comes first. This high level of attention and service begin with each client being greeted with an "aloha" and a smile.

Lex Brodie is a master at setting expectations and then clearing the bar with room to spare. Employees are trained that a customer's expectations are part of their experience. Employees should always strive to exceed those expectations.

Scott Williams, Executive Director of Marketing, will tell you that "We fix cars, but care for customers. Our primary business is the people business. If you do everything right, you are going to have customers coming back to you. That's the best part of your base, your loyal customers who attract more customers."

Whether you are an individual seller or someone responsible for identifying and meeting expectations of a customer to ensure repeat and referral business, make sure you understand what the Bar of Expectation looks like.

It's Business, Not Personal... Until it Hits Your Pocketbook

When a seller consistently misses the bar of expectation, a decision-maker will shop for a new SalesMaker. Losing business can happen faster than gaining new business because relationship-building takes time. Service that sinks a sale can happen in a second.

Customers take service issues seriously, often more seriously than a company who sees it as "just one more problem." All business relationships are personal to the person whose pocket book is being affected. When expectations are missed and frustrations not resolved, the customer's decision to move on and not renew creates a financial consequence that is very personal to the SalesMaker because it is felt in the most personal place—the pocket book.

Exceeding Expectations Means Doing More than is Expected

When SalesMakers perform to a customer's expectations, they fit in. When they exceed expectations, they differentiate themselves in a way that sets them up for a higher frequency of renewal and referral business. How can a SalesMaker ensure they always clear the bar of expectation? By going the extra mile!

Two thousand years ago a teacher, who was also a carpenter by trade among other things, began to teach many things. One of His sayings was, "If someone asks you to go one mile, go with them two." From this ancient saying we get a new standard of excellence in service that means to do more than is asked. Said another way, do more than is expected.

> The big rewards come to those who travel the second, un-demanded mile." Bruce Barton, Former U.S. Congressman

Step up before you are asked, take initiative, anticipate the customer's needs before they have them, think ahead, go the extra mile. In doing so, you will close the next sale while you are still servicing the first sale. Author and inspirational speaker Mac Anderson says that "Great service is giving more than the customer expects, consistently."

What does the bar of expectation look like in the service arena? Here is a reference list of service expectations that produces one of three outcomes which include the SalesMaker missing, meeting, or exceeding a customer's expectations. As you read through these, give yourself a grade on a scale of 1-10 based on how your service behavior performs on each of the following expectations. Then ask your customers to do the same. If you give yourself a 1, that means that you rarely perform that service behavior. Give yourself a 10 if your answer is always. If you are somewhere in the middle, give yourself a 5 and let's see how you do.

Misses Expectations	1-10
Being late or unprepared.	
Letting problems go unresolved.	
Taking the business for granted.	
Calling only when you want an order.	
Failing to notice signals of dissatisfaction.	
Forgetting to watch over the little things.	
Showing your frustration to the customer.	

Meets Customer Expectations	1-10
Paying attention to details.	
Keeping your promises to the customer.	
Showing up on time, informed, and prepared.	
Calling back even if you don't have an answer.	
Following up after the order has gone through.	
Uncovering a need before you ask for an order.	
Listening, and then following the customer's instructions.	

Exceeds Customer Expectations	1-10
Making good (and then some) on mistakes that were made.	
Asking for feedback on how to improve your service.	
Putting the relationship above the transaction.	
Going the extra mile and letting the customer see you do it.	
Breaking company policy to make your customer happy.	
Surprising your customer with gestures of appreciation.	
Remembering what is important to the customer and acting on it.	

How did you do? For every area you scored below a 10, you know you have room to grow. Customers rarely expect perfection. They do however expect that you meet expectations. If you are unsure of your customer's expectations, ask them in a way that is consistent with the relationship research you read earlier. For now, pick a few of the 21 areas of service expectations for which you just graded yourself and work on improving the ways in which you provide service. With a little time and effort, you will be meeting and exceeding the bar of customer expectation and be on your way to increasing your renewal and referral business.

"The bar of expectation is usually hidden within plain sight."

Increase your Relationship Equity

The relational dynamics that exist between sellers and their customers are like a bank account balance that is always going up or down, similar to Stephen Covey's "Emotional Bank Account" metaphor. In the SalesMaker's service accounts, every service event and conversation represents an emotional transaction being made that acts like a deposit or withdrawal. When expectations are met and exceeded in the relationship, emotional deposits occur and relationship equity is increased. When expectations are missed, withdrawals occur and relationship equity is reduced.

"Relationship equity can save or sink a sale when a problem arises, and problems always arise."

> "The close of a sale is not the end of the sale, but the beginning of a new relationship. Delivering on the promise of good service from the first sale is what kick-starts selling for the next sale."

With every interaction, an emotional transaction takes place to either increase a SalesMakers' relationship equity or reduce the confidence the customer feels toward them and the company. Consistent deposits lead to a strong foundation in the customer/SalesMaker relationship. Consistent withdrawals will lead the SalesMaker and their company toward relationship bankruptcy with the customer.

Each new relationship is opened with a starting balance. In sales, that starting balance is the "benefit of the doubt" that is a small amount of trust based on what was promised during the presentation phase of the sale. As a SalesMaker delivers or exceeds expectations on those promises, their balance in the service bank account grows. If a seller does not deliver, or follow-up, or forgets key service items, the balance decreases. Below are a few dynamics that impact the SalesMaker's Service Account.

> "The customer's service experience with the SalesMaker is the emotional currency in the relationship, and that currency can increase or decrease."

Principles of the SalesMaker's Service Account

> "Practices are many and principles are few. When you practice the principles of the SalesMaker, dollars will follow you."

1. The customer's service experience with a SalesMaker creates an emotional reaction that becomes currency in the SalesMaker's Service Account.

2. Relationship equity increases when deposits are made. Deposits are any service behavior that meets or exceeds expectations.

3. Relationship equity decreases, and a withdrawal is made when service expectations are missed and the customer experiences disappointment.

4. Deposits and withdrawals are usually made "in the little things." Little things become big things when they are not taken care of.

5. Relationship equity takes time to build, but can be lost in an instant. Relationship equity, when withdrawn from a SalesMakers Service Account, comes out faster than it goes in because of the negative emotional and financial impact it can create for the customer.

6. Where a high equity balance exists, a negative service experience will create a withdrawal, but recovery can be faster.

7. Where a low equity balance exists, a negative service experience can result in slower repairing of relationship equity or no recovery at all.

8. Once trust is broken or the relationship enters bankruptcy, it may be more financially expedient for a company to replace the seller on the account than wait for the business to come back or hold out for another chance with the customer.

How are deposits or withdrawals made in the SalesMakers Service Account? Below are lists of service behaviors that increase or reduce the equity balance. By becoming more aware of what makes for deposits, the SalesMaker can work toward ensuring higher top line, share, and commissions for themselves and their company. By avoiding the service behaviors that reduce relationship equity, the SalesMaker can continue to grow and not retract their financial influence with the customer. The higher the relationship equity, the more likely the SalesMaker will be in position to receive renewal and referral business.

> "Relationship equity is won and lost in the small things; and so are dollars."

Insights into What Increases and Decreases Relationship Equity

in the SalesMaker's Service Account

Increase your service competencies and watch your dollars grow.

Equity Deposits	Equity Withdrawals
Consistent follow up.	Disappear after you get the order.
Probe for your customers' interests.	Fail to find their hot buttons.
Thank the customer for the business.	Fail to show appreciation.
Listen for what the customer is feeling.	Fail to hear what is not being said.
Be prepared for meetings with an agenda.	Attend meetings without an agenda.
Understand your customer's expectations.	Fail to discover the service hot buttons.
Catch mistakes before your customer does.	Drop the ball and let the customer find out.
Find out what is important to your customer.	Pitch the business before you probe the need.
Collaborate to problem solve before you close.	Be more of a closer than a partner.
Make your customers feel special.	Make them feel like one of many.
Put yourself in their shoes when problems arise.	Fail to empathize with your customer's pain.
Compliment your customer about their business.	Complain about your company.
Make up for service mistakes in a meaningful way.	Ignore the impact of a mistake and let it reoccur.

Offer options when the customer makes demands.	Quote the customer your policy and say "no."
Be available when the customer is looking for you.	Be inaccessible when they have a need.
Ask for more business when the customer is happy.	Put your selling goals above their service priorities.
Put in extra effort and deliver more than is expected.	Be average like everyone else.
Do your homework and research before each meeting.	Show up unprepared.
Take responsibility when problems arise and fix them.	Pass the buck.

Once people have suffered repeated disappointment in a relationship, it becomes hard to undo what's been done. In personal relationships, people may be inclined to hang on and hope for the best. In business relationships, customers are more prone to move on rather than hang on because there is always a competitor close by who's been waiting in line for their turn at the business. In servicing a repeat customer, if the ball is repeatedly dropped, an opportunity isn't missed. It just passes to the competition.

Turn Withdrawals into Deposits

Service balls are bound to get dropped at times. If a SalesMaker spends enough time in sales, they will witness how a dropped ball in service can cost them the sale. When the unavoidable happens and a ball gets dropped, there are a few specific steps the SalesMaker can take to turn an equity withdrawal into a relationship deposit. The following illustration shows a few simple steps the SalesMaker can take to save a relationship, turning a withdrawal into a deposit in the SalesMaker's Service Account.

Equity Withdrawals Can Turn Into Relationship Deposits

5

FOLLOW UP
Tell them what you did.
Tell them how you feel.
Tell them how you fixed it.
Then, surprise them by telling
how you'll make it up to them.

4

RESOLVE THE ISSUE
Find out what happened behind the scenes.
Find out why it happened and how you can prevent it
from happening again & fix the problem.

3

MAKE A PROMISE
Ask what they'd like to see happen.
Offer possible solutions.
Tell them what action you'll take.

2

EMPATHIZE & APOLOGIZE
Reiterate the problem so they know you understand.
Communicate that you understand and apologize.
"If I were in your shoes, I'd feel the same way."

1

HEAR THE CUSTOMER OUT
Let the customer vent - Don't interrupt.
Take responsibility - Don't pass the buck.
Ask questions until you understand what they are saying.

R E P A I R

Steps to Catching Dropped Balls...
WHEN THE CUSTOMER COMPLAINS!

Reputation Management is Relationship Management

Reputation Guarantees a Return Result

Bad News Travels Fast

Where does an unhappy customer go when they leave you? Are they lost? Of course not! Are they orphans? Not for long. Customers don't just disappear. They disperse their dollars in a new direction when they are disappointed. When their needs are not being met by one company, they select another.

> When you create a happy customer, you are creating a positive memory to which your customer will return. That's loyalty. Once you create loyalty, the customer is yours to lose."

But the story isn't as simple as a tale of one lost customer. When a customer leaves a company because they are unhappy, they tell as many as nine other people about their dissatisfaction. Why will a customer not take the time to confront bad service but still complain about it after leaving a company? It's because people don't keep their pain to themselves. When people have a sad or frustrating story, they need to vent. It's typical human behavior to share our pain points with others. In fact, in the media news business, there is an old saying, "If it bleeds, it leads." Bad news just seems to travel faster than good news. This is *not*

> News of bad customer service reaches more than twice as many ears as praise for a good service experience." White House Office of Consumer Affairs

good news for companies with unhappy customers who can now share their unhappiness with way more than nine people at one time through social media.

Social Media Can Hold Your Business Hostage

Social media can be paradise or hell for companies when customers give reviews online. The "speed to the street" for both the positive and negative is extremely fast. With the click of a button on a website or an App, the ascension or decline of reputations accelerates. Reputations travel faster, further, and can make a significant impact on a company's bottom line in cyber space.

I recently hired a company to paint my house and had a very good experience with them. After expressing my satisfaction to them, they asked me to go onto a popular social media review site and post a comment about my happy experience with them. The business owner explained to me that an unhappy customer who was friends with his former business partner had posted some unwarranted negative comments about his painting company, and those negative reviews were costing him business. He went on to explain that only more good reviews would cause the bad posts to be pushed out of view. Companies are held accountable more today than ever before to a customer's expectations and held hostage if that customer has a bad service experience.

Web and social media spaces are filled with both happy and unhappy customers. Never before in business history has there been so much visible accountability for the service a company provides. There's an FBI saying that says, "Our victories are private, but our mistakes are public." Today's instant-access social media platforms reach thousands of customers. One mistake can mushroom into thousands of hits online with the tap of a finger on an App.

Unfortunately for businesses that are negatively impacted by poor reviews, a new potential customer's first stop is often to see what the rest of the world is saying about them online. Through online reviews and posts, a company's reputation can be created or destroyed in a short period of time. For SalesMakers, it is not as quick because one-to-one contact with customers is what creates the memories that form reputation. And, reputations for individual SalesMakers don't often make the company review pages. Nonetheless, there has never been a time in business history where the financial benefits or consequences of service are felt so rapidly.

> "The rise of the citizen review site is a sobering development. No longer are you on top of the mountain, blasting your marketing message down to the masses through your megaphone. All of a sudden, the masses are conversing with one another. If your service or product isn't any good, they'll out you." David Pogue, Scientific American, 2011

One thing we are all guaranteed is a reputation. Regardless of how good or poor your service is, you will be remembered for the service signature you leave behind. Like footprints in the sand, leaving impressions behind is unavoidable. What will you be known for? Will it be follow-through, quick response, friendliness, integrity, your ability to ask great questions, intuition, or something negative?

Everyone is guaranteed a reputation for something. Some reputations grow sales and commissions while others sabotage a SalesMaker's efforts. A reputation in sales is a memory of you or your company held by another person that is perpetuated and spread among others. You are going to be remembered by the customer for service, one way or another. Make it an excellent memory by providing excellent service.

Reputation is defined as "the opinion of others; the overall quality or character as seen or judged by people in general." In ancient Rome,

> "If reputations went on resumes, we'd all be more careful in how we treat our customers."

"character" was the total sum of the parts that made up the character of a person. The Greeks viewed reputation more like a "stamp," or how something was perceived on the outside. Whether you view reputation as a character quality on the inside or a perception of the outside, we all carry one. Authors John C. Maxwell and Les Parrott, P.H.D. have said, "For most of us, a reputation is something we either have to live up to, or live down." That couldn't be truer in the marketplace.

Here are a few reputation principles to keep in mind:

1. Reputation becomes an emotional stamp that when triggered, reminds a customer to feel a certain way toward a SalesMaker or their company.

2. A positive reputation can put a SalesMaker in first position when business becomes available.

3. A negative reputation can keep a SalesMaker out of position when dollars are being spent.

4. A reputation tells people how to think of us when we are no longer in the room.

For most of us, the first time we learned of "reputation" was on the

> "Once an impression is made, it solidifies into a reputation with a customer. This reputation becomes a governing factor in how a customer thinks, feels, and behaves toward us."

playground or in the hallways of the school we attended growing up. Someone came to us and told us what they thought of us. Or, someone came to us and told us about what someone else thought of us. The opinion of others was simply their perception of who they thought we were. We quickly learned that if that opinion got spread and shared by others, it led to a reputation. And that reputation, whether positive or negative, made us into someone that others wanted to be around or someone that others wanted to avoid. The power of reputation, whether in grade school or the marketplace, has the same impact.

As kids, if we had a bad reputation, the worst-case scenario was that our feelings could be hurt. Our parents taught us that "sticks and stones can break my bones but words can never hurt me." In business, however, what a customer, supervisor, or marketplace thinks of us can either help or hurt business.

A SalesMaker's reputation as to what a customer, supervisor, or marketplace thinks of them can lead to increased or reduced dollars. In business, dollars are how companies keep score. You can change how people perceive you in the marketplace. You, as a SalesMaker, have the ability to influence how a customer, supervisor, or marketplace perceives you based on the consistency with which you deliver and present yourself.

> "You can't build a reputation on what you are going to do." Henry Ford

Here are a few things for which a SalesMaker wants to be perceived. If you feel you've earned the right to say you are remembered for these qualities, put a check mark next to the qualities of reputation that resonate.

1. _____ I have a **REPUTATION** for always delivering!

2. _____ I have a **REPUTATION** for always being prepared!

3. _____ I have a **REPUTATION** for always being reachable!

4. _____ I have a **REPUTATION** for always following through!

5. _____ I have a **REPUTATION** for always being resourceful!

6. _____ I have a **REPUTATION** for always being trustworthy!

7. _____ I have a **REPUTATION** for always going the extra mile!

8. _____ I have a **REPUTATION** for always being a good listener!

9. _____ I have a **REPUTATION** for always having a good attitude!

10. _____ I have a **REPUTATION** for always communicating clearly!

11. _____ I have a **REPUTATION** for always resolving problems quickly!

12. _____ I have a **REPUTATION** for always saying "Yes" more than "No!"

13. _____ I have a **REPUTATION** for always being attentive to details!

14. _____ I have a **REPUTATION** for always having a good sense of humor!

15. _____ I have a **REPUTATION** for always being easy with which to do business!

16. _____ I have a **REPUTATION** for always making a client feel special!

17. _____ I have a **REPUTATION** for always being knowledgeable in my field!

18. _____ I have a **REPUTATION** for always showing appreciation for the business!

19. _____ I have a **REPUTATION** for always providing a quick turnaround on client requests!

20. _____ I have a **REPUTATION** for always being more interested in the client than the order!

21. _____ I have a **REPUTATION** for always making what is important to a client, important to me!

Regardless of what your reputation is today, you can always build on it by removing the behaviors that negatively impact it and by increasing the behaviors that positively feed it. If you are not sure of your reputation in the office or the marketplace, ask for feedback from those around you by giving you an A, B, C, D, or F grade on the above twenty-one statements. It can be risky and a little uncomfortable, but you are guaranteed a learning experience and a way to quickly improve the perception of others around you.

> "A reputation, once broken, may possibly be repaired, but the world will always keep their eyes on the spot where the crack was."
> Joseph Hall

Your Reputation is Your Brand

How important is a brand to generating repeat and referral business? According to the 2015 Global State of Multichannel Customer Service Report, "62% of global consumers have stopped doing business with a brand or organization due to a poor customer service experience." Customer experiences create a memory to which they want to return, or avoid in the future. Customers remember moments from their experiences with you that greatly influence whether you get some business or no business at all from them.

> "How you handle the relationship with the customer is what will create your reputation with them and make the decision as to whether they buy from you again or turn to another company."

You are the Brand to the Customer, Not Your Company

The SalesMaker is the front line of a company's brand. In one-to-one direct sales, the customer buys from the SalesMaker before they buy from the company. That is why the customer buys into the SalesMaker before they buy into the company product. The reverse is also true. When a customer leaves a company, they leave a relationship with a SalesMaker first. Many customers don't like confrontation so they speak in code with statements like, "our needs have changed"; "the competition was cheaper"; "we'll call you when we're ready to reorder," and other similar statements. A customer's service experience with a SalesMaker is what forms the first position of perception in the mind of the customer. If a customer does not buy into the SalesMaker, it is unlikely they will buy into the company. As the front line of what creates a reputation for a company, a SalesMaker is the first position of the brand in the eyes of the customer.

> "It takes 20 years to build a reputation, and five minutes to ruin it. If you think about that, you'll do things differently." Warren Buffett, CEO Berkshire Hathaway

In the context of the level of customer service a SalesMaker provides, a *service brand* is also the brand of the company. A customer service brand is defined as: A past emotional experience anchored with an event and embedded within the memory of a customer. When that experience or emotion is recalled, it causes a customer to remember and emotionally relive what the business experience with the SalesMaker felt like. If the experience was good, the customer will want to return and refer others by remembering and retelling their positive perception. If the customer had a bad experience with a SalesMaker, they will want to retreat from the idea of returning to a relationship associated with a negative experience.

As the front line of service in direct one-to-one sales, the SalesMaker is the brand. Whether a SalesMaker has a separate customer service department or not, they will reap the rewards or consequences from the experiences the customers have related to service.

If I were to ask you about a good or bad experience you have had with a company or seller, you could no doubt recall that experience. You may not remember every detail, but you'll remember enough to recall whether that experience was positive or negative. The same is true for the customers we serve. Recognizing that the SalesMaker's level of service is responsible for creating the reputation that becomes the company brand in the eyes of the customer is essential to understanding what creates and loses business.

Customers Remember Moments, Not Just Conversations

According to Lee Resources, the cost of a customer with an unhappy perception is that "91% of unhappy customers will not willingly do business with you again." A customer's perception is based on the memory of their experience, whether good or bad. A bad experience creates a brand that reproduces like a good experience does.

How a SalesMaker handles an unhappy customer will determine whether a customer recommits to the relationship or seeks a new one elsewhere. The words a SalesMaker uses with a customer have the power to either restore or end a relationship that's been damaged by poor service. Words have the power to create a reputation and brand for the SalesMaker that is positive or negative. The right thing said at the right moment can lead to another order and increased share of business. The wrong words can lead to lost business not just at the moment, but permanently.

Tom Asacker, motivational speaker and author says, "Customers will not remember what you said, but they will remember how you made them feel." The weight of right and wrong service decisions by a SalesMaker in the moment can lead to financial rewards or financial consequences because customers remember moments, and they can work for or against a company.

According to Esteban Kolsky, Researcher & Customer Strategist, "if a customer is not satisfied, 13% of them will tell 15 or more people that they are unhappy. On the other hand, 72% of customers will share a positive experience with 6 or more people." Derek Sivers from CD Baby was right when he said that "customer service is the new marketing." Once a customer has an experience with a SalesMaker and the company they represent, they spread the word and that "word-of-mouth" marketing comes with a personal recommendation.

All customers have a love language. For some it is convenience, competence, friendliness, free stuff, and so on. My #1 service priority is "time." Time is in short supply for most families and business executives. When I run into a challenge and need customer service, I measure my experience by the speed and quality of the service resolution.

I'm not alone. According to Forrester Research, "77% of US online adult customers say that valuing their time is the most important thing a company can do to provide them with good service." I dread having to pick up the phone and call a customer service hotline for fear of how much time it will take out of my day and the potential for that experience to leave me unsatisfied.

Timing can Make the Difference Between Meeting, Missing, or Exceeding Expectations

Timing is also very important when it comes to meeting and exceeding a customer's set of expectations. Great service is especially valued when provided at the right time. If a SalesMaker anticipates and addresses a customer's needs before it arises, they are thought of as "thoughtful." If a SalesMaker responds to a customer's need after it emerges, their actions may still be considered timely. However, if a SalesMaker delays in meeting a customer's need after the expectation has been voiced, the SalesMaker is late and being late for anything creates new challenges to be addressed. There is never as great an opportunity to strengthen a relationship than when a customer is in need. A SalesMaker who steps up to meet that need in that moment builds trust. A positive memory is created. So is a good reputation.

To today's customers, meeting needs in a timely manner is as important as time itself. Time is in short supply, not just for business-to-business customers, but for consumer and retail customers. Handling a customer's service issues in a timely manner and delivering on time will ensure that relationships are strengthened and business returns.

An example of handling service in a way that strengthens relationships while creating repeat business is Dell Computers and their Service Repair Division. My Dell laptop once took a back flip off a table. Within one week of calling Dell's Service Department, Dell had shipped me a box to send them my computer, repaired my computer, and shipped it back to me. The best part was everything was covered in the amazing warranty I had included in my laptop purchase.

The speed of service, convenience, and courtesy with which my account was handled created a terrific experience between us. I won't just remember Dell for the one experience I had with them, but I will remember to buy the extra warranty so I can have the same experience again in the future. Having Dell meet my needs in a timely manner made me a very happy customer. Dell made their next sale with me by servicing the first sale well.

Since that experience I have bought more Dell computers and have recommended Dell to many others with whom I shared this experience. Dell delivered on the first purchase and guaranteed my second purchase, and many more, through my word-of-mouth recommendations in the retelling of my happy customer service experience.

> "There is proven ROI in doing whatever you can to turn your customers into advocates for your brand or business. The way to create advocates is to offer superior customer service."
> Gary Vaynerchuk, The Thank You Economy

Relationship Insights Lead to Consistent Return and Referral Business

The SalesMaker's ability to connect with a customer is in direct proportion to their relationship knowledge of that customer. Where return revenue is dependent on an ongoing relationship, the strength of service and the depth of relationship knowledge a SalesMaker has of their customer is what will help them drive repeat orders, top line, and share. Insights gathered during fact finding can lead to a sale. Connection made during relationship building leads to recurring sales. While a SalesMaker's

> "Connecting on sacred ground shows us that what connects us is far more important than the things that separate us."

focus on the front end of a new relationship may be focused on dollars, there can be no doubt that once the relationship is formed, the dollars can become a byproduct of that relationship.

Renewal and referral business is not only dependent on having a good relationship with customers, it is also dependent on the connection a SalesMaker and customer share. In fact, the more common points of connection a SalesMaker has with a customer, the more likely the relationship will be strong and have a high equity balance in the SalesMakers service account.

When a personal connection is made that transcends the financial transaction, a business relationship can turn into a friendship. Over time, friendships can transcend even the business relationship. Going beyond the transaction, the SalesMaker grows in the knowledge of their customer. Below are a few questions a SalesMaker can pursue as a means to learn more about their customer beyond the sale. With each insight, the possibility of forging a deeper connection emerges.

The following questions will help you develop a deeper relationship with customers. As you enter each area of conversation, remember that some ground is sacred to the customer and where you find the heart, you will find the keys that unlock what they treasure. Another reward a SalesMaker discovers when building relationships with customers is not always in the financial arena, but often in the friendships that eventually follow. The financial benefit for the SalesMaker and the company they represent must always be present; however, it becomes the byproduct of the relationship.

While some sales made by the SalesMaker may be one-time occurrences, others are recurring, or include referral sales. What connects one sale to the next is always a relationship. At the heart of a great SalesMaker lies an ability to probe past the surface needs of the sale and connect relationally with the customer in a way that transcends the transaction. The SalesMaker goes to higher ground with the insights gathered in the sacred journey toward relationship. These insights will help the SalesMaker close the sale as they get to know the people behind each sale. Greater relationship knowledge can lead to a growing partnership. How well do you know your customers? Are you connected beyond the sales? Here is a quick quiz to help you evaluate the depth of your relationship knowledge.

Customer Relationship Quiz Questions	Yes/No
Do you know what gets your customer excited?	
Do you know what will make your customer renew and refer business?	
Do you know what makes your customer withdraw?	
Do you know why your customer buys what they buy?	
Do you know who else your customer buys from and why?	
Do you know who influences your customer in their buying decisions?	
Do you know what your customer values the most in the relationship?	
Do you know what one word your customer would use to describe you?	
Do you know your customers desires of today and dreams of tomorrow?	
Do you know what causes your customer to "trust" or "distrust" a vendor?	
Do you know what shared interests you and your customer have together?	
Do you know who else your customer enjoys doing business with and why?	
Do you know what caused your customer to buy from you and not another?	
Do you know what you could do to increase your value in your customer's eyes?	
Do you know if your relationship is strong enough to break the tie when a competitor is being considered?	

> "Returning and referral business will require relationship knowledge that transcends the transactional."

If you are in a business that thrives on renewal and referral business, then you are in a relationship selling environment. Knowing what makes your customer's hearts sing or sink can help you not just make more sales, but more memories for forging deeper relationships. That is what sales is all about, forming relationships in the greatest business in the world—the people business.

Making the sale isn't the end of the sale, but the beginning of the relationship between the customer, the company, and the SalesMaker. As you've learned in the Law of Relationship, how well you service your customers will determine your level of connection, relationship equity, and ultimately reputation which will drive your renewals and referrals up or down. Providing good service may seem as simple as meeting a customer's needs but it is more than that because a SalesMaker isn't just managing a transaction, but a relationship. When developing a customer relationship, it is not just relationship equity that goes up or down, but dollars for the company and commissions for the SalesMaker. Being more informed of your service gaps and blind spots will help you to eliminate costly behavior.

On the following page, you will find a Sales Maker's notes and action items from their C.I.A. exercise. As you read the Law of Relationship, I am sure there were present and past customer experiences that came to mind. As you engage the C.I.A. process, consider how you can leverage your newfound knowledge and insight into saving lost business, shoring up a weakening relationship, or begin a new relationship with a customer. The Law of Relationship says, "SalesMakers clear the bar of customer expectations with room to spare, setting themselves and their companies up for renewal and referral business." Once you put your insights into action, you will be not only meeting but exceeding more customer's expectations, and be well on your way to growing your renewal and referral business.

C.I.A. CONTRIBUTORS

The LAW OF RELATIONSHIP

Dana Young, Dell EMC

Emi Hart Sorenson, Yelp

Kevin Yim, Hawaiian Airlines

My name is **Dana Young** and I have been with **Dell EMC** for 17 years. I attribute my success to recognizing that I'm never the smartest person in the room, and I compensate in two ways—perseverance and being intentional about innovation. What I love most about my job is the flexibility and empowerment to pursue personal passions.

1. As hard as it is for a customer to invest in a new relationship, it is much harder for them to invest in repairing a relationship. Repairing means correction is needed, and that includes relational confrontation and conflict—two things that customers will avoid if they can.

2. In a world where the efficiency of communication has grown exponentially over the past decades, the implications of word-of-mouth reactions to customer service experiences have grown exponentially as well. The reality in sales relationships must be considered in this because human nature tends to loudly complain, but quietly praise. We hear far more often the bad than the good. Hence, a focus on service is more critical today than ever before.

3. Relationship equity (the aggregate deposits you've accrued in a relationship with a customer) provides two things: It can cover unexpected withdrawals that might occur completely outside the SalesMaker's control, and it is there for planned withdrawals, such as asking for a favor to cut a purchase order a week early to make an end-of-quarter cut off. It's important to always be aware of what you have in your relationship account.

4. Everyone is guaranteed a reputation for something, and you can't build a reputation on what you are going to do. Did I move my reputation in the direction I wanted to today? I will be aware of my actions and how they influence my reputation with others.

5. How you make the customer feel is more important than what they hear you say. That's simply true because of the way our brains are wired—memory is much stronger from the *feeling* of an interaction than the *content* of the interaction.

6. Work hard on developing the capability to anticipate customer needs. The ability to anticipate a need and meet it before the customer has to spend time explaining it delivers a large deposit of relationship equity.

My name is **Emi Hart Sorenson**, and I have been in marketing for 20+ years as a professional event planner, entrepreneur, social media influencer and a Senior Community Director for **Yelp** in Honolulu. I build vibrant, engaged communities, and attribute my success to my ability to clearly communicate, negotiate and clarify expectations, consistently over-deliver on my promises to partners, and most importantly, create authentic connections. I love my career at Yelp because it allows me the ability to produce unique and emotional experiences that make people's lives happier and more positive. Here is a summary of what connected me in the Law of Relationship.

1. "The customer's feelings, their finances, and with whom they invest their dollars are intrinsically linked. With every purchase, they are voting with their wallets based on how they feel toward their SalesMakers and the service they are experiencing." Great relationships are about asking, interpreting, and truly understanding your customer so they feel valuable at multiple touchpoints. In today's marketplace, you

have to go beyond what consumers expect or you won't create enough momentum to break through the noise.

2. I am always trying to explain to others what great customer service looks like, and *The Tale of the Lost Customer* was the perfect example of a purely transactional relationship that ended when the seller started taking the customer's business for granted. Customers don't want to be just a sale; they want a truly authentic connection and service experience.

3. "The Relationship Gap: In personal relationships, we are judged by what we say first and do later. In business relationships, we are judged by what we deliver based on the spoken and unspoken promises of the product and person who sold the customer." This principle of service deliverables is in-sync with my personal rule of thumb which is, "Never make a promise I can't deliver on." And whenever possible, I do my best to over-deliver on what is expected with gratitude and enthusiasm. Relationships are built on trust, and the quicker you can build the trust bridge, the faster everyone enjoys the fruits of a true win-win relationship.

4. "After spending countless hours with customers hearing about the good, the bad, and the ugly, I concluded that the difference between the best and worst service providers resided in the SalesMaker's ability to uncover a customer's spoken and unspoken needs, identify and meet expectations after the sale, and adapt their sales and service behavior to make and keep the customer consistently happy." Through my job at Yelp I've met so many amazing business owners, and time and again, the ones that truly thrive both on and offline deliver an excellent product experience and understand their customer by always listening with an open mind. This allows them to turn negative feedback into positive results by constantly fine-tuning their formula. Consumers are extremely savvy; they do their research and want to find businesses who know how to deliver value, service and magic.

5. "When SalesMakers exceed expectations, they differentiate themselves in a way that sets them up for higher frequency of renewal and referral business. How can a SalesMaker ensure they always clear the bar of expectation—by going the extra mile!" Going the extra mile can mean so many different things these days. Often I see businesses try to compete on price, but that's not always sustainable and I'd prefer to see

a business deliver value through emotional output. Whether it's their passion for making each food dish magical, shaking each customer's hand and learning about their lives, or loving on their customers with free hugs (I've see this work), true emotional output is free, but to your customer, it's priceless and this is what creates a brand zealot. SalesMakers who become service zealots for their company make repeat business possible with customers.

6. "Knowing what makes your customer's hearts sing or sink can help you not just make more sales, but more memories for forging deeper relationships. That is what sales is all about, forming relationships in the greatest business in the world—the people business." This is my favorite quote from the chapter because "the people business" is why I love what I do. When I first started my job at Yelp, my boss at the time told me that when you build a community or business, it's like pushing a snowball up a mountain. It's hard at first, because you are the only person who's pushing that snowball. As you get higher and higher up the hill, it gets larger, so you will have to find others to help you get it to the top. Long term success is about building relationships with others by helping them push their snowballs up the mountain as well, and in turn, they will help you get your snowball to the top too. The great news is that your hard work and efforts will eventually pay off, because once your snowball is at the top of the mountain, it will roll down effortlessly and there's nothing that can stop it.

My name is **Kevin Yim** and I have been with **Hawaiian Airlines** for six years. I attribute my success to believing that no matter how successful my last effort, there's always more that could have been done, a better result, or a more efficient way to do that work. What I love most about what I do is that the diversity of work keeps it interesting and the diversity of people I meet is invigorating. Below you will find a list of my takeaways and insight from the Law of Relationship.

Relationships are the basis for continued business with the customer, or at the very least, a source of word-of-mouth advertising and referrals. As I reflect, the idea that "retention through attention" is the key to ensuring repeat business.

In the airline business, which has become heavily commoditized, the best comments we can receive are from guests who said we made them feel special in an environment that is more conducive to guests being treated like just-another-person-in-a-crowd; that we recognized a need and fulfilled it before the need was expressed, with empathy and humanness. When done correctly, people are willing to pay a price premium to travel with us, over another commoditized provider. When we don't spend enough time attending to guests' needs, we garner another type of fan—the people that like to pile-on the negative commentary on social media. Repeat customers are won one-by-one through attention, but enemies are created by the dozen in this age of social media.

An action I can take is to ensure frontline service providers understand how their roles create repeat customers, and, in turn, contribute heavily to the bottom-line financials. Conversely, ensuring that all social media commentaries, good and bad, are made available to every employee so that everyone can see where the entire operation is performing well, and where that person can make a positive difference in someone else's day. Other helpful takeaways I received from the Law of Relationship include:

1. Doing more than what's expected, even when expectations are high, is the key to winning and keeping business.

2. Pay attention to the details—what you may think is a relationship going well, may be headed south because you took for granted too many parts of your relationship.

3. The customer judges you by your actions, not by your intent. It's not good enough to try hard, it only matters that you've actually done well by the customer

4. In the airline business, the emotional stakes are very high. Often, travel to Hawaii is wrapped up in high-stakes special occasions, such as weddings, honeymoons, special anniversaries, or a very special family trip. When things go poorly, employees can't act as if it's just another day, with another problem. For some customers, that one service failing is the thin line between a dream wedding, or a disastrous experience. Sometimes, relationships can't prevent a weather delay or a lost piece of luggage, but the rapidity and quality of the service intervention makes all the difference to that person.

5. Hawaiian Airlines is not the kind of airline that most people fly very frequently, therefore, we don't have as many opportunities to impress our guests with our service (or let them down, depending upon how you see

it). However, if the most powerful form of advertising is word-of-mouth, then each and every service interaction must be executed flawlessly. Our business is similar to the "Emotional Bank Account" metaphor, but it's like a bank you only visit once a year, so deposits and withdrawals are high stakes. We can never take for granted that the customer will weigh the good and bad service actions and it will all net out in your favor. There can be no "net balance" mentality in our service game—the board is only set to binary scoring: Was the most recent expectation exceeded?

Put the 7 Empowering Laws of the SalesMaker to Work And Convert your Insights into Income

Now that you've completed the Law of Relationship, it is time to convert learning into earning. The first step is to return to the sections of this chapter that you highlighted, underlined, or made notes from. Of the key points that you connected with, pick three that resonate the most with you. Following the simple formula for transformation found in the C.I.A. process in the introduction (Connection, Insight, Action), identify and write down that which resonated with you. Then, identify the insights you gathered, and finally, decide how you might put them into action. Reading, doing, believing in, and incorporating three sales insights into your daily routine will create a transformative impact on your sales volume and sales commissions.

Here is how I will convert my insights into income:

C = Connection: As I read, the following content, principle, or idea that connected with me was:

_____

_____

I = Insight: As I reflect, the idea or insight I received is:

_____

_____

A = Action: The action I will take to convert my insight into income will be to:

_____

_____

Chapter 4

The Law of Discovery

Anyone can ask questions, but it takes a SalesMaker to *craft* a question into a close.

I never planned for a career in sales. In fact, I don't know many people who have grown up wishing that they would one day go into sales. It's ironic because sales is a most noble profession with highly professional individuals making five, six, and seven figure incomes.

Anytime someone persuades or influences another person to do, feel, say, or buy something, they are selling. Many people are in sales, yet don't know it. I was in sales from a very young age and did not know it.

At nine years old, I became a paperboy for the Chicago Tribune. I learned early on what it meant to make a sale by asking for a subscription, then keeping my customers sold with the service I rendered. Paperboy was my morning job, and I learned to sell Fingerhut products door to door in the afternoon. By age 14, I sold a local retailer on the idea of hiring me (until they learned that I had to be 15 with a work permit for them to hire me). At 15, I worked at Burger King, where I sold and served my way to a series of raises and was eventually promoted to assistant manager while still in high school. I worked in fast food until I was 20 years old when I started in outside sales.

Prior to entering broadcast sales, I was communicating and closing my way through life, unintentionally. I was selling and closing with the tools that I had picked up unconsciously. My selling strengths back then included my work ethic, listening skills, and desire to constantly learn. I didn't know then that the highest paid SalesMakers develop certain skill sets that include crafting questions, leading customers through discovery, and learning how to convert a question into a close.

My first official job in the selling profession was as an Account Executive. I was so proud. My paper delivering days were over. I no longer had to work in fast food, and I was now a respected professional—but still did not know very much. I was concerned that I might be put in a position to sell things that people may not want, and that made me uncomfortable. I had many false assumptions about the sales profession.

My wife is in sales, as well. She owns an advertising agency that does very well because she is a great salesperson. She says that "sales" is a four-letter word to many people, and I couldn't agree more. Having discovered SalesMakers who have honed their skills and sold their way into earning high incomes, I've learned that they spell sales with four letters, as well. However, their four letters are: L.O.V.E. The first thing that I fell in love with about sales was the idea that I could develop my selling skills, hone my craft, and how good I became was entirely up to me based on how hard I was willing to work at it. My classroom was my car during the day. My customers were my selling experience in the marketplace, and my paycheck was my reward. I could earn as fast as I could learn.

Discoveries of a Seasoned SalesMaker

Many things in life are dependent upon factors that are out of a person's control, but in sales I was in control of the speed at which I could learn.

Many other aspects of sales were attractive also: The freedom to pick and prospect customers; the income potential; the relationship building opportunities; and so many others. Have you asked yourself why you love the profession of sales? Consider making a list of reasons why you love sales. I have found that a question can unlock more than a customer's motivation, it can unlock a SalesMaker's motivation also.

Here are a few other discoveries I made as I matured into a seasoned SalesMaker:

1. Persuading people with facts and figures doesn't make a sale, but moving them with emotion does.

2. Building rapport isn't accomplished through charisma, but by genuinely caring for people.

3. Connecting and relationship-building isn't about talking. It's about listening.

4. Selling isn't about pushing the unwilling. It's about leading those who want to follow.

5. A signed contract isn't the result of closing, but the by-product of the right questions being asked.

6. Servicing isn't something you do after the sale, but what you do to make the next sale.

I was ignorant of many things in my first year in sales. But, like any beginner, I didn't know what I didn't know. I had a lot to learn if I was to be successful in sales. I learned early on about influence and the persuasive power of a properly posed question. There are inherent powers that exist within the framework of sales questions. In the hands of a seasoned SalesMaker, some of those powers create an environment of discovery with a customer that is necessary to close a sale. What follows are 12 strategies a seasoned SalesMaker uses to leverage the powers inherent within a question. Consider highlighting a few of the following abilities you may want to add to your SalesMaker's skill set.

Conversational Powers of a SalesMaker

Seasoned SalesMakers are able to leverage questions to:

1. **Create Appetite.** The SalesMaker has the power to use questions to create interest where none may exist.

2. **Lead the Conversation.** The SalesMaker has the power to set conversational direction and steer a customer by using questions.

3. **Learn about the Customer.** The SalesMaker has the power to use questions to uncover areas of interest using the 5-W Brothers, (Who, What, When, Where, & Why).

4. **Produce Passion.** The SalesMaker has the power to elevate the desire to purchase by probing deeper into areas determined to be hot buttons.

5. **Disarm Dissatisfaction.** The SalesMaker has the power to disarm unhappy or uncomfortable customers by using questions to probe needs, pain points, or problems. When a SalesMaker changes a customer's focus, feelings change. Change the thought and the emotion will follow.

6. **Inspire the Customer.** The SalesMaker has the power to create an atmosphere of discovery and wonder using questions that target a customer's curiosity and interests.

7. **Propose Perspective.** The SalesMaker has the power to create a new perspective using questions.

8. **Uncover Motivation.** The SalesMaker has the power to uncover a customer's hard-to-find or hidden motivations by asking relevant follow-up questions to discover the "WHY" that is driving the purchase decision.

9. **Reduce Resistance.** The SalesMaker has the power to use questions to reduce resistance during a sales call.

10. **Switch-Pitch the Mood in the Room.** The SalesMaker has the power to use questions to shift a conversation's emotional energy and focus.

11. **Elevate Rapport.** The SalesMaker has the power to create connecting moments while probing a customer to uncover shared interests and common ground.

12. **Neutralize Disinterest.** The SalesMaker has the power to turn an uninterested person into an interested prospect by discovering something of importance that will connect the prospect's interest to the product.

> "The art and science of asking questions is the source of all knowledge."
> Thomas Berger

Discovery is a Place to which Seasoned SalesMakers Lead Customers

Not every SalesMaker makes a million dollar income in a single year, but many make millions and more throughout their careers because they become experts at leading customers through the process of discovery. *Discovery is not just a process a seller leads a customer through; it is the place to which the SalesMaker takes the customer to.* In the *place of discovery*, a SalesMaker learns a customer's purchasing preferences, level of passion for the purchase, price sensitivities, and their predisposition to "think it over." While probing during discovery, a SalesMaker learns how a customer thinks, why they think the way that they do, and what will move them to decision.

Uncovering needs is only one of the skills the SalesMaker utilizes during the discovery process. Strategically crafting questions and developing a questioning roadmap creates an environment that allows for discovery. The environment that allows for discovery is essential to the sale because it shapes the emotional atmosphere in a way that sets up the close. It is often intangible assets filled with emotion that most influence a sale in one direction or the other.

Here are seven intangible assets that the discovery process contributes toward converting a conversation into a close:

1. **Discovery is the place where customers find their "Yes".** Where does a sale first get made? Is it while rapport is being built, benefits are being discussed, or at the closing table? The answer may surprise you. All of these steps play into a customer's decision to purchase. Discovery takes place at the intersection where sales information turns into personal

revelation. It's when a customer's "a-ha" turns into an "Oh, yes!" Personal moments of revelation give birth to inspiration that produces confidence in the customer to move forward with a purchase. At the intersection of inspiration and revelation, the customer chooses to commit, but customers don't always get there on their own. It's the SalesMaker's job to guide customers to that intersection. It takes a SalesMaker's skill in the art of questioning to lead the customer through a discovery process that converts information into inspiration making a personal revelation possible. A SalesMaker's ability to lead a customer to self-discovery is critical because the moment of decision is always made inwardly before it is announced outwardly. Being told something intriguing may create interest, but discovering something on your own creates inspiration and inspiration is where discovery takes place.

> "Wisdom begins in wonder."
> Socrates

2. **Discovery is the place where permission to purchase is granted.**
   When making personal or business decisions, it is normal for people to search their inward monitor for permission, a sign, or a signal that indicates it is safe to proceed. Deciding to buy goes beyond logic and emotion. It often comes down to a gut instinct. The emotional environment that discovery creates is where the internal "go-ahead" comes from. Discovery is where internal conflict is resolved and comfort is found as the SalesMaker leads the customer through a series of questions, pauses, and considerations to those gut feelings. Without going through the discovery process, a customer is less likely to recognize the "go-ahead" on the inside that turns into a "yes" on the outside. Discovery is where the customer finds their "yes."

3. **Discovery is the place where interest is created and increased.**
   It's very important to lead a customer through the discovery process by posing questions they may not have thought to ask themselves. An ultimate goal of the SalesMaker is to get customers to ask themselves the right questions. When this happens, customers are likely to close themselves as the conviction to purchase comes

> "A question is a knock at the door of possibility. The SalesMaker who finds a door of interest will eventually find a way in."

from within. SalesMakers must help their customers discover the right answers within because curiosity can carry the sale when the customer starts probing. Discovery questions can create interest as well as unlock areas below the surface of interest. Good questions lead to intelligent insights and information that is helpful in solving a problem, satisfying a need, and giving birth to new desires.

4. **Discovery is the place where positive emotions are created for the purchase.**

SalesMakers use the place of discovery to create an emotional environment conducive to closing the sale. This environment is created by asking the right question at the right time. A close is a question and a SalesMaker is a dealer in emotions that create the questions. Picture a dealer at a poker table. The cards the dealer holds are questions. In sales, the table is the conversation between the customer and the SalesMaker. The SalesMaker is the dealer, but what they are dealing is emotions. Now imagine that each card dealt to a customer poses a question that creates a predictable emotion or response. A SalesMaker can deal a sense of wonder, interest, desire, rationale, comfortability, confidence, appetite, or awareness for a customer to go from discovery to decision. Just as the house has already figured the odds on a game, the seasoned SalesMaker can often predict how a customer might respond based on the question, or sequence of questions they ask once interest and intent are established. A well posed question has the power to create and evoke emotions that can help the customer connect to making a commitment. With every question the SalesMaker poses, a customer responds. Based on the emotion within the response, the SalesMaker can piggy back on the customer's positive reaction with another question that brings them closer to the close.

> "The important thing is not to stop questioning. Curiosity has its own reason for existing." Albert Einstein

> "The sale is made during discovery when the ebb and flow of emotions takes place, not when the money changes hands."

5. **Discovery is the place where the fear of buying is overcome.**
Everyone has emotional deficits, fears, and doubts. When making big decisions, fear, doubt, and second guessing naturally come into play. Often, the bigger and heavier the decision, the more doubt and concern a customer needs to overcome. During discovery a SalesMaker helps a customer overcome the concerns surrounding the purchase while creating the confidence to move forward with the purchase. It is during discovery that a customer is inspired to take the leap of faith, overcome the fear of buying, and proceed. A SalesMaker walking a customer through the discovery process turns big decisions into little decisions and big steps into baby steps that are not as intimidating. At the place of discovery, the SalesMaker is able to help the customer find their courage, which is not the absence of fear, but the willingness to move forward in spite of it.

> Courage is not the absence of fear, but the willingness to move forward in spite of it."

6. **Discovery is the place where a customer's hidden motivations are revealed.** Every customer has a story to tell that reveals why they are considering the purchase. An astute SalesMaker is always in search of the customer's story because they know that lying dormant within that story is the secret to making the sale. That story is almost always anchored in the past, relevant in the present, or carries within it a future hope. The customer's story is significant to the sale, sacred to the customer, and needs to be heard by the SalesMaker. During discovery, questions become keys that unlock the secrets to the sale, but a SalesMaker has no way of knowing which questions are most meaningful until after they are asked. Diane Sawyer, one of television's great interviewers has said, "I love the early process of asking questions about a story and deciding which questions matter most."

> The most effective conversation a customer can have with a SalesMaker is not the result of an information exchange, but a shared experience."

The importance of a question is often not known until after it is posed and then observed as to how it impacts the one hearing it. The process of discovery is where the emotional responses of a customer can be observed, catalogued, and then converted into follow up questions that advance the sale. Probing deeper into an area that has created a customer's positive reaction can help make the sale. The opposite is also true. Probing deeper into an area which reveals a customer's negative emotional reaction can sink the sale. Discovery is about impact for the customer, not the seller. As the impact is observed, the SalesMaker reads the mood and knows where to probe more and less. Discovery is far more than soliciting information; it is the creation of a positive experience for the customer.

7. **Discovery is a place where trust, influence, and relationships are built.** Crafting and then posing good questions is how a SalesMaker creates an environment of discovery. The idea of moving people to decisions and persuading them through the use of carefully crafted questions did not begin with the sales profession. Sages long ago developed the craft of communicating and convincing audiences with just an idea.

> "The most effective conversation a customer can have with a SalesMaker is not the result of an information exchange, but a shared experience."

Aristotle, the ancient Greek philosopher and scientist, believed that there were three modes of persuasion that included logos, pathos, and ethos. Logos is the Greek word for knowledge, and one who used logos to persuade used knowledge, rationale, and demonstrable evidence to make their points. Pathos, the second mode, is used to persuade someone with passion as a means to move and arouse interest with emotion. The third mode, Ethos, is the moral competence and expertise of the persuader used to develop trust in a relationship. To establish trust one must believe in the character of the one persuading. Aristotle believed that one must utilize at least one of the three modes in order to successfully persuade others. He thought ethos or trust was the strongest because it overpowered logos and pathos.

Trust is the Tipping Point that Closes the Sale

Trust is the magical force behind influence that aids a SalesMaker in leading a customer through discovery to decision. While great trust may exist between a SalesMaker and a customer, it is not uncommon to create more than a connection and a closed sale, even a relationship to which SalesMaker and customer returns. With great trust comes the responsibility to steward the customer's interests and desires. A seasoned SalesMaker excels by learning to leverage all three forms of persuasion while communicating.

> "Trust makes the transaction possible and a relationship probable with a customer."

SalesMakers Communicate Like the Masters

Leading a customer to and through the discovery process is a communication art form that can be learned. Masters in the discovery process are the most influential voices in a conversation, and able to covert an uninterested prospect into a vested customer. They can weave their way through trouble and arrive at the close. The most successful SalesMakers learn to craft questions, create interest through probing, showcase a product's strengths, and bring to light both obvious and hidden needs. Leading a customer to a decision is not something done periodically, but regularly and systematically. How SalesMakers speak is a specialized skill developed by habitual repetition.

> "Customers won't be led where they don't want to go. To get them to follow, you must first find out what they need, where they are headed, and then lead them to what they want."

Socrates was another great Greek philosopher. He was known for brilliant debates and penetrating thought. His greatest communication skill was his ability to influence people by the questions he posed. He once said, "I know nothing except the fact of my ignorance." Being ignorant in his mindset is what made him wise because it caused him to be curious, and curiosity led him to ask more and better questions.

Socrates labored to establish an ethical system based on human reason rather than theological doctrine. He pointed out that human choice was motivated by the desire for happiness. He believed that the more a person knows, the greater their abilities to reason and make choices that bring true happiness.

Knowledge, options, and the power of choice are still at the center of many successful decision making processes even today. For Socrates, Athens was a classroom and he went about asking questions of the elite and common man alike, seeking to arrive at political and ethical truths. The most successful SalesMakers become Socratic in their thinking and masters in the art of communicating with questions.

> To ask the 'right' question is far more important than to receive the answer. The solution of a problem lies in the understanding of the problem; the answer is not outside the problem, it is in the problem." Jiddu Krishnamurti, The Flight of the Eagle

As a master communicator, Socrates had many students seek him out to gain knowledge and an edge on life. If Socrates had a class for students in sales, I can imagine the following conversation taking place between him and one of his students whereby his student asks him, "What is the secret to becoming successful in sales?" Socrates then proceeds to have the student follow him into a lake in waist-high water. Socrates then pushed down and held the student under the water. After a period of time, he let the student rise up and asked, "What do you want?" The student replied, "The secret of sales success, great Socrates." Socrates once again held the student under water for a time and once again let him rise. He asked, "What do you want?" The SalesMaker student replied, "I want to know the secret to becoming successful in sales." Again, Socrates held the student under water, but for a long while. When he finally let the student rise up for air, he asked him again, "What do you want?" Gasping for air, the student replied, "Air, air, I need air!" Socrates would then have said, "When you learn the secrets of how to create and ask questions as much as you want air, you'll know the secret to sales success."

Why is leading a customer through discovery so important to closing more sales? Roy Williams, author of *Advertising in America: What works, What doesn't, and Why* wrote a memo entitled, "Win the heart and the mind will follow." It says, "The heart doubts declarative statements because they tell us what to think and believe; whereas evocative statements pull responses from inside of us. Lead a person to an answer and they will usually discover

> Successful people ask better questions, and as a result, they get better answers." Anthony Robbins

it. Lead a person to the truth and they will cling to it. We own every truth that comes from inside of us and that is why it is rare for an argument to overturn something we have realized.

Socratic SalesMakers Learn to Think in "Questions," Not Declaritive Statements

SalesMakers retrain their brains to think in questions, not statements. It is difficult to do, but well worth the effort since it could mean the difference between earning an average income, or a high income. The more time a SalesMaker invests in thinking in questions rather than declarative statements, the quicker they will form the habit of crafting questions that lead a customer to decision. Successful SalesMakers become Socratic thinkers by investing more of their talking time asking customer's questions rather than telling them everything they know about their product. Asking versus telling may seem counter-intuitive to most people's natures. Retraining your brain to focus your talking time on asking questions versus making statements requires a mindset shift, a strategic approach, a toolbox of questions, and the decision to put the other person first. Further, becoming a Socratic SalesMaker involves more than learning how to ask good questions. It requires asking the right questions.

SalesMakers Communicate in Questions

As SalesMakers develop this Socratic ability, they become able to lead the customer with questions and their powers of persuasion increase. Whether you are new to sales or seasoned, the following process will be helpful in developing advanced questioning skills. Here are a few steps that helped transform my style of communication from telling to asking, and to leading instead of pushing when closing:

1. **Connect** with customers by placing yourself in the customer's shoes. Ask yourself the questions a customer might ask before, during, and after a purchase.

2. **Collect** and document questions and concerns asked by all of your customers. When you know all the questions, objections, hurdles, and concerns most likely to be heard, you should be able to develop intelligent responses in advance.

3. **Create** a SalesMaker's Navigational Roadmap of Questions that sequences questions to convert conversational dialogue into closing language. This library of probes is a go-to catalog of questions that can be used to create interest, uncover needs, spark a sense of discovery and wonder, advance a sale, and consummate a transaction.

4. **Craft** questions into closes using communication tactics and strategies. These tactics, tools, and strategies make up the SalesMakers Questioning Tool Box.

SalesMakers Identify with Customers by Placing Themselves in the Customers Shoes to Ask the Questions the Customer Would Ask

Do you have the ability to think like the customer thinks and feel like they feel so you can see what they see? A SalesMaker's ability to see through the eyes of a customer allows them to develop a buyer's perspective. It is a powerful mental asset to be able to identify with a customer and lead them toward the close. In order to develop the buyer's perspective and think from the other side of the table, SalesMakers ask themselves questions as if they were the ones making the purchase.

When SalesMakers ask the right questions, trading places emotionally and intellectually with customers, they are able to see what the customers see and think like the customers think. They do this so they can feel what the customer feels. A SalesMaker walking a mile in a customer's shoes is better equipped to take them to the place of discovery because they will have already been there. A SalesMaker can learn everything they need to know about a customer in order to connect emotionally, communicate intellectually, and close financially by mentally trading places during discovery.

"SalesMakers help customers think through, talk through, and walk through the journey from confusion to clarity, and from consideration to closing."

To experience what the customer experiences, it is helpful to connect with the purchasing process. One who can sort and sift through the mental and emotional obstacle course in their own buying decisions will be better equipped to help a customer navigate the mental machinations and internal tug-of-war faced while journeying from discovery to decision. Once the SalesMaker connects with the purchasing process, it is easier to walk the customer through it because they have already gone where they are trying to lead the customer.

I recently purchased an investment property and had the pleasure of working with a stellar SalesMaker. It was a big financial decision and some of my reservations against moving forward included concerns about the future of the housing market, questionable tenants, the return on investment, risks I might face, and an inclination to wait. My realtor, Peggy, helped me work through my thoughts and concerns. She was more than a seasoned SalesMaker; she was a recent buyer herself. I knew when talking to her that she could understand what I was going through because she had just walked a mile in my shoes and closed on a new property herself. She was extremely competent and there was virtually nothing she could not overcome. She was a true barrier remover because she knew where my thoughts and emotions were heading before I ever felt or voiced them. Even if you are not a seasoned SalesMaker, you too can determine in advance how to help your customers in their decision-making process by knowing the questions they may ask themselves while navigating the purchase.

SalesMakers help customers think through, talk through, and walk through the journey from exploring to buying. You and your customers may not consciously encounter every question in a buying cycle, but knowing the internal questions that can push a sale through or prevent it from happening will make you a better buyer and a better SalesMaker. You will identify more quickly with customers by relating to what they are thinking and feeling. The following are a dozen customer motivations that drive decision making and a few questions the SalesMaker can use to put themselves in their customer's shoes.

> "Judge a man by his questions rather than by his answers." Voltaire

Driver	Internal Questions Customers May Ask Before Buying
MOTIVE	Why do I want/need this?
DESIRE	How much do I want this?

FEAR	What concerns might cause me to put off the purchase?
CHOICE	What are my other options?
BENEFITS	How will this purchase help me or solve a problem for me?
SATISFACTION	How will I feel about this decision after I make the purchase?
PEER PRESSURE	What will others think if I make this purchase?
CIRCUMSTANCES	What factors brought me to the point of acting today?
BENEFITS TO OTHERS	Who in my world benefits by this purchase?
RISK OR LOSS	What will happen if I don't make the purchase?
RELIABILITY	Will there be good service and follow through after the sale?
TRUST	Can I rely on what this person is telling me or should I shop somewhere else?

> "Knowing in advance the questions a customer will ask during a purchase makes the SalesMaker better prepared to assist them in navigating their decision."

SalesMakers Create a Navigational Roadmap of Questions

A SalesMaker's Navigational Roadmap is a quadrant of questions designed to help navigate each of four areas of discovery: 1. Past & Present; 2. Motive & Meaning; 3. Barriers & Barometers; and 4. Decisions & Deadlines. By following the roadmap, buying interests are discovered, needs are uncovered, and an open path toward the purchase materializes. SalesMakers must intentionally craft and choose the questions that appear in their Navigational Roadmaps. There

"A seller without a 'plan to close' is like a traveler wandering aimlessly. Every journey requires a plan. A Roadmap of questions provides a plan to follow, a path to walk, and a promised outcome if you stay on that path. The SalesMaker's Navigational Roadmap is a GPS to the close."

"Thought-provoking questions posed during discovery can lead the customer to experience insight, curiosity, and a sense of wonder."

"People make decisions based on today's need, yesterday's experience, and tomorrows hope."

"Sales success is more dependent on good probes posed by a SalesMaker than product benefits presented."

should be no accidental questions. Each question must be deliberate with an assigned purpose to elicit a specific emotion, solicit specific information, and be capable of walking the customer through discovery to the close.

The questioning strategies are not solely for the purpose of gathering facts, but for unearthing the emotions buried within the customer that will drive the sale (the Customer's "WHY"). As the SalesMaker poses questions the customer may not have thought to ask themselves, inspiration can be converted into motivation to move forward.

The progression of questions will reveal what a customer has purchased in the past, what their purchasing preferences are in the present, and how the customer will use and experience the product in the future. When a SalesMaker uncovers how a customer is imagining their experience with the product, this intelligence can be used to escalate the desire for the purchase.

The goal is to lead the customer through each area of probing, but not necessarily ask all of the 21 questions that appear in the four quadrants. In fact, a customized approach is best depending on the situation.

The SalesMaker's Q4 — Quadrants of Questions

PAST & PRESENT

What did the customer have in the past? What do they have now? The past can often be a path to the future because knowing what a customer decided before and the "why" that drove the decision can provide a hint of what they will or won't do again.

FAMILIARITY	What do you have now / in the past?
PREFERENCE	What do you like about it?
DIFFERENCE	What would you like to change from what you have?
CORRECTION	What will you do differently this time?
CONTEXT	Where did the idea come from that made you want what you want?
MEMORIES	What in your previous experience reminds you of today's purchase?

MOTIVE & MEANING

What is driving the customer's intent to act now? When customers take action they are either taking initiative based on an expected event or responding to an event that has already taken place. By knowing what is driving a customer, a SalesMaker will have uncovered a hot button. Their motives to act now can include replacement, improvement, or a new acquisition.

TRIGGER	What was the impetus to cause you to come in today?
URGENCY	Why is it important now to no longer put off the purchase?
MOTIVATION	Are there any other reasons why this new purchase is important to you?

| IDEAL | When you envision the perfect purchase, what does it look like? |

BARRIERS & BAROMETERS

What could prevent the customer from acting today? What prevented them from acting prior to today? What is their current temperature toward the purchase, hot, cold, or lukewarm?

ROAD BLOCKS	Is there anything standing in your way from getting what you want?
CONSIDERATIONS	What issues do you need to consider before making a decision?
APPROVAL	Is there anyone you need to consult with before deciding?
TEMPERATURE	If you could put a number on your gut feeling, (on a scale of 1-10), where are you on the purchase?

DECISIONS & DEADLINES

DEADLINES	What is the timeline for what you are looking to do, and why? (What is the customer's timeline for processing vs. purchasing?)
TRADE-OFFS	With this purchase, what are the trade-offs you are making? (Will the customer be giving up time, money, or other resources in exchange for the purchase?)
FINAL OBJECTIONS	Are there any remaining issues we need to address today?
CONSEQUENCES	What happens if you don't make the purchase? (What will be the outcome, good or bad, if the customer does not move forward?)

PERSONAL	Who does "not moving forward" impact? (What is the negative or positive outcome of the customer's decision?)
BUDGET	What is your comfort level financially speaking?
TERMS	What terms are most acceptable to you? (Define monthly payments, down payments, term of payments, credit application, cash up front, etc.)

A strong questioning sequence will lead the customer to uncover what you want them to know while selling themselves during their internal process of discovery (the a-ha moments). What you ask them (and how you ask them) will determine whether they feel safe and comfortable during their time with you. Great SalesMakers develop the ability to create a gravitational pull between them and their customers by leading them to learn, uncover, and discover for themselves how the sale will bring them the satisfaction they seek. The byproduct of a strategically-developed questioning sequence is a strong influence with the customer in an environment that is emotionally charged in favor of the purchase.

"The greatest obstacle to discovery is not ignorance—it is the illusion of knowledge." Daniel J. Boorstin

The SalesMaker's Quadrants of Questions

SalesMakers customize their questioning sequences in ways that fit their style and connect with their customers. Take a moment to rework, reword, and recraft questions for your industry using previous examples of the SalesMaker's Navigational Roadmap.

PAST & PRESENT

FAMILIARITY

PREFERENCE

DIFFERENCE

CORRECTION

CONTEXT

MEMORIES

MOTIVE & MEANING

TRIGGER

URGENCY

MOTIVATION

IDEAL

BARRIERS & BAROMETERS

ROAD BLOCKS

CONSIDERATIONS

APPROVAL

TEMPERATURE

DECISIONS & DEADLINES

DEADLINES

TRADE-OFFS

FINAL OBJECTIONS

CONSEQUENCES

PERSONAL

BUDGET

TERMS

SalesMakers Craft Questions into Closes to Become Masters of Their Trade

Anyone can ask questions, but it takes a SalesMaker to *craft* a question into a close. Every profession and trade has masters. In the sales profession, SalesMakers earn high incomes because they've become Masters in the art of leading, influencing, and crafting questions into closes. They wield the wands of persuasion and influence to draw others to them with their ability to craft questions that lead toward the close. Tom Hopkins, also known as Americas #1 Sales Trainer is a master craftsman who teaches the importance of creating and crafting questions that close the sale. He has taught questioning strategies to millions of sales people around the world. Learning to craft questions into closes will be paramount to your success.

A question, for a SalesMaker, is a closing tool used to navigate a course to the final closing sequence. Without questions to advance the sale, the SalesMaker is only having a conversation. One of the most important skills for a SalesMaker is the ability to probe, pose, and position strategically ordered questions that lead to a closed sale. In this next section, you will find ten questioning strategies you can draw from to develop your customized "Questioning Tool Box."

Successful SalesMakers do more than ask general questions, they become craftsmen by learning to create custom questions that move people to decisions. A sales tradesman is one who works with an end in mind—a closed sale. A sales craftsman is one who works for the enjoyment of developing mastery in their skill and takes delight in the development of long-term relationships. They are craftsman in the profession of sales.

My grandfather was a master craftsman who could fix anything. He could fix machines, fabricate metal into usable parts, and even build homes. Learning to survive in his early years gave him the work ethic, and willingness to figure out how to fix, or make anything he or his family needed.

While most children grow up at home and become formally educated, my grandparents never got that chance. They were both taken from their homes during World War II as teens and forced to work in German work camps. My grandmother was a wise communicator and connected quickly with others, eventually becoming an interpreter between those in the work camp and the German officials in charge of the camps. She was a wizard of words, but my grandfather became a wizard of another sort—a craftsman.

Americans liberated them with other survivors in the camps on D-Day 1945. They eventually found their way, through missionary sponsors, to the town of Sandstone, Minnesota. Armed with nothing more than determination to survive, they raised a family of seven kids as first-generation immigrants in America. During my grandfather's lifetime, he was a farm worker, a factory worker, a mechanic, a carpenter, a home builder, and a general craftsman. Times were tough, but he thrived wherever he went by dedicating himself to mastering whatever he put his hands to. I don't think there was anything he couldn't fix or figure out.

While a Craftsman may carry a tool box, a SalesMaker uses questions as the tools of their trade. Anyone working in sales will use questions to close a sale, but a craftsman develops an inventory of questions they can draw from in order to convert customer no's into yeses. Learning to craft questions with excellence is another distinction between a SalesMaker who practices the art form in their career vs. a seller using questions to only close the next sale.

SalesMakers Use Questions to Capture the Attention of Their Customers

The power of a sales question is in its ability to attract the attention of others. In the chapter on the Law of the Close, we discuss "Seven Things the Mind Can't Resist." One of the seven is a question about something a customer cares about. This question is irresistible. Like a perfectly pitched fast ball that finds its way into a catcher's mitt, a question posed instantly finds its way into the mind. But not all questions are created equally. Some move customers toward the "Yes" more effectively than others. Once a SalesMaker has captured a customer's attention, they can create interest, steer a conversation, uncover needs and problems, and lead the customer using the power inherent in a carefully-crafted question.

Questions are tools of the trade for the SalesMaker. Armed with the new knowledge the answers to those questions generate, one can craft, create, and wordsmith questions to qualify a customer, discover a need, close sales, and reveal opportunities for repeat and referral business.

All master craftsmen have a few things in common. They are students of their trade. They are resourceful, able to craft and create using tools around them and skills within them to advance in their trade. Learning to become a master craftsman in the art of questioning takes time, practice, a willingness to take risks, and explore new areas, and above all else, persistence.

Every SalesMaker develops a closing signature comprised of go-to questions used in sequences that move customers from one point to the next during the course of a conversation. The SalesMaker's Tool Box contains many resources, and the SalesMaker knows that using one tool for all jobs won't guarantee success. Instead, a number of tools are utilized to work and weave their way through the sale with the customer.

The most seasoned SalesMakers develop a library of questions and questioning tools to help them navigate and advance in any sales situation. Following is an inventory of questioning tools and techniques that move people to decision. These may be used frequently but not necessarily on every sales call. They should be customized for specific applications and situations. Even more important is to understand the psychology behind the words of each questioning tool. For example, what is the intended outcome, and why do the questions work the way they do? Understanding why a specific questioning tool can be effective in a given situation will allow for the crafting of customer questions that advance the sale. As you read through the SalesMakers Questioning Tool Box, ask yourself these three questions:

1. What is the expected reaction of the customer to the question being asked?

2. Why does the question being asked create this reaction by the customer?

3. How could I customize this question for my industry to help advance more sales?

In order to comprehend how a questioning skill might make more sales, you will need to engage in a process that sales sages employ to become a master of their craft. Masters in every profession become masters by the way they think, and how they practice thinking. Mental role playing, thinking through sales situations and conversations with customers before they happen, crafting multiple responses, questions, and other mental scenarios, help move a customer along in the sales process. Forecasting possible outcomes through mental role play is the work of all Master SalesMakers.

Mental preparation allows SalesMakers to process a conversation before it happens by enacting it in their minds. The idea of visualization is used

> "We must first see ourselves asking the right questions before we can lead a customer with questions that will close."

in business, sports, and anywhere you find top performers. Mental role playing, or visualization is a three-step process. SalesMakers first think it or, imagine something. Next they envision saying and doing it. Then, they actually say or do it. They must think and envision asking the right questions before they can lead a customer. When they play it out in their minds, they are better equipped, and more prepared to use their arsenal of questions to move customers from interest, to discovery, and on to the close.

When you see it you can do it. When you hear it you can say it. And when you mentally practice it on the inside, you will be able to professionally perform it on the outside.

The SalesMakers Tool Box of Questions

As you read through the following SalesMakers Questioning Tool Box, pick three of the Ten Tools that resonate with you and work with them until you become comfortable and confident using them. Once you become comfortable and confident using them, add more.

The following are questioning tools found in the SalesMakers Questioning Tool Box. They are advanced questioning tools crafted to help advance any sales situation. Each should be customized for your industry and created in your own words so when they are delivered, they are coming from your voice, not mine. Consider picking three of the following questioning strategies and engage the C.I.A. learning process in making them you.

10 Questioning Tools to Help the Customer Find Their "Yes"

Tool #1: The Interest Building Question

Interest Building Questions focus on what the customer cares about and can amplify a desire into a decision. They are questions that probe into an area where the customer has exhibited a positive emotional reaction. By continuing to probe an emotionally-charged area, the customer's interest builds, and desire escalates to decision.

For example, if a life insurance customer exhibits interest in a whole life policy and emphasizes a specific amount, the SalesMaker might ask a follow-up question to uncover why the customer prefers one over another. In the probing process, they may uncover that the customer's neighbor had a similar policy and that relationship is what caused the customer to explore insurance to begin with. Now the SalesMaker has context of the customer's motivation and can refer back to the amount and type of life insurance knowing that it is a priority on the shopper's list.

Another example could be a SalesMaker walking a husband and wife through the dining set section in the furniture store. The SalesMaker observes the wife making positive comments about a particular dining set, sitting down to experience what it is like to be seated in that particular set, but casually walking past other sets. The astute SalesMaker will pick up on the customer's emphasis on one set over another and ask her why that particular set has drawn her attention. The customer's answers will not only give the SalesMaker insight into what will make the customer say "yes" today, but will open up the door to ask trial closing questions to advance the sale.

Tool #2: The Trial Closing Question

Trial Closing Questions are used to test the customer's willingness to move toward the close. An example of a trial closing question could be, "John, we've covered a lot of details on what you would like to see happen. Would you like to discuss delivery options?" Tom Hopkins, America's #1 "How To" Sales Trainer recommends an Alternate of Choice closing questioning strategy as another form of trial closing. As Tom has taught for years, an Alternate of Choice Question is a question with two answers. Either answer confirms the customer is still moving toward the purchase. An Alternate of Choice question which also becomes a trial closing question with options might sound like this, "John, we've covered a lot of details on what you would like to see happen, would you like to discuss delivery options for the first week of the month or the third?" Both questions test the waters on a customer's willingness to advance.

Tool #3: The Strength-Based Positioning Question

Strength-Based Positioning Questions are purposely posed to position a product's strength or to highlight a major benefit. They are followed by questions that peak customers' interest or advances the sale. For example, *"John, KXYZ Radio has reduced the risk factor in advertising by uncovering what delivers results and what does not. Would you be interested in hearing about how ABC Plumbers (John's competitor) created $25,000 in new revenue using KXYZ Radio?" Or, "John, using a famous personality to endorse your product will accelerate brand recognition, top* *of mind awareness, and results. Would you be interested in exploring an endorsement program with one of our personalities or handle the creative conception yourself?"*

Tool #4: The Switch Pitch Question

Switch Pitch Questions can change the direction of a conversation, refocus the discussion to get it back on track, displace negative emotions, neutralize resistance, or pivot in a way that points the way to the close. Switch Pitch Questions start with a transitional phrase or question and can create a pivot in the right direction.

Take Them Back: *Before I forget, can you please remind me again what you said earlier about how you would prioritize the neighborhoods?*

Give Them Feedback: *Based on what you said, may I provide you feedback by showing you two other options (if you can stay with me for a moment)?*

Bring Up A Negative: *Before we go any further, tell me what you don't like.*

Hit The Pause Button: *Can I hit the pause button for a moment to circle back around to the beginning and ask you: what is driving the need to get this particular brand? Did you have a good or bad past experience?*

Ask For Help: *I need your help; I'm uncertain what you mean. Can you please explain that to me again but in a different way?*

Acknowledge The Point: *That's an interesting point you just made. It reminds me of something I need to show you. Can we look at my screen for a moment to see another option you might find interesting?*

Thank Them: *Thank you for bringing that up. I also want to bring up two other things that you may want to consider before you decide which direction to go. There are two things that cause customers to experience buyer's remorse in my business. Would you like to know what they are?*

Tool #5: The Targeted Probing Question

The Targeted Probe is designed to be either an open-ended question that gives the customer the freedom to express themselves, or a closed-ended question designed to solicit a specific answer. Open probes are safe, exploratory, and often reveal the "why" (customers motivation) behind the purchase. Closed probing questions require a more intellectually based answer that is direct or factual. A closed probe question can be answered with a "yes" or "no" response, where an open probe always invites the expression of thought and feeling. Both types of probes play an important role during the discovery process.

All probes are investigatory in nature and designed to uncover a customer problem, pain point, or passion surrounding a purchase. Using open and closed probing questions is the easiest way to walk a customer through the discovery process. Simple probing questions can start with Who, What, When, Where, and Why. We call these questions the 5 W-Brothers and there are many examples of them in the SalesMakers Questioning Roadmap. Here are a few examples of both types of probes.

> "When a SalesMaker uncovers the customer's 'WHY,' they discover the way to the close."

- Open Probes: *Tell me about your business! How would you articulate our progress so far? What does your dream vehicle look like? What does the ideal house remind you of when you walk in the door? What events have led you to making the decision you arrived at today?*

- Closed Probes: *What color do you prefer for the purchase? Who, other than you, will make the final decision? Do you want to finance this over 15, 20, or 30 years? Is this life insurance policy for you, your spouse, or both? How much are you hoping to save per month with a new mortgage? Are you planning to buy an extended warranty or take your chances?*

Tool #6: The Magic Wand & Wish Question

Magic Wand Questions are designed to be dreamy and take a customer from intellectual processing to emotional imagining. They take us from what we think to how we might feel or dream about an ideal situation. Here are a few examples:

- *Suzie, if you had a magic wand and could make a dream house appear, what would it look like? How many rooms does it have? What is your favorite room? Describe for me what you see.*

- *Janet, if a genie in a bottle appeared and you could ask for anything, what type of kitchen remodel would be on your wish list? Can you pretend with me for a moment and paint me a picture of the ideal remodel?*

- *John, looking back, if you could turn back time and change anything about the first heavy equipment hauler you bought, what would it be? How would you do things differently? If you could go back in time and give yourself advice, what would it be?* (This is an example of "rewinding the tape" and asking John his woulda, coulda, shoulda questions.)

Tool #7: The Summary Closing Question

Summary Questions are designed to review the points of importance the customer identified during discovery. followed by additional probing or call to action. Summarizing points of interest communicates that the SalesMaker was listening, is focused on the customer's priorities, and nothing is being left out that is important to the customer. Summary Questioning is a customer-centric way for the SalesMaker to circle back around in a conversation to ensure they've thoroughly captured the customer's likes and dislikes during the discovery process. Here is an example of using Summary Questions to review what a customer likes and doesn't like while advancing the sale.

- *John & Jill, to confirm (or review) the items most important to you, you said you wanted your new counter tops to be blue Quartz, with a full back-splash. You liked the extended warranty, and having it installed before Thanksgiving was very important. Would you like me to indicate on the paperwork to have the leftover pieces of the quartz counter top turned into hot plate pieces, cutting boards, or smaller coaster-sized pieces?*

- *John & Jill, there were some things I gathered during our discussion that you wanted to avoid. Can I clarify with you what those things are before I process the paperwork? (Pause for customer agreement) With the new Quartz counter tops you didn't want the limited warranty but the extended, you didn't want straight edge but bull nose corners, and finally, you wanted to avoid paying interest the first six months if we could make that work. Is there anything else I need to be aware of?*

Tool #8: The 360 Degree Question

360 Degree Questioning is where a SalesMaker will ask a question and answer it during the probing or discussion process with the customer, and then follow it with a question that will uncover critical information or create momentum that advances the sale. The SalesMaker's "asked & answered" question might sound like this:

- *John, when I first took this job, I used to wonder, "What would I choose when deciding on a policy for myself, whether to save a little now and risk more in the future or invest more now so I could guarantee the future!" After thinking through that question, I realized that guaranteeing the safety of my family was non-negotiable and that's when I became a customer. John, what are the non-negotiables for you?*

- *John & Suzie, my wife and I also had to ask ourselves the future portfolio question. "Do we bite the bullet now and invest more in our future where the principal multiplies, or spend the principal now where it can't grow in the future?" We discovered our answer by focusing on the future gains instead of the present sacrifices. By sacrificing a little more today, we guaranteed a larger nest egg in the future. Which guarantee is more appealing when you look down the road, the return in column A or column B?*

- *John, whenever I am making a purchase I ask myself, "What would Scott do if he was in this same situation?" As I thought of it, the answer that came to me was, "Why save a little and risk being unhappy when I can stretch a little and get what I really want for a few bucks more?" So I made the leap, skipped the buyer's remorse, bought what I really wanted and never regretted it. If money was not an issue, where is your gut leading you right now?*

Tool #9: The Elimination Question

By design, Elimination Questions create clarity in the customers mind by removing unnecessary information and resistance from the discovery process. Making big decisions can be challenging for many people, and one of the ways to reduce unnecessary complexity and stress for the customer is to help them identify and vocalize what they don't want. Arriving at the right decision for a customer can be challenging, but by eliminating the "absolutely not" items, the right answers often bubble up to the surface. The SalesMaker who can utilize the art of elimination has another strategy for helping the customer find their "yes." It is not uncommon for a SalesMaker to be surprised by how a customer might answer an Elimination Question. Some customers are more passionate about what they don't want than what they do want. Here are a few examples of Elimination Questions:

- *Sally, before we go on, is there anything about this process you want to avoid? Are there features you want to avoid having on your new copy machine? What is unnecessary to the purchase?*

- *John, knowing you for the short time I have known you, I can tell that you are a man who knows what he wants. On the other hand, you must also know what you don't want. What do we need to stay away from on the options list?*

- *Suzie, before we go any further, is there anything you hate that I should be aware of? What makes the alarm bells go off for you?*

Tool #10: Return the Volley Questioning

Customers ask many questions during the discovery process. One of the best ways for a SalesMaker to convert a customer's question into a closing opportunity is to "Return the Volley." Like in the game of volleyball, when the ball is volleyed, it is hit and returned to the other side. In the same way, when a customer asks a SalesMaker a question, the SalesMaker "Returning the Volley" serves the question back to the customer in a re-formed question. Here is an example of a simple return serve and a return serve with two options offered as a way to advance the call.

- **Customer Question:** Does this table come in finishes other than Mahogany?

- **SalesMaker's Response:** If I am hearing you right, you are asking if there are other finishes available. What is your favorite finish?

- **Customer Question:** Does this table come in finishes other than Mahogany?

- **SalesMaker's Response:** Are there other finishes besides Mahogany available (pause)? If this table is available in the finish you'd prefer, would you like me to check on delivery options for *this* month or *next* month?

Of the ten tools in the SalesMakers Questioning Tool Box, which techniques did you find yourself gravitating toward? I want to encourage you to work with the three that fit you best and work with them for the next 30 days. After you have developed a level of confidence and competence using the first three, add three more and work with those until you are ready to adapt the next three. Through mental role play and a little time, patience, and practice, you will be able to wordsmith custom questions that will lead to higher sales not just one time, but throughout your entire career.

In the Law of Discovery, you've learned about the powers inherent in questions to close sales, the importance of taking a customer through and to the place of discovery, and how master communicators think in questions and not statements. You've been equipped with 21 questions that make up the SalesMaker's Road Map of Questions and 12 different questioning techniques you can apply. Most importantly, you have discovered that Masters in the art of Discovery do not become Masters overnight. They are built one day, one skill, and one learning experience at a time. Now is the time to change your trajectory upwards, and you can do that by engaging the C.I.A. learning experience.

> "The best sales questions have your expertise wrapped into them." Jill Konrath

Whether you are new to sales or seasoned in the art of communicating and questioning, the sooner you get started, the quicker you will become a craftsman in the art of questioning, and be able to create and customize questions and questioning techniques specific to your style. The Law of Discovery says, "Anyone can ask questions, but it takes a SalesMaker to craft a question into a close." My hope is that you get started today in crafting questions into closes.

C.I.A. CONTRIBUTORS

The LAW OF DISCOVERY

Natalie Phanphengdy, Google
Carl Ishikawa, New York Life

My name is **Natalie Phanphengdy** and I am a Sales & Onboarding Specialist at **Google** for small and medium businesses. I attribute my success in sales in part to my ability to ask the right questions. I love selling because it gives me the opportunity to improve my customers' business. Here is a summary of my observations, ideas, insights, or sales nuggets that connected with me as I read.

1. The idea that every customer has a hidden motivation connected with me most. My sales role is to cold call businesses and sell an online advertising platform. I often learn about a customer's pain points from their experiences with online advertising and lead generation tools. Learning their experiences is learning their stories; which unlocks many secrets to the sale. It illustrates the client's emotions and fears. From reading about the place of discovery, I will create questions to unlock my customer's needs, wants, and concerns and this will help me to build trust with them.

2. SalesMakers learn to communicate like the masters using well-crafted questions. By improving myself in the art of communication, I will be able to use strategic questions to discover opportunities during probing that help my customers learn about my product and help me close the sale.

3. "Thinking in questions was an interesting read. This will be the biggest challenge for me because I tend to get impatient with my own thoughts. I've learned that retraining my brain will be beneficial in my professional growth because it will cause me to rely more on questions than statements. I will use the SalesMaker's Question Tool Box and put myself in my customer's shoes. This will also help me better anticipate their needs.

4. The SalesMaker's Q4 is very helpful. I will incorporate these four probing areas into my selling system but customize them to my product and customers.

5. Reading about mental preparation reminded me of my days playing volleyball. Our coach set 30 minutes to visualize before each volleyball game. Every time we visualized, we played great! I've never considered it for my sales calls, but it makes sense. Just like sports, I will mentally prepare myself before game time. Moving forward, I'm going to definitely visualize between each dial and mentally role play to be prepared.

6. There were three questioning tools in the SalesMaker's Questioning Tool Box that I can incorporate to my business. Helping my customer emotionally experience the benefits of ownership before they buy will be helpful and I can do that with questions. I also like tool #9, the Summary Closing Question. It's such a great tool because it can potentially force a "yes." In my sales calls, clients share their negative experiences with similar ad platforms. I like this tool because it causes me to circle back and confirm their likes and dislikes and then close the sale.

My name is **Carl Ishikawa** and I have been with **New York Life** for 28 years. My work ethic combined with my ability to connect with customers, build relationships, and add value to them financially is what I credit my success to. My purpose is to help others protect and grow their financial futures. Here are the salient points that grabbed me in the Law of Discovery and how they can and have helped me throughout my career.

1. If the SalesMaker ASKS & LISTENS, the buyer will tell him/her everything that he/she needs to know in order to serve the customer and close the sale. The questions in the SalesMaker's Roadmap are a great navigational tool for going from a first meeting to a closing

meeting with a customer. I will incorporate a few of these new questions into my probing process.

2. The SalesMaker must create a positive and exciting experience during the Discovery Process. The powers inherent within a question reveal all the ways in which a question can help a customer and help the sale. I will work to match a specific questioning skill I need to tap into depending on the type of customer I am working with.

3. The Questions in the Discovery Process reveal the physical twitches in a prospect that may help the SalesMaker with the Sale. These Physical twitches may otherwise be concealed by the buyer, not necessarily intentionally. Asking the right question at the right time will reveal the customer's true motivation for exploring the purchase.

4. The SalesMaker's questioning strategies are very useful and easy to apply. Once a SalesMaker can relate to a customer's needs & desires by going through the discovery process, they are able to suggest solutions. The 360 Degree Questioning process can be used to demonstrate solutions that are working for customers in similar situations.

5. Other questioning strategies I have found to be very effective after decades in one-to-one selling were Tool #1 The Interest Building Question, Tool #6 The Switch Pitch Question, and Tool #9 The Summary Closing Question. All three of these are go-to questions that help me close the sale.

Put the 7 Empowering Laws of the SalesMaker to Work And Convert your Insights into Income

Now that you've completed the Law of Discovery, it is time to convert learning into earning. The first step is to return to the sections of this chapter that you highlighted, underlined, or made notes from. Of the key points that you connected with, pick three that resonate the most with you. Following the simple formula for transformation found in the C.I.A. process in the introduction (Connection, Insight, Action), identify and write down that which resonated with you. Then, identify the insights you gathered, and finally, decide how you might put them into action. Reading, doing, believing in, and incorporating three sales insights into your daily routine will create a transformative impact on your sales volume and sales commissions.

Here is how I will convert my insights into income:

C = Connection: As I read, the following content, principle, or idea that connected with me was:

_____

_____

I = Insight: As I reflect, the idea or insight I received is:

_____

_____

A = Action: The action I will take to convert my insight into income will be to:

_____

_____

CHAPTER 5

THE LAW OF THE SIXTH SENSE

The SalesMaker leverages Timing, Intuition, and Emotion (T.I.E.) to lead the customer to commitment, and then closes the sale.

There was an enormous deal on the table. On a scale of 1-10, it was an 11. In fact, the sale would not only have been the largest sale made by anyone that month, it would be the largest sale of the year. A sale this size would single-handedly lock in our success for the year. The customer was in the travel industry and numerous people from my company had been working to build a proposal with deliverables to which everyone would be agreeable. Today's meeting was to be a mere formality.

What had already been agreed to in concept, structure, and pricing was to be presented and approved by all parties. All the decision makers were at the conference room table. The staff at my company had worked tirelessly for weeks building the program. The customer was the only one in attendance from his company, but as we were all about to learn, one can be the majority when they wield the power to say yes or no.

It is important to note that I was a bystander more than a participant in the meeting. I was attending because I was managing five radio stations, which would be part of this promotional travel program. What was expected to be a meet-and-greet followed by a shaking of hands turned into an endless negotiation driven by the customer. The more the customer asked for, the more our company conceded. Getting a "yes" from the customer felt farther and farther away with every passing minute. One request turned into another, and there was no end in sight. We had been set up by the customer and were ill prepared for the negotiation. He knew it—and so did we.

Once the concessions spiraled out of control, I knew what had to be done and how to do it, but the timing had to be right. We needed a "reset" in the meeting, the negotiation, and the terms. I could feel the confidence level of the customer escalating with one demand after another as one concession turned into another. The level of desperation on our side of the table got deeper and deeper; over-promising on a deal we couldn't afford to lose.

I waited as long as I could before interrupting the conversation and taking control of a meeting that was not my meeting. It was a gutsy move on my part, as I was with two supervisors who outranked me and a number of sellers who did not report to me. But I knew in my gut what had to be done. My Sixth Sense told me to take control of the negotiation, but how and when to do it had to be spot on. The stakes were high!

My Sixth Sense was telling me what to do and say, how to do it, and that now was the time to take action. There was only one thing to do—end the meeting!

Using a frustrated voice tone, elevated speech volume, and exasperated body language, I motioned with my arms and said to the customer, *"I'm now uncomfortable with this program and I don't know if we can deliver all that you are asking. I think we should all go away and rethink this deal."* You could hear a pin drop in the deafening silence as I took the deal off the table. The customer looked stunned. In that moment of silence that seemed to last an eternity, nobody moved or said a word. In response, the customer gathered his belongings and left the building. I had gained control of the meeting, but to those left in the room, the deal seemed dead. Ten minutes later the customer called from his car and said "Yes" to our original proposal with a few minor concessions. It was the biggest sale of the month and the year. It would contribute significantly to our organization's success.

What closed the sale? Was it a gutsy move, a calculated plan, or something else that pointed the way to a successful outcome? The answer is found in the SalesMaker's Sixth Sense! When a SalesMaker discerns what to do, their Sixth Sense communicates a sense of timing, intuition, and emotion to close the sale.

What I sensed in the room—that others may not have—was the customer's unwillingness to let go of the deal. His success that year would be too closely tied to what we were offering.

I like to remember the Sixth Sense with the acronym T.I.E. which stands for timing, intuition, and emotion. What may appear to be a courageous or risky close to some is natural to the SalesMaker with a well-developed Sixth Sense. A SalesMaker acting based on their Sixth Sense may appear to be uncertain to an observer, but their behavior is actually driven by inward certainty.

In hindsight, it is always easier to look back and reverse-engineer a split-second decision to determine when and how to close a sale. I knew early in the meeting where the momentum was going after the first few "asks," having been alerted by my Sixth Sense. I also could feel that we had lost control of the meeting, and knew that we needed to bring the customer and negotiation back under our control. My trained intuition perceived it would take a "final concession close" or a "take it off the table close" to correct the course of the meeting.

My Sixth Sense has been developed from my experience, training, and sales radar (gut).

It is easier to judge timing and read the emotional atmosphere with only one or two influencers in the room because there are fewer variables. However, as more influencers enter the environment and impact the sales atmosphere, the variables increase. Hence, the SalesMaker's Sixth Sense plays an even more important role in making the correct in-the-moment decision to close the sale. This is not guess work, nor is it blind luck. It is the culmination of timing, intuition, and emotion converging that provides the Sixth Sense to make the right call that closes the sale.

You Will Earn More with a Developed Sixth Sense than Without it

The SalesMaker with a developed Sixth Sense is able to discern the exact moment to act. They can sense obstacles, predict outcomes, and anticipate multiple scenarios simultaneously, while adjusting and adapting to shifting dynamics that may present themselves on a sales call. This awareness and trained sense allows the SalesMaker to see and secure closing opportunities that others may miss. With a trained Sixth Sense, the SalesMaker is able to read the intangibles in the atmosphere to leverage timing, intuition, and emotion to better help their customers and increase their commissions.

The ability to exercise and maximize T.I.E. in any sales situation can have a dramatic impact on the outcome of a meeting. Some have a more natural ability to exercise T.I.E., while others require more training. SalesMakers who become students of T.I.E. can develop their Sixth Senses and seize more and higher income opportunities because they recognize more closing opportunities.

Examples of Timing, Intuition, and Emotion While Communicating

Consider a professional speaker who makes their living giving speeches. Their ability to read the room is paramount to keeping their audience engaged. A speaker may change his program mid-stream, utilizing a tactic to reengage the audience if they sense the audience is fatiguing or tuning out. At the right time, the speaker may use a personal story the audience can relate to or get them to stand up and do an exercise with another seminar participant.

Why would the speaker do this? What is the speaker's Sixth Sense communicating?

There may be nothing tangible in the atmosphere to the casual observer, yet the speaker senses that the emotional environment has changed. The speaker must react to retain the attention of the audience. How did the speaker sense the shift in the room? The audience's body language, facial expressions, and other atmospheric feedback indicated that the audience was becoming disengaged and tuning out. A trained speaker with a developed Sixth Sense knows how to read and then lead the shifting emotional environment in the moment and make an adjustment that keeps the audience engaged through the end of the speech.

Here's another example: A SalesMaker is interviewing a couple in a needs-analysis meeting. After a few minutes, the SalesMaker's Sixth Sense tells him that the husband wants to leave, while the wife is excited to learn more about the purchase options. The SalesMaker with a developed Sixth Sense sets their standard sales questions aside, turns toward the husband who is wearing a ball cap, and begins talking about baseball. Why did the salesperson shift their attention to focus on the husband even though the wife was enthralled with the discussion about the purchase? The SaleMaker's Sixth Sense was communicating that the husband had to get interested fast, or the meeting would end and all the ground gained in persuading the wife would be wiped out by the husband after the couple left the showroom.

How did the SalesMaker save the sale? By reading the emotion in the room, discerning what to do, and when to do it. The SalesMaker with a developed

Sixth Sense acknowledged what their sense of timing, intuition, and emotion were communicating to them and made an adjustment before the sale was lost. The SalesMaker's T.I.E was at work!

There are five qualities of a SalesMaker's Sixth Sense embodied with Timing, Intuition, and Emotion.

1. **The Sixth Sense of the SalesMaker requires awareness.**

   Two business machine sellers with equal experience go on a sales call. One recognizes the customer is ready to buy and wants to ask a closing question to advance the sale while the other continues talking aimlessly. Why does one seller feel it is time to close the sale while the other misses the clue to close given by the customer? It's the Sixth Sense of T.I.E.! One is aware and looks for it, while the other is oblivious. Becoming aware that there are clues to close is the first step in capturing them.

2. **The Sixth Sense of the SalesMaker is subjective.**

   What a seller perceives determines what they see, sense, and hear. Their "read" will determine how they lead on a sales call. *Reading the room always precedes leading the room!*

   A sales manager and new seller at a car dealership are sitting with a customer. They hear the wife say to the husband, "Honey, since I'm going to be driving the van, I really want the white one with tan leather interior. It cleans up easier with the kids." The new seller thinks if they find a white van with tan interior that the sale is made. But the sales manager reads something different, he sees the need for convenience with the kids so makes it a point not to just talk about easy clean-up of the seats but also the side doors that open automatically, the DVD entertainment system, and other features that will make a mom's life easier. Both the seller and manager see and hear the same customer, but one proceeds differently than the other. What is the difference? How they leverage T.I.E. to close the sale! SalesMakers who look for and then accurately leverage the dynamics of the T.I.E. will always close more sales than sellers who do not. Where one SalesMaker may see an opportunity to close now, the other may believe it is better to wait for more positive stimulus before proceeding with the close.

3. **The Sixth Sense of the SalesMaker is instinctive.**

   Doors of opportunity open and close during sales calls. One seller senses that they need to move things along while another feels they should remain in an area of customer interest. One seller thinks it's time to ask for a decision while the other wants to probe more to get to the root of the issue at hand. Having a trained eye for using T.I.E. always comes down to a gut feeling. Often we don't know if our instincts are right or wrong until we meet with success or failure. A sense of right versus wrong timing is often not revealed until it is too late, meaning the opportunity has passed us by. The right action on a sales call at the wrong time is still the wrong action, so instincts play a major part in knowing how to leverage the SalesMakers Sixth Sense of T.I.E.

4. **The Sixth Sense of the SalesMaker becomes a voice of guidance.**
    How the SalesMaker blends Timing, Intuition, and Emotion is the sales chemistry they create in any given situation. The most competent SalesMakers know how to leverage T.I.E. to *set, direct, and manage the mood of the sale.* Developing a strong sense of T.I.E. will not only increase your sales prowess, but your commission statements as well.

5. **The Sixth Sense of the SalesMaker is used by the Pros.**
    Selling is not the only profession that leverages the power of T.I.E. in their trade. Professional speakers, counselors, even comedians have a sense of what to say, when to say it, and how to say it the right way. In any field where the ability to communicate is paramount to success, you will see the T.I.E. of the Sixth Sense at work.

    iHeart Media has the largest national reach of any radio or television outlet in America with more than 850 AM & FM radio stations across the U.S. reaching over 250 million people monthly. For all its greatness in size and strength, the company is most proud of its in-house talent. The morning teams on a radio station are on the air 4-5 hours each week day providing information and entertainment for their listeners. How do they keep their listeners coming back for more day after day? They use their talent, tools, and their Sixth Sense of T.I.E. to merge a myriad of elements to captivate and hold a person's attention. Listener phone calls, contests, traffic updates, and chances to win tickets to the world famous iHeart Music Festival create an environment that delivers ratings and revenue. Do you have a favorite radio station? Take a moment to reflect on your experiences. Perhaps you'll relate to these:

- Is there an example you remember when a zinger was thrown from one host to another at the right time that packed a punch? That was the Sixth Sense of T.I.E. at work.

- Do you remember being moved emotionally to be happy, sad, interested, or disgusted with what was being talked about on the air? That was the Sixth Sense of T.I.E. at work.

- Have you ever been tired of listening to a radio station and ready to change the station, when all of a sudden your favorite song played or the DJ said something that reengaged you? That was the DJ following their Sixth Sense of T.I.E. that pulled you back.

If you answered yes to any of the questions above, you've experienced how those in other professions use and leverage T.I.E. every day.

Your Sixth Sense is the X-Factor

Not all radio personalities are great. Genius is often found in the intangibles, something often called, "The X Factor." If you were to ask program directors what comprises a great morning team, they would include attributes such as chemistry, commonality with the life group, an uncanny ability to connect emotionally with the audience, a reputation for credibility, entertainment skill, and an ability to read a moment. Many of these qualities are intangible yet recognizable when we experience them.

One thing is for certain, your favorite morning show host seems to have a sense for knowing what to say, when to say it, and how to say it in a way that resonates with you. He or she uses their Sixth Sense of Timing, Intuition, and Emotion to enhance your mood while you listen. They create a magnetic pull between you and them that keeps you coming back for more. If you've ever stayed in your car long after you've arrived at your destination just to hear what your favorite radio person was going to say next, you understand. If you utilize Facebook, Facetime, or hang out at the water cooler comparing the funny comments or jokes you heard on the air, you know what it's like to experience a broadcaster's Sixth Sense that blends chemistry, content, credibility, timing, humor, and intuition. In the same way, what separates one seller from the next

> "It's not just what you say, but how you say it and when you say it that matters most."

is their ability to use the Sixth Sense of T.I.E., "The X Factor." In successful communication, the use of the Sixth Sense—which is made up of T.I.E.—will help you if you work with it, or hurt you if you ignore it.

Be Intentional in Using your Sales Sixth Sense

You are already using T.I.E. to some degree. Timing is a sense of when or when not to do something. Intuition is an instinctive ability to speak from the gut that tells you what creates success or sabotage for your efforts. Emotions are created to move customers in one direction or another.

Since birth, we have all learned to develop our sense of T.I.E. to one degree or another.

- A baby cries and taps into the emotions of a mother in order to get a bottle.

- A teenager learns, through success and failure, how (and when) to approach parents in hopes of receiving a positive response to a request.

- An employee knowing when and how to ask for a raise uses an instinctive sense so it is not met with a standard company deferral or negative response.

- A person in love plans the right place, time and way in which to ask someone to marry them.

- A jewelry sales person knows which questions to ask and hot buttons to hit in order to make someone buy two carats instead of one.

- A public speaker knows when to pause and when to laugh to connect emotionally with their audience.

- A sales person observes a customer in their showroom for the first time and uses their T.I.E. to avoid the most typical response of "I'm just looking!" The SalesMaker with a trained Sixth Sense of T.I.E. will look and listen for the right moment and the right words to say so as to not sabotage their introduction for a "leave me alone and let me look" response.

T.I.E. is all around us and shows itself in success and failure every time communication between two or more people occurs. Effective use of the Sixth Sense is easier to observe than it is to teach, yet we all know it when we see it. Learning it takes time and living up to your potential practicing the Sixth Sense of T.I.E. will pay dividends in your pursuit of communicating, connecting, and closing the sale.

Why is This True?

T.I.E., for all we know of it, is still elusive. The correct use of T.I.E. in one situation can be the wrong use in another because of its contextual nature. A SalesMaker can do everything right and not make the sale. Why? The answer is always hidden in T.I.E., the SalesMakers Sixth Sense.

Timing

> When (Timing, Intuition, & Emotion) intersect with the RIGHT "ask," a close becomes the key that opens the door to the sale.

If you saw that Walmart was selling winter jackets in July, would you think that their timing was off? Or if you heard Christmas music on the radio in May, would you think someone at the radio station screwed up? What if you knew that Leon Day in the United States is June 25th? LEON day is the half way point in the year to Christmas. LEON is NOEL spelled backwards. If you are listening to the radio on June 25th, you may hear a Christmas song. If you know it's Leon Day, you may enjoy signing along to holiday music in June, but if you don't, the music will feel out of sync with the time of the year and you'll probably switch the station. Contextually speaking, playing holiday music on Leon Day is met with wonder and warm holiday wishes for many. Play it a few days later and it will sound out of season. Why? Because it's bad timing, it just doesn't fit. Timing is entirely about context. Good timing in one moment could be bad timing the next.

Timing Creates Consequences, Good and Bad

I am a novice investor. I have done well in real estate, but not always in stocks. During the down turn I bought real estate and it's doubled in value. If I sell now, I make money. If I wait too long, I could lose money. Knowing when to hold and when to sell is a timing issue. I also bought stocks that were the right stocks, but I bought them at the wrong time and lost money. There are financial benefits or consequences for recognizing a moment and missing one. Investors will tell you to buy low and sell high. It sounds so easy. Yet, many main stream American investors lose money every year in the stock market. Why? In a word, timing.

In the same way, sales are won or lost every day, along with the revenues they represent, because someone missed something and now it's too late. Wins and losses in the sales arena are often the result of timing. A SalesMaker's judgement on how they leverage timing is critical.

Timing Requires Recognition of a Moment

Have you ever sped up through an intersection thinking you could make it through the yellow light, only to find yourself driving through after it has just turned red? Maybe you've been at a stop light and were slow to go on green, but thankful you waited because a driver went through the intersection on red.

Timing Requires Wisdom

Timing can make or break your career. Mike Murdock, a motivational teacher and preacher, once described wisdom as the ability to "discern a moment." King Solomon from biblical times once wrote about the seasons of life and said that there is a "time and season for every activity under heaven." In the same way, there are seasons of a sale. There is a time to probe and a time to pitch. There is a time to close and a time to consider. There is a time to listen and a time to speak. And there is a time to act and a time to wait. Do you recognize that there is a right time and wrong time to advance the sale?

Here are examples of how your right and wrong use of timing can cause a customer to react toward you:

Right Time vs. Wrong Time to Close

At the Right Time:		At the Wrong Time
The customer goes along	vs.	The customer resists
The customer is comfortable	vs.	The customer exhibits fear
The customer is confident	vs.	The customer is hesitant

The customer asks questions	vs.	The customer is silent & looks concerned
The customer is excited	vs.	The customer puts up road blocks
The customer is interested	vs.	The customer is disengaged
The customer is trusting	vs.	The customer is skeptical
The customer is moving forward	vs.	The customer is pulling back
The customer body language is open	vs.	The customer's buying posture is closed
The atmosphere feels comfortable	vs.	The temperature feels cold

"The right thing at the wrong
time is the wrong thing."
Joshua Harris

Timing can Feel Elusive, But Right Timing can be Seized

Timing is like the wind; it comes and goes. If you are to seize it, you must sense it. The right sense of timing may feel elusive, but it can be caught. If you've ever left a conversation and thought to yourself, "I wish I would have said this when they said that," you know that you missed the moment, and you can't go back. Have you recognized a cue to close the sale but waited a minute too long and the customer changed the subject and you just knew that you missed your chance to close? Timing is often recognized in hindsight. But what if you could recognize it when it is happening, what would you be capable of? When you know what to look and listen for, you will better discern good timing from bad timing and know when to advance the sale. The customer often gives cues that they are ready to close. Do you know what customer cues to close look like? Do you know what you are looking for? Here are a few cues for knowing when it is the right time to close.

- There are physical, emotional, and verbal gestures of heightened excitement and curiosity. It's time to realize the sale is heading in the right direction and get ready to close.

- There is a hint of interest and excitement in the air. It's time to remain in the area of customer interest so you can convert and expand on the customer's interest level.

- There is a feeling of energy moving in the direction of ownership. It's time to ask the customer about options they may select for the purchase.

- There are questions the customer is asking as if they already owned the product. It's time to answer their questions with questions that will advance the sale.

Sales are Lost When the Cues are Missed

Sales can be lost when the customer is ready to buy but the seller is not ready to close. There is an unwritten rule in sales that when the customer says yes, stop selling. This rule exists so sellers don't talk past the moment of decision and un-sell what has been sold. There are a number of reasons why a seller might miss the moment. A few may include:

SELF-IMPORTANCE: The seller is overly focused on talking rather than looking and listening.

SELF-ABSORBED: The seller is unaware the customer is ready to buy.

SELF-CENTERED: The seller is listening with their ears, but not their heart.

SELF-FOCUS: The seller is focused more on themselves than the customer.

SELFISHNESS: The seller is moving at their own pace, not the pace of the customer.

In most cases, customers will tell us when they are ready to buy if we listen and look for the clues. To do that, our focus needs to be on the customer and not ourselves. The SalesMaker closes when the customer is ready to close, and not a minute before. Closing too soon can cause the sale to backfire.

> "Knowing when to close is half the battle. The other half is knowing how."

When is the Right Time to Close?

In poker, a "tell" is a body movement or facial expression that can communicate what you may do next. In the same way, there are "tells" a SalesMaker can spot to know it is the right time to close. Here is a list of buying signals that act as clues to close for the SalesMaker. These should trigger the SalesMaker to move the customer to and through the buying decision.

Clues to Good Timing

The customer starts to ask questions:

- Is that available for delivery by...
- Does the price include...
- What other options do you have?
- What happens if...
- Could you include...
- Can you match so and so's price of...
- Customer repeats a question.
- Customer asks about features.
- Customer asks for more detail.
- Customer starts negotiating.

The customer's body language (non-verbal clues):

- Leaning in & reaching forward.
- Nodding of the head up & down (not side to side).
- Handling & wanting to experience the product.
- Facial expressions of interest, excitement, and so on.
- Openness of posture: arms open or out, palms up.
- Hands forming a triangle.

The customer starts talking past the sale:

- I think we could use that to also...
- If I bought this, could I...
- I want to be able to _____ with my (product)
- This is going to be much better than...

Other Clues that can indicate a buying signal:

- Customer's guard drops, relaxes.
- Customer starts joking.
- Customer becomes more open with sharing information.

SalesMakers Know When to Speed Up And When to Slow Down

A number of years ago my wife, myself, and our two young boys took a Disney cruise. During the cruise, we visited the port of Pompeii, Italy. My wife walked with our five-year-old and I pushed the baby jogger with our two-year-old in it. We were walking on an old road with many cracks and the pavement was uneven.

I found myself looking back many times to realize I had left my wife and son way behind me. I wasn't walking in step with them. I was going faster than they could manage. When I went too fast, I left them not only physically but emotionally behind as well.

If you have a tendency to be impatient like me, then you know what it means to manage your pace and be aware of your sense of timing during a conversation, demonstration, or presentation. Although you are giving the same presentation for the 1000th time, the customer is experiencing it for the first time. Understanding how to walk in step with the decision-maker is critical to understanding how timing can make or break a sale.

A military march is an image that reminds me of what it means to walk in lock step with our customers so we don't go too fast or too slow. The SalesMaker must adjust their cadence to that of the customer if they are to avoid leaving them behind. I have to always remind myself to do this because I sometimes like to move too fast.

Here are the six steps to walking in lock step with your customer to ensure you are always leveraging your sixth sense of timing:

1. **Cadence**: When the customer steps, I step with them. Selling at the customer's pace ensures they don't get bored by going too slow or frustrated by waiting for you.

2. **Patience**: When the customer slows down, I slow down with them. A customer getting quiet is the time to let their heart catch up with their

head and experience the "a-ha" moment that tells them you have the right solution for their needs. There are times in a sale where pausing is critical to the sale.

3. **Decision**: When the customer asks questions about terms, I load up on trial closing questions to advance the sale. I will give you multiple ways in which to casually and confidently ask for the order in the Law of the Close.

4. **Curiosity**: When the customer gets interested, I pause and probe to discover what interests them and why. A customer showing curiosity tells the SalesMaker it is the right time to probe. In the Law of Discovery, you learn over 21 questions to assist you in uncovering a customer's obvious and hidden motivations for the purchase.

5. **Preferences**: When the customer wants to move forward, I provide them product options to choose from. When a customer begins choosing options, it is the best time to close.

6. **Involvement**: When the customer starts asking questions, I walk through the open door of opportunity by giving them options they can say yes to. A customer's queries are the time to provide information in the form of feature-benefit selling and then provide options from which they can choose.

Intuition

> "Intuition is the voice within. She is the muse that instructs us, influences us, and inspires us."

What is intuition? Is it knowing what is going to happen before it happens? Is it the muse within, giving you insight into a particular situation? Or maybe it's a second sight that allows you to see what others don't see? Intuition is all of these things because it comes from within. In sales, intuition is a knowing, a perceiving, and is designed to help us to adapt or adjust based on what we are seeing and reading so we can successfully make selling decisions that lead to success. The SalesMaker who works to develop and exercise their intuitive sense daily will fare better than the ones who don't. What are some of the characteristics of intuition?

1. **Intuition is "knowing."** Sylvia Clare, author of Trusting Your Intuition said, "Intuition is a sense of knowing how to act spontaneously, without needing to know why." Some people express intuition as a gut feeling. Others say with conviction that they "just know" things but can't tell you why. The dictionary defines intuition as "a thing that one knows or considers likely from instinctive feeling rather than conscious reasoning."

2. **Intuition is a feeling.** Malcolm Gladwell, the New York Times Best Selling author tells an opening story of a statue that didn't quite look right in his book titled, BLINK. The J. Paul Getty Museum in California had researched a 6th century marble statue for its authenticity and decided to purchase it. However after a year of researching and being on the brink of buying it, an Italian art historian took one look at it and knew in the blink of an eye that it was not authentic although he could not put his finger on why he felt the way that he did. It was a hunch, gut instinct, an intuition that led to proving the statue was not authentic. This instinctive feeling led the museum to saving millions of dollars. Feelings are not always right, however they should be listened to if for no other reason than to confirm facts before acting. Intuition is one of the ways in which life speaks to us. The art expert who spotted the fake had an informed intuition after decades of working in his field, what I call "experiential intuition."

3. **Intuition can be wrong.** Anytime we are making decisions based on how we feel, subjectivity enters in. Sales skills may be able to be broken down scientifically, but selling is an art that requires finesse and style. So much of working with a customer is feeling our way through the navigational course of a customer's needs, wants, emotions, objections, and sometimes ultimatums. A SalesMaker with an advanced intuitive sense reads the situation right much of the time, but even the most experienced can get it wrong. Anyone who has ever been betrayed by their feelings before knows that the heart is not always right. What feels right doesn't always make for right. That's why informed intuition is important. Here is an example of a man who followed his gut instinct but may have listened to the wrong voice:

   There was once a man who lived by the river. A radio report came on one day and said that the town was flooding and it was time to evacuate. The man thought to himself, I'm not leaving. I am a God fearing man and He will take care of me. As the water rose, a boat came floating by and those in the boat said, "Jump in, we're here to save you." The man said, "No, I'm a church going man. God will save me." Finally, a helicopter flew by and dropped a rope. "Hey YOU down there," said the folks in the helicopter, "grab the rope; we're here to save you." The man said, "No thanks. I pray every day. God will take care of me." Well, the water rose and the man found himself standing in front of God and being very upset, he asked God "How could you let me die? I am a good man, try to do right, and go to church. I prayed every day, why didn't you help me?" God replied, "I sent you a radio report, a boat, and a helicopter. What the heck do you want from me?" Besides being an amusing story, it also points out that God is not to blame for everything bad that happens. It is clear that the man misapplied his knowledge and in so doing silenced his more primal instinct of survival. The moral of the story is that intuition is not right all of the time, but can be a good guide most of the time if it is developed properly.

4. **Intuition can be acted upon or ignored.** Have you ever felt there was something you should have said during the sale but didn't, and those unuttered words could have saved the sale? Or did you ever feel something strongly but ignore the feeling? We can choose to act on a feeling or ignore it. My son Bailey played high school baseball for Mid Pacific which is known as the best baseball school in Hawaii. The program, the coach, Dunn Muramaru, and the team are legendary for discipline, methodology, and wins. During one of the home games, my wife and I watched Bailey batting when a fast ball hit him on the back. He took his base, advanced through the inning and made it home. On the ride home, my wife asked Bailey how he was feeling after taking a fast pitch into his back and he replied "I'm fine. I knew the ball was going to hit me." My wife asked Bailey why he didn't get out of the way and he said, "If I wear it, I get on base." Bailey KNEW how to "read the ball" off the hand of the pitcher's finger tips and KNEW it was going to hit him, but chose to ignore his instinct to get out of the way. Intuition can be ignored or followed. Whether we are right or not when we choose to ignore our intuition is not known until after the fact. As the saying goes, "wisdom is known by her children." SalesMakers who are intentional at developing their Sixth Sense will be right more often than not.

Sales Intuition is More Practical than Mystical

Sales intuition is the ability to read, learn, lead, adapt, and know what to do in a split second decision when a sale is on the line. In relating to the above story of Bailey, information regarding sales decisions needs to be observed in an instant like a batter would read a fast pitch off the fingers of a pitcher. An intuitive SalesMaker perceives opportunity, resistance, or roadblocks, and adjust accordingly. In the same way, the SalesMaker can sense the meaning of a moment and leverage their intuitive knowledge to plot a course that takes their customer from their current position in the sale to the close.

Have you ever heard a customer say one thing but you just knew they meant another? Or maybe they threatened to walk away from the deal but you knew they were trying to negotiate for a better deal. How did you instinctively know?

Intuition is like having your Spidey senses communicating with you under the surface to tell you which road will advance the sale and which will lead to a road block. Think of sales intuition as a sort of closer's GPS. Intuition is your Global Positioning Satellite of senses that brings billions of bits of information together. That information helps you to make split second judgement calls.

Scientists over the years have stated that the conscious mind can process as many as 50 bits of information per second, but the unconscious mind or intuitive mind can process millions of bits of information in the same time period. With all the studies debating the power of the unconscious and conscience minds, one thing is for sure; we all know what our insides are telling us when they tell us.

As mentioned above, feelings are not always right, but they are always valid because we are experiencing them. The same is true for our customers. Because of this, it's vitally important for SalesMakers to be able to use their instincts to read and sense what their eyes and ears may not be telling them. Follow your intuition, but always leave room for adjustments. Although your sales GPS might be off from time to time, it is better to follow what you feel is right versus ignore the correct move your insides are communicating to you.

"A SalesMaker's developed intuition is always more reliable than one that is not developed."

If you've ever trusted your instinct and you were wrong, you can identify with the self-doubt that exists within every person's intuitive sense. I like what Albert Einstein said about intuition.

"The intuitive mind is a sacred gift and the rational mind is a faithful servant. We have created a society that honors the servant and has forgotten the gift."

SalesMakers Develop their Own Sales Gps

Without the ability to make split-second decisions to advance the sale, your level of performance, prosperity, and potential is handicapped. Intuition is the part of the SalesMaker's sixth sense that combines previous experience with present circumstance and learned skills.

Intuition may feel mystical, but it is something you can learn and develop. Without the development of your intuitive powers, reaching a high level of sales success is not possible. In fact, you are almost guaranteed to be relegated to an average five figure income, with six and seven figures out of reach. Practicing The Law of the Sixth Sense will help you harness and hone your intuitive abilities so they are at your beck and call when you need them most.

Below are examples of split-second sales decisions the SalesMaker processes internally and intuitively. By training yourself to answer these questions from your customer's perspective, you are well on your way to developing your own Sales GPS.

Six "Sixth Sense" Intuitive Questions for the SalesMaker:

1. How does the customer feel right now?

2. Are they following where I lead, or do I sense resistance?

3. What questions are they asking of me that are convertible into a close?

4. What are their questions, fears, or issues that will keep them from moving forward?

5. Has their interest level escalated into an identifiable hot button?

6. What secondary issue question can I ask them that will advance the sale?

This may seem like a lot for a SalesMaker to process in a split-second decision. However, what may feel slow and clunky at first will speed up and feel confident as you get the hang of it. A good start to developing an intuitive sense begins with asking yourself the right questions. If you are able to mentally role play and put yourself in the moment with a customer, you know that intuitive guidance was present, although you may not have been aware of it until now. There is nothing magical or mystical about Sixth Sense knowledge or its application. The SalesMaker who tunes into all that is being communicated will pick up on what their Sixth Sense is saying to them. The SalesMaker who learns to ask themselves the right questions will activate their Sixth Sense.

What Voice are you Listening to?

Now that we've established that intuition is more practical than mystical, let's talk about where it comes from. Knowing where the voice of intuition comes from is always helpful in sifting and sorting through what to listen to and what to ignore. Sometimes we need an outside source to listen to. At other times, it may be wiser to listen to the inner voice. To know yourself is to know the source of your intuition.

1. **Intuition comes from your experience.** Intuition in the moment is contextual, and you are the context. The sum of our experiential knowledge, our past, and our training, all converge on the intersection where our intuition speaks to us. Experience can be an influential voice that sways our intuition. Have you ever taken the time to evaluate where you've been, what you've experienced, and what you've learned? If not, take a few minutes to answer these questions and listen for the muse within to share how the past may be an asset to assist you in the future. When you hear this voice, you will know you're listening to intuition. Jovi Santiago, General Sales Manager for iHeart Media said," We have too much experience not to listen to ourselves."

   > "A painful past can be a tormentor that haunts us. But a properly applied past experience can be a mentor that guides us."

2. **Intuition comes from your strengths.** Your natural gifts or talents are dominant voices that color the lens you see the world through. What are your natural gifts or strengths? If you ask a school teacher what she sees, she sees how the world can be made better through education. Ask lawyers and they see how legal strategies can help or hurt cases. If you ask SalesMakers what they see, they will show you a path

to the close. One of my strengths is what I call "strategic sight." I can often see the end before I begin. This helps me to be a better planner. This strength serves me well and whenever I observe someone planning something, my intuitive sense speaks to me about whether the plan is sound.

Wayne Gretzky, nicknamed "The Great One," is in the Hockey Hall of Fame. Known for his prowess on the ice, the story of Wayne Gretzky is a great example of intuition. A reporter asked him one day what made him such a great hockey players and he responded, "I skate to where the puck is going to be, not where it's been." The SalesMaker's intuition is the ability to read where the customer wants to go and have the "know-how" to get them there. To be able to subconsciously and intuitively discern, educate, and lead a customer toward their desired outcome is a combination of natural and developed sales intuition.

3. **Intuition comes from your mindset.** We all see the world through our own lens. We hear the world through the voice speaking the loudest to us in the moment. If there is a pain or need in our lives, that is on our mind and that pain or need frames what we see, hear, and perceive. It can also point us to a solution to what we seek. Whatever we are focused on, that is our mindset, and our mindset feeds our intuition. Some believe that God speaks to us through the context of pain and pleasure. C.S. Lewis once wrote, "God whispers to us in our pleasure, talks to us in our conscience, but shouts at us in our pain." Sometimes intuition only makes sense to us and nobody else. Maybe because it's only happening on the inside of us. Our mental filters help us develop our intuition over time.

DILBERT © 2013 Scott Adams. Used By permission of ANDREWS MC-MEEL SYNDICATION. All rights reserved.

Six Areas the SalesMaker Needs to Be Intuitive

SalesMakers who are intentional in practicing the art of applied intuition know the six signals they need to read in order to succeed in sales. These six signals are intuitively discerned yet can be subjective. As mentioned before, every profession has an X Factor, an invisible or unknown force that can assist in generating an outcome of success. Intuition is part of that X Factor. The intuitive SalesMaker sees and senses what others may not by keeping their antennas up and their receivers on. Here are the six signals the SalesMaker reads:

1. The customer's **readiness to buy**. There is a point of decision in every sale. The atmosphere is charged either way, but only an intuitive SalesMaker can tell which way the wind is blowing. Being able to read the moment provides the SalesMaker with the strategic knowledge of what to do in the future based on what is happening in the present.

2. The customer's **willingness to buy**. A customer can have all the information on a product, and even be persuaded that owning it is in their best interest, yet still not buy. The SalesMaker intuitively knows how hard to push in order to move the customer from resistance to willingness.

3. The customer's **unspoken motivating factors for the purchase**. The SalesMaker has the ability to know what the key driver for the purchase is. The driver is the motivation. Steering or guiding someone with what motivates them is easier than creating motivation on a sales call. A SalesMaker can sense what is driving the customer to buy.

4. The customer's **need or want for the purchase**. The SalesMaker's sniff test reveals whether the customer is casually looking because the product is something they want, or if they are on a mission because it is something they need. What is the sniff test? It is the ability to identify a "must buy" from a "want to buy" situation.

5. The customer's **level of confidence in the product and trust in the seller**. Confidence can be spotted by the words said; however it is also a feeling in the air. The intuitive SalesMaker has the ability to know when there is faith or fear, confidence or hesitation toward moving forward.

6. The customer's **emotional state**. The temperature in a sale may be set by the desire of the customer but it is read by the SalesMaker. How well the SalesMaker reads the emotional state of the customer will tell them whether it is time to close or probe more and look for a better door of opportunity.

Emotion

> "Follow the heart, for it is the first indicator
> of where the customer wants to go."

Why are emotions such an important part of the sales process? I mean, what does it matter if a customer likes me or not, as long as they like my product? Here are a couple of sales truths: 1) Customers usually buy into you before they buy into your product. 2) Until you can learn to lead your customer emotionally, they will not follow you financially.

In sales, trust is the primary currency that wins the business. Without it, making sales is almost impossible. A SalesMaker's ability to portray themselves as authentic, helpful, and knowledgeable can enhance the buying experience for a customer. Just as a SalesMaker wants to enhance the emotional aspect of buying they also want to avoid creating the wrong emotions on a sales call.

> "Customers follow those who make them feel good as they journey from deciding to buying."

Financial Commitment Follows Good Feelings

Is being able to recognize and capitalize on emotions important on a sales call? Whether we like it or not, how we handle a customer sets the tone for the relationship. It also impacts the likelihood of whether they will or will not follow us to the close.

SalesMakers skilled in the art of creating emotional environments that are conducive to buying know how to set a mood. One way they set the mood for buying is by uncovering or creating desire, and then magnifying it. One way to magnify an emotion is to spend more time probing and discussing an area that excites and interests the customer. This escalates the interest level the customer is already feeling and elevates the desire for the purchase. The opposite is true also. The more time a SalesMaker spends creating coldness or conflict on a sales

Persuade

call (albeit unintentionally), the more unlikely it is that there will be a closed sale. There are words, actions, behaviors, and specific skills we can learn that increase positive emotions on a sales call. They will bring the customer and the purchase closer to us. There are also things a SalesMaker can do to push a customer away.

Whether you are new to the profession of sales or a seasoned SalesMaker, deliberately crafting a selling style unique to you that creates closeness with the customers and avoids conflict will decide your level of success. It is critical that the SalesMaker becomes aware of what creates momentum and what breaks it in the sales arena so they can increase one and reduce the other. Knowing what you are doing that is helping or hurting your chances toward closing the sales will help you to intentionally create the buying atmosphere you want.

Customers will Buy or Bolt Based on How You Make Them Feel

Setting, directing, and capitalizing on the emotional mood in the room can make or break the momentum of a sale. The SalesMaker has the ability to solidify or sabotage a sale based on the emotional undercurrents their behavior creates. The most important part of communication is often to hear what isn't being said by the customer. The SalesMaker also needs to know what invisible communication they are emoting toward the customer.

My publisher tells a story of a meeting with a financial planner that not only missed the emotional signals, but ignored the alarm bells he was giving off as a prospective customer. The financial planner was asked repeatedly to skim through the material and skip to the end, but was too locked into their sales process to read what was happening right in front of him. This particular seller missed the emotional clues while ignoring the customer's verbal and non-verbal communication and in so doing, sabotaged the sale. In this sales situation, my publisher became so frustrated that he stood up and walked out of the room. What could have been a sales making moment for this financial planner became a sales breaking moment. Why? Because he could not read what was happening, and he ignored the emotion the customer was emitting. Not only did he not have a trained eye, but he had deaf ears to the temperature in the sale he was creating. This seller was emotionally incompetent and in sales, emotional incompetence can cost you dearly. Paying attention to your customer's positive and negative emotions during the sales process can mean the difference between closing or killing a sale. I wonder how many millions in sales are lost each year

176

because a seller fails to recognize what is going on around them and adjust their behavior in a way that helps the sale instead of killing it?

The SalesMaker who can create, regulate, and modulate emotions during the sale will make more sales and avoid the pitfalls and potholes that can typically sink a sale. Here are a few practical examples of emotional momentum-makers and momentum-breakers you have control of.

Momentum Makers		Momentum Breakers
Listening *Creates connection.*	vs.	Interrupting *Creates an emotional separation.*
Asking questions *Demonstrates concern.*	vs.	Talking too much *Demonstrates carelessness.*
Talking about them puts *Focus on the Customer.*	vs.	Talking about you appears *Self-focused.*
Focusing on customer needs is *Solution oriented.*	vs.	Overselling on product features is *Product oriented.*
Affirming the customer's choice *Creates confidence for purchase.*	vs.	Telling the customer they are wrong *Creates offense.*
Uncovering the buying motive puts *Customer's priorities first.*	vs.	Pitching the product before knowing the need puts *Your Company's priorities first.*
Leading the customer w/ questions *Lead to interest and "a-ha" moments.*	vs.	Pushing the customer by telling & overselling *Creates doubt and fear to push them away.*

Closing w/ trial closing questions	vs.	Asking for big decisions too early
Warms up the customer emotionally.		*Hard closes and backfires financially.*

These are just a few of the emotional outcomes our behavior can create. Being aware of your behaviors is a first step toward creating positive emotions and eliminating negative ones.

The Sixth Sense Leverages the Power of Two Opposite Emotions: Pain and Pleasure

"Every customer carries within them a visible and invisible need. The visible need is why they are meeting with you. The invisible need is why they will buy from you."

"That's what great SalesMakers do. They are problem finders, problem solvers, and their customers love them for it."

Everybody hunts for something and hurts from something, and that includes your customers. The two things in shortest supply for most Americans are time and money. Time poverty and money shortage are two of the biggest challenges most people face. When you can help someone cure their pain points in either of these two areas, you are solving problems. Financial rewards follow problem solvers. If one SalesMaker cannot satisfy a pleasure or remove a pain, the customer will find someone who will, usually a competitor. Make no mistake, if you are a SalesMaker, you are in the pain removal or pleasure creating business.

What Does Problem Solving have to do with Emotions?

Two of the most powerful emotions are pain and pleasure. We spend most of our lives pursuing one and avoiding the other. Whether deliberate or not, we are typically in pursuit of one or the other, and so is your customer. The astute SalesMaker learns how to convert a customer's problem into currency that closes the sale. Let me give you a few examples:

1. **Every customer carries within them visible and invisible needs.** The visible needs are why they are meeting with you. The invisible needs are why they will buy from you. The first home my wife and I built was perfect. But, a week after we moved in, so did the bugs. Every neighborhood has its unique set of insects. In Hawaii we have roaches and centipedes. It didn't take long for my wife to put her foot down and scream for a solution. When the bug spray company arrived, I acted like I was negotiating with them but they knew I wasn't going to let them leave without ordering bug spray service. Why? They were there to solve a problem for me and remove a pain point for my wife. Ask a bug man what problem he solves and he will tell you he is in the bug removal business. Ask a husband and he will tell you his wife can't sleep at night knowing there are bugs in the room. Happy wife, happy life. Customers tell SalesMakers what they need to know, but not everything they know. Find the invisible need, then come up with a solution to solve the need and you will be close to closing the sale. In the Law of Discovery, I shared with you a strategy for how a SalesMaker can do a deep dive during probing to uncover the hidden or invisible need of a customer. There are tactical questions a SalesMaker can use to unearth hidden needs which are often hiding below the surface.

2. **Not solving the problem will cost you the sale.** Years ago I traveled to the Midwest on a scouting trip to purchase property. My goal was to create an extra income stream that would pay for my kids' education. I was very specific with the Realtor® about what I was looking for. After all, I was buying a plane ticket and planning on spending the day with him and then making some final decisions. Our day started off together in the lobby of the hotel where I was staying. Unfortunately, the Realtor® proceeded to show me none of the types of properties I had asked for. When I asked the agent where the listings were that I had asked for, he said that we would be seeing those properties as well. As the day went on, most of our time was spent looking at properties I would never buy, and I told him that. Our day ended with me going back to my hotel feeling like I had wasted a lot of time and money to travel to that city and meet with that agent. The next day I got back on the plane, left with a bunch of money still in my pocket and never

called the Realtor® again. I showed up with a problem that needed solving and I even told the agent how to solve it, but he ignored my need and my instructions even though I clearly communicated my feelings. He was more focused on trying to get me to buy what he wanted to sell versus selling me what I would buy. He put his problem ahead of mine and lost the sale. If this Realtor had picked up on the emotional mood he had created, he could have made an adjustment and saved the sale. Instead, he sunk the sale by being emotionally ignorant. Whether his emotional receiver was broken or he was indifferent, I do not know. Unfortunately for sellers who do the same, their emotional incompetence is costing their company revenue and their family unnecessary losses in commissions.

3. **If you don't find a problem, it is unlikely you will make a sale.** Customers will tell you that they are looking for or thinking about buying something, but in reality, few people are going to waste their time window shopping for cars, cabinets, life insurance policies, and other items that they are never going to buy. Kelli had a son that went to the same preschool as our son. She was a life insurance agent and asked to meet with us. I knew where this meeting was going but I am a trained sales professional so I wasn't worried. Kelli asked all the right questions. I held my ground and didn't give her any buying signals. I didn't know I had a problem before my wife and I met with Kelli. But Kelli brought to the surface some life issues Kate and I had never considered. It didn't take me long to realize that while I was only in my 30's, I had a safety and security problem for my family—they were unprotected should something happen to me. Kelli brought an unseen problem to the surface by painting for me a picture of the next 30-40 years, and then presented a number of solutions that could solve my problem. If you are wondering if we bought a life insurance policy from Kelli, the answer is yes, of course we did. I had no intentions of buying anything, but she showed us a problem and then presented a solution. That's what great SalesMakers do. They are problem finders and problem solvers, and their customer's love them for it.

By now, you have discovered that the sales senses of timing, intuition, and emotion are not mystical but instead identifiable. The SalesMaker's Sixth Sense is practical and applicable in everyday sales situations. You have also discovered how improving your sales sense for timing, intuition and emotion will increase your sales volume.

A book or seminar can't impart a Sixth Sense to you. It can't be downloaded but it can be developed in the field and during interactions with other people, not just in a sales setting. Now that you know what to look, listen, and feel for during the sale, you can quickly pick up on communication cues that will help you persuade and influence more effectively.

The Sixth Sense is in operation all around you, all the time. It is taking place every time communication occurs between two or more people. Strengthening your sense of the T.I.E. will make you better in the areas of relationship-building, conflict resolution, motivating others, and closing more sales.

No longer is the next level of sales success elusive. No longer is the X Factor unidentifiable. It is close by. It is within your reach and within your power to develop it, and then leverage it. When you do, you will function in a state of instinctive sales behavior that effortlessly listens to and reacts to the T.I.E. automatically.

Where can you learn to grow your instinctive sales skills? The Law of the Sixth Sense points the way. It says, "The SalesMaker leverages Timing, Intuition, and Emotion (T.I.E.) to lead the customer to commitment, and closes the sale."

The following C.I.A. will highlight key takeaways by a SalesMaker like you who wants to grow in their knowledge of their Sixth Sense. As you read the insights and action plan below, consider how you might accelerate your sales by leveraging what they've learned.

C.I.A. CONTRIBUTORS

The LAW OF THE SIXTH SENSE

Gaylord Escalona, Microsoft Xbox

Bryan Heathman, Made for Success Publishing

My name is **Gaylord Escalona** and I am a Senior Category Manager for Xbox with **Microsoft**. I have over 25 years of accomplishments in sales and marketing roles. I attribute my success in generating positive topspin and clarity, by respectfully and authentically helping others achieve profitable results. Here is a summary of my observations, ideas, insights, or sales nuggets that connected with me as I read.

1. With a trained Sixth Sense, the SalesMaker is able to read the intangibles in the atmosphere to leverage timing, intuition, and emotion to better help their customers and increase their commissions. I find that while working with teams and groups, this dynamic is at work whenever I am communicating. I will make sure I am aware of the intangibles during conversations so I can increase my ability to leverage timing, intuition, and emotion. As I build upon my knowledge and experience to influence, hone and improve my skills, my confidence in using my intuitive instincts will grow.

2. Timing, Intuition, and Emotion work together to form my Sixth Sense. My Sixth Sense can help me reach a shared understanding with my business partners, more quickly and efficiently.

3. The most competent SalesMakers know how to leverage T.I.E. to set, direct, and manage the mood of the sale. This is a communication art form that will help me not just in persuading others, but in all forms of communication with family, friends, coworkers, etc.

4. Every customer has a visible and invisible need. If I can find both, I can close them by solving their problems. By paying attention to the customer's emotional state I will be able to read where their emotions are leading them and this will equip me to better help them.

My name is **Bryan Heathman** and I have worked in various sales capacities for almost three decades. As the **CEO of Made for Success Publishing**, I derive great satisfaction from hearing the stories of highly accomplished professionals ranging from fighter pilots to Olympians to Sales executives. Pursuing "success" can be a fickle beast, but can be truly experienced by developing a sixth sense related to selling, which the author calls Timing, Intuition and Emotion (T.I.E.).

In my line of work, I've met sales professionals who have what I call "natural born sales abilities." I can count these individuals I've met personally on one hand. Scott Hogle is one of these people, and having watched him work has given me an incredible respect for the processes he uses in selling. Few people take the time to document their success formulas. Scott has unpacked what comes natural to seasoned sellers in the Law of the Sixth Sense so it can be learned and developed by newer sellers. The Law of the Sixth Sense is one of the most powerful resources I've encountered to help move from having a subjective sense to an instinctive sense in a selling situation. Here are impactful pointers gleaned from the Law of the Sixth Sense.

1. **Timing**: When studying comedy, the timeless adage people teach is that "timing is everything." In a sales situation, this is incredibly true. Being able to recognize the exact moment when your line of questioning shifts from information gathering to closing is essential. Tip: Make a copy of the chart called "Right Time vs. Wrong Time to Close," and keep it in front of you while you are selling. In no time your sales timing will come naturally, enabling your to bring a sale to a close on an intuitive level.

2. **Intuition**: Learning to trust your intuition is fundamental to expanding your intuitive sales senses. Memorize the signals in the "Clues to

Good Timing" chart and you'll have a sales intuition you can trust for your entire sales career. Your feelings can be trusted. Can you memorize 6 things? Sure you can! Memorize the 6 Sixth Sense Intuitive Questions and watch your close ratios skyrocket.

3. **Invisible needs**: Moving your awareness from subjective feelings to instinctive questions is one of the most powerful tools in this book. By working to uncover invisible needs that your product or service addresses makes the difference in your sales productivity. These can be some of the toughest customer needs to identify. Strive to move conversations to a close by solving the unspoken need and you are on your way to addressing your buyer's emotional needs. What can you do to read what the author calls the "tells" in your next sales call? Review the emotional Momentum Makers again and make it part of your sales toolkit.

4. **Time poverty vs. money shortage:** Sales success in differing regions of the country or world hinges on knowing what motivates people. In North America, knowing that buyers generally are time starved or cash constrained is an essential fact to know. If your product or service can save time, the cost of your solution becomes a secondary consideration in the sales cycle. Confidently move forward knowing that often your pricing is a secondary consideration in closing a deal.

Put the 7 Empowering Laws of the SalesMaker to Work And Convert your Insights into Income

Now that you've completed the Law of the Sixth Sense, it is time to convert learning into earning. The first step is to return to the sections of this chapter that you highlighted, underlined, or made notes from. Of the key points that you connected with, pick three that resonate the most with you. Following the simple formula for transformation found in the C.I.A. process in the introduction (Connection, Insight, Action), identify and write down that which resonated with you. Then, identify the insights you gathered, and finally, decide how you might put them into action. Reading, doing, believing in, and incorporating three sales insights into your daily routine will create a transformative impact on your sales volume and sales commissions.

Here is how I will convert my insights into income:

C = Connection: As I read, the following content, principle, or idea that connected with me was:

_____

_____

I = Insight: As I reflect, the idea or insight I received is:

_____

_____

A = Action: The action I will take to convert my insight into income will be to:

_____

_____

CHAPTER 6

LAW OF THE CLOSE

Everyone sells, but it takes a SalesMaker to Close the Sale.

Everyone sells, but not everyone is in the Sales profession. Sales is persuasion, and when you are persuading, you are selling. If you are in sales, your income is dependent on your ability to close the sale.

Have you ever asked someone for something? If so, you made what's called an "ask" and when you are asking, you are selling. If you've ever successfully convinced someone to give, gift, or lend something to you, you closed the sale. Even if you didn't sell a product, it doesn't mean you did not persuade, or sell someone on doing something.

Whether you consider yourself in the sales profession or not, you are in the persuasion business. To sell means to influence, convince, persuade, or move someone from point A to point B in their thinking or doing. To persuade another is to move them in their beliefs, actions, and decision making in the direction you wish to influence them. If you are successful in your persuasion, or when you make an "ask" of someone and they agree or give you something, it's said that you "closed the sale."

SalesMakers are successful because they train themselves to communicate in a way that closes the sale. Don't be mistaken; we are all selling someone something, somewhere, all the time, from the cradle to the grave. But while everyone sells to influence those around them, it takes a SalesMaker to close a sale where a product or service is exchanged for money. Whether you are any good at selling or not is dependent on your ability to close. Whenever you are persuading, you are selling. When you are closing, you are a SalesMaker.

> "A SalesMaker's income is dependent on their ability to move people to decisions with their words."

Everyone Sells, But Not Everyone Closes

Do you remember your first sale? Your second sale? Or, are you still waiting to make your first sale? Whether you're struggling or succeeding in the sales profession, the Law of the Close will help you sell your way to higher commissions. It will help you dramatically increase influence, sales volume, and income. It will help you improve your communication skills in persuading others.

The first sale I ever made was pure luck. It was my first week in sales and I tripped into the order. It was a warm call set up by my manager. Armed with five minutes of product knowledge training and nothing else, I went on my first sales call. Was I naturally good or just lucky?

I'm pretty sure I didn't close anything on my first sale. The customer bought, but not because I closed the sale. The customer said yes and I was stunned. I didn't know what to do. My instincts told me that I needed to have the customer sign something. So I took out an order form, not knowing how to fill it out, wrote a paragraph in the middle of the form of what the customer said they wanted and asked them to sign it. Luck was with me—the order went through!

As an unqualified 20-year-old salesperson with little life experience, selling to established business owners, I hoped and prayed they didn't realize just how unqualified I was. Back then, my stereotypical view of sales people was that their job was to force people to buy things. That is the view of sales for some people today. I did not have a pushy personality, so I dreaded my imminent failure until I realized I could "ask" my way to the close.

When I learned there was a way to close with simple questions, and that those questions could create comfort and confidence on the sales call for both the customer and me, I was thrilled.

The first close I learned was the alternate of choice. It's where you give the other person two options, both of which advance the sale. Customers like options. Every time I asked closing questions, I gave two options. If they kept choosing one of the options, I was selling.

Today, I believe that asking questions is the most under-rated closing technique. If sellers who now only ask yes-and-no questions switched to offering options, their closing ratios would explode. More than ever we live in an age of online options, ubiquitous information, and the democratization of choice where we can have just about anything we want, when we want it. Customers can't be pushed into buying, they must be invited. Given options whether online or in person, they buy.

> "Customers can't be pushed into buying, they must be invited."

If You do Everything Right But Don't Close, You Don't Eat

With the Law of the Close, I will share with you practical ways in which you can level up in your ability to communicate, convert, and close your customers in a conversational and comfortable manner. To succeed in sales, you need to close. If you don't close, you don't eat. You can be an expert in every other area of the sales process but if you can't close, you will not survive. You have to learn the turns, twists, and techniques of the science of closing. This includes a deep knowledge of word choices and sentence structure. How you say what you are going to say and the order in which you say it, while intuitively feeling your way through the sale, is the art of selling. With the Law of the Close, you will be equipped with new insight that will help you weave your way around the twists and turns of closing the sale. My hope for you is that you don't just learn "how to close," but why the closes work the way that they do. Armed with this knowledge, nothing will stop you from creating your own closing vocabulary.

Let's start with what a SalesMaker looks like. I want to paint you a picture of a highly-trained, highly-competent, and highly-practiced SalesMaker. First, think of the best sales person you've ever encountered. How would you describe the way they made you feel? You probably didn't even recognize that you were being sold by what was very likely a SalesMaker. Great sales people never make their customers feel like they are being sold. They effortlessly glide from first contact, to discovery, and then gently move past objections, and on to the final decision.

The SalesMaker who can communicate, convert, and close handles seven aspects of closing very well:

1. **Comfort**: SalesMakers create confidence, comfort, and a sense of control for the customer by leading them with questions. They provide options at every turn so the customer feels in control. The customer never feels pushed, only invited to move forward by making their own choices.

2. **Shared Experience**: SalesMakers connect themselves, their customers, and the product together to create positive emotional experiences as they journey together toward deciding and buying.

3. **Ownership Experience**: SalesMakers paint pictures in the customers' minds so they can experience the emotional charge of ownership before they buy. SalesMakers know how to talk past the sale putting the customer in the middle of the ownership experience before they actually make the purchase. Realtors place buyers in the kitchen and master bedroom, auto dealers place buyers in vehicles, radio sales people describe what a commercial will sound like before it airs, and business machine sellers talk about ease, capabilities, and convenience before the first copy is made. They do all this with questions and storytelling even before they do it in reality.

> The more comfortable people feel during their time with you, the more likely they will buy you, your product, and your company. The more uncomfortable they feel, the more likely they will retreat from you."

4. **Relationship**: SalesMakers build influence and grow in relationship equity by speaking to what is important to their customers, and then super-serving those needs and interests.

5. **The Golden Rule of Sales**: SalesMakers create a closing atmosphere by selling their customers as they would want to be sold. A SalesMaker's priority is to read and learn their customers early, before they lead them to the close.

6. **The Why Shows The Way**: SalesMakers discover the customer's purpose and passion for the purchase. SalesMakers know that the discovery of the customer's "why" leads the way to the close.

7. **Connection**: SalesMakers create a personal closing vocabulary in their own words by crafting their own closes so when they speak, their words connect, communicate, and close.

The Right Words Empower You to Wield the Wand of Persuasion

SalesMakers use words to create wealth. This is also true for speakers, preachers, teachers, presidents, and sales people. If you knew how to communicate to the customer in a way that created a magnetic pull between you and them, how different would the selling and buying experience be for both of you? If you could create connection, accelerate relationship-building, uncover needs, answer every objection, close more sales, and resell customers almost every time, how would this new skill set impact your level of confidence, influence, and income? If this ability was within reach, what would stop you from taking a hold of it? If you knew you could not fail on a sales call, who would you call on today? If you could double your closing ratio for setting appointments, closing sales, getting referrals and renewals, would that be worth a few hours a month of your time? What price would you be willing to pay to be able to provide for you and yours above and beyond anything you ever thought possible? If the wand of persuasion could be put into your hands, what price would you be willing to pay? These keys to attaining this wand are waiting for you to grab. But there is a foundational key required in order to access higher levels of income, influence, and relationships for your life. That foundational key is within your reach. In fact, it's simple. You've done it before. Become a student again and study your vocabulary every day.

Closing Requires You to be in the Business of Words

Making millions during the course of your sales career by employing the principles of the SalesMaker is possible if you are willing to commit to becoming a student of what creates sales excellence. Learning new words and the language of the SalesMaker is how you can begin to level up in your income, influence, and sales volume.

How important are words? Consider that with words, the world was created. With words, the couple at the altar says "I do." With the right words at the right time said in the right way, treaties are signed, hearts are won, worlds are conquered and territories expanded. Elections are won, followers follow, and sales are closed. Never underestimate the power your words can wield to create positive change for yourself and others.

> "With the right words, the SalesMaker yields the wand of persuasion. Never underestimate the power your words can wield to create positive change for yourself and others."

Here is what Kevin Hall, a friend of mine and an author of *ASPIRE: Discovering Your Purpose Through the Power of Words* had to say about the impact of words. "Words are like passwords. They unlock the power. They open the door. They can also shut the door. Used correctly and positively, words are the first building blocks for success and inner peace; they provide the vision and focus that show the way to growth and contribution. Used incorrectly and negatively, they are capable of undermining even the best of intentions. This is true in business, in personal relationships, and in every other walk of life. There is a language of success and a language of distress. There is a language of progress and a language of regress. Words sell, and words repel. Words lead, and words impede. Words heal, and words kill. By truly understanding what words mean in their purest sense, we are able to unlock their importance and divine value and put ourselves in position to develop a new leadership vocabulary that looks up, not down, and inspires, motivates, uplifts, excites, and propels. When words are used properly, they sing out to the human heart."

Beautifully written, nobody articulates the power of words better than Kevin. Kevin is what I call a "wizard of words" in his own right and a master at using language to create an environment that motivates and inspires people to create breakthrough moments and memories. In the same way, a SalesMaker recognizes the power inherent within words to move and motivate a customer toward decision. Like Kevin said, "Words are like passwords. They unlock the power. They open the door. They can also shut the door." This is the power a SalesMaker wields when closing the sale.

SalesMakers are Always Learning New Words to Communicate Better

The first time I traveled internationally was to Paris. Stepping off the plane and into the airport was an exhilarating but terrifying experience. For the first time in my life, I was lost. I couldn't read one word or one sign that showed me the way to the bathroom or to baggage claim. I was a stranger in a foreign land who didn't know the language. That is how the first few years of sales can feel. You are not just learning the language of sales, but also of your industry and that of your customer group. If you are new to sales, learning this new language of the SalesMaker will take time. Be patient with yourself. Increases in income and influence come as you grow in your sales communication skills.

When my sons were in elementary school, they started bringing home vocabulary words each week that needed to be learned, memorized, and then tested on Friday. In second grade they had five words per week. By the third grade they had ten words a week. By the fourth grade, that

> "If you are going to invest a lifetime in a career, isn't it worth developing the language of success for that field?"

number went up to 15 words a week. And by the 5th grade, they were up to 25 words a week. (If elementary school students can learn new vocabulary words every week, so can SalesMakers who are willing to study.) By the 7th grade, they were studying words I had never heard. If you've been a parent helping your kids with their homework, you know what I mean. There is nothing more humbling than having your kid ask you what a word means and having to answer, "Google it."

Learning the language of the SalesMaker will help you to understand how words impact the emotional dynamics of conversations. You can memorize your way to mastery just like a second grader becomes an A student—through practice. But memorization isn't enough. It's only a start. To achieve sustainable growth in your career, you will need to put into practice what you learn and improve with each sales experience, whether it's good or bad.

Six Principles of SalesMaker Success

Whether you are learning the language of sales or improving your game as an already successful SalesMaker, here are 6 timeless principles to keep in mind:

1. **If closing words, techniques, or skill sets feel fake to you, they will feel phony to your customer.** Most people can spot a phony. Until you work with your new vocabulary and techniques to make them yours, they may sound phony to others. New sales skills feel uncomfortable at

first, but like learning a new language, the more you work with them, the more comfortable you become.

The first time I learned words to help me close the sale, the words I heard were not relevant to my product or industry. I had to work to adapt them to my product, my industry, and my own style of speaking.

Here's the rule of thumb that the great motivational speaker, Jim Rohn taught, "Don't try to export something you haven't imported yet." The best way to go from feeling funny about using new words to feeling natural using them is to write them out in your voice. Work with them. Practice them, and make adjustments based on how people respond to you when you use them. Repeat what works and fail forward on what doesn't.

2. **People will follow you as long as they feel you have their best interests at heart.** A breach or disconnect happens when customers feel you are trying to manipulate them for personal benefit rather than motivate them for their own benefit. Can't we all tell from the relationships we encounter in our lives who is there to help us and who is there to help themselves? All of us have intuition and when someone is trying to manipulate us, our internal alarm bells sound.

> "The right words and motives create connection, closeness, and a closing atmosphere. The wrong words with self-serving motives create distance."

Have you ever had the experience where you are listening to someone who is saying all the right words but you can sense they are only thinking of themselves? A SalesMaker's motive is to always make the purchase meaningful for the customer and not just profitable for them. Self-serving motives carry a scent and customers can sniff it a mile away.

3. **People buy for their reasons, not yours.** If I were to ask you why people buy your product or why they do business with you, you could likely give me a quick list of ten feature-benefit statements why you, your product, or your company are great. However, if I were to ask happy customers why they bought from you or your company, that list might look very different. People buy your product for how it makes them feel and the value it delivers to them—their reasons, not yours. Investing time probing the area of their passion and purpose will create

more closing momentum than anything we can say or do. Sales guru Jeffrey Gitomer said it this way, "The more time you spend talking about me, the more I like you. The more time you spend talking about you and your company, the less I like you."

4. **People follow when we are meeting their needs and moving in the direction they want to move.** The SalesMaker finds out where the customer wants to go, then gets out in front to lead them. A disconnect in the sale happens the moment we start to lead the customer in a direction they don't want to go. If you find yourself pushing and not pulling a customer with your words, you are doing it wrong. It's important to pay attention to whether or not someone disconnects from you. Are you able to read the moment when the customer stops listening? Physically they are present with you, but emotionally they've left the conversation. SalesMakers are sensitive to the emotional atmosphere and can read when they are leading but the customer is no longer following. They then make the necessary adjustments in order to get the customer reengaged.

5. **Closing may come down to a moment of decision, but the journey to a YES requires walking down the road of collaborative discussion.** Selling products with large price tags may not be a one call close. The size of an investment and significance of a purchase can make for a longer selling cycle. As a rule of thumb, the larger the purchase, the longer the selling cycle. The bigger the life decision and investment required, the more important the collaborative selling process is to closing the sale. When customers come to you for your expert advice, they're already half sold. They may need further education or to convince themselves they're making the right decision. When we are making big decisions that we have to live with for years to come, we want a guide to help us navigate through the decision-making process. A helping hand is always preferred over a hammering closer.

6. **Trust is the deal-maker or the deal-breaker in a relationship.** The right words without the right heart make it impossible to build lasting rapport. If you connect early, you can always close the sale later. But if you close before you connect, it is difficult to remake a first impression. Trust is the linchpin that makes building rapport, relationships,

and renewal business possible. In the absence of trust in you, the customer will seek out someone else.

As you continue in your journey toward improving your closing skills, taking these six principles of the SalesMakers success to heart will ensure you reach your potential as a Master Closer.

Do You Have the Triple Threat Talent Set of a Closer?

In the final three sections of this chapter, you will learn how a SalesMaker communicates strategically, converts emotionally, and closes conversationally. These three abilities are trainable, attainable, and within your reach, but they require commitment and practice.

Actors who have three talents are often thought of as those with a triple threat talent set. For example, if an actor can act, sing, and dance they are a triple threat. Their abilities to land acting roles and succeed in a very competitive career are much easier than for those without those three talents. When closing, the triple threat talent set for a SalesMaker includes the ability to communicate strategically, convert emotionally, and close conversationally. Following are the ways in which a SalesMaker practices and perfects all three.

SalesMakers Communicate Strategically

If you knew you could walk into a room and wield the words of influence to move, persuade, and close anyone on anything, what could you be capable of in the sales profession?

The best communicators tug at our hearts and capture our minds. That is why we are so willing to follow where they lead. It's not magic. Their words create a momentum of influence during conversation that allows them to persuade people into feeling, believing, or doing something. They have a developed skill that allows them to win us over emotionally and then convince us intellectually.

It has always fascinated me as to why 300 million people would put their trust in someone without business experience to run the largest economy in the world. In one word, the answer is communication. When you think back to the greatest U.S. presidents in your lifetime, which come to mind? Would you have on your list communicators like John F. Kennedy, Ronald Reagan, Bill Clinton, or Barack Obama?

Regardless of your feeling toward presidential performance and the people who held the office, there can be no doubt that winning candidates are likeable and have an exceptional ability to communicate in a way that makes us feel good, believe in them, and want to follow them. I like what Roy Williams, author of the *Wizard of Ads* had to say about how communicators win people over, "Intellect and emotion are partners who do not speak the same language. The intellect finds logic to justify what the emotions have decided. Win the hearts of the people, their minds will follow." Great communicators always win the hearts and then the minds.

I recall watching a debate between John McCain and Barack Obama in the 2008 election. I observed McCain give an answer to the moderator's question, and then Obama give the same answer—but so much more eloquently. McCain might have been right with his answer, but Obama won the moment.

Great communicators are strategic in their methods to win us over. Who in your life has won you over? Who do you follow? I think you will discover that the common thread in each of these answers is that the people you follow are great at communication. We follow great communicators. Therefore, SalesMakers must be professional communicators in every sense of the word. The best SalesMakers work to not only to become professional communicators, but polished as well. The more polished and prepared they become in their skill sets, the more effective they are at persuading and moving people to decision.

> "The way SalesMakers transform and become a better version of themselves is by improving the way they think and speak."

Your communication skills and character will determine your level of confidence and your level of contribution toward others.

- If you knew you could walk into a room and wield the words of influence to move, persuade, and close anyone on anything almost all the time, what would stop you from going to the next level?

- If you had the power of persuasion to overcome customer fears, create comfort on a moment's notice, and solve needs with the products you represent, how great would your contribution to society be?

- If you possessed the communication tools of the ages that could capture the attention of your listeners so they are better off when they leave you than when you found them, wouldn't you want to use them to help others?

What would you attempt to do if you had the words that could connect, communicate, and close almost every sales call? Who would you help with your new found level of influence? SalesMakers wield the words of wise communicators in a way that doesn't just close, but contributes in serving the customers and the interests most important to them. In the following section, you will find practical ways that will equip you to win others over emotionally and convince them intellectually.

SalesMakers are Purposeful in their Communication

SalesMakers communicate differently than other people. They sound different and are strategic in their communications. They communicate with purpose and use the tools of communication to reduce customer concerns and fears while building excitement and passion for purchases. The SalesMaker's communication is focused, intentional, and preplanned with a desired end in mind. When SalesMakers communicate, they listen differently than others in normal, casual conversations. SalesMakers hear differently, too, because they are listening for specific things they can use to help the customer and close the sale. As they are strategic in speech, they are also strategic in what they set their attention to.

In conversations, the SalesMaker is more focused on asking questions than making statements. SalesMakers are not casual about how they deliver product data, features, and benefits. They pick and choose the most important over the less important knowing that the attention span of customers is not long enough to digest a large volume of information. They converse with purposeful, strategic messages because their goal isn't the transfer of information, but the persuasion of people from point A to B. Communication tools are powerful weapons in the hands of the savvy and skilled SalesMaker.

Here are a few communication tools the SalesMaker uses to influence outcomes and wield the wand of persuasion during a conversation:

1. **The SalesMaker communicates with clarity.**
   Nike, one of the world's best known brands has long been known as a world leader in advertising. I once saw a picture of a Nike shoe in a magazine that sported the following ad copy, "Tell me what it is, tell

me what it does, and don't sing the national anthem while you're doing it." The point to me was clear which I interpreted to be, "get to the point and don't oversell me." There are occasions when I see advertising messages with lots of ad copy, but they are not communicating clearly. The ad copy seems to go on and on but isn't saying anything—it lacks clarity. With over 25 years of experience in advertising, I know that if I am struggling to make sense of the messaging, others are too. Where clarity is absent, connection is impossible and closing unlikely. One hallmark of every great communicator is clarity.

As an example, there are generally three lengths of ad copy in broadcasting: 15-, 30-, and 60-second commercials. As a rule of thumb, the best ad writer starts by writing a 15-second commercial. Then they add copy to make up a 30- or 60-second spot. This discipline forces the communicator to do three things very concisely: 1. Tell the customer what it is. 2. Tell the customer why they want it. And finally, 3. Tell them how to get it—also known as a call to action.

When communicating with customers, you should be able to make your point, make them want it with a persuasive statement, and then convert to a closing question all in 3 to 4 sentences. It can be done. It has been done. And you too can do it with a little practice. The next time you want to communicate something important, consider writing out a persuasive argument that you can state in 15 seconds or less. When you are prepared, you will be better understood, and will communicate with clarity.

There are two tactics you can use to leverage this technique to create your new sales language:

- Write out the 10 strongest feature-benefit statements of your product and complete each one with a question framed to advance the sale.

> "If you can't make your point in 3 or 4 sentences, you have not thought through what you want to say and will risk others tuning you out."

- Write out the 10 most common questions customers ask about your product. For each customer question, write 3 or 4 sentences that answer the question while advancing the sale. In doing so, you will avoid sales speak that does not lead to advancing or closing the sale.

2. **The SalesMaker communicates with anchoring questions.**

   If you've anchored a basketball hoop into the ground, you know that once anchored in cement, it is not coming out. Our beliefs and perceptions once anchored can be like that cement, unmovable. Customers who mention, articulate, or even go on and on about a product's features have often cemented in their minds a belief or strong opinion about your product or service. The SalesMaker can capture this moment of a customer's inner conviction and steer it into closing momentum by asking the right questions about it. The next time you are hear an opinion, strong belief, or full force conviction expressed, instead of agreeing with the person or making a statement about what has just been said, considers asking one of the following questions as a way of anchoring the customers belief:

   • Can I ask you why you feel that way?

   • Why do you feel so strongly about that feature?

   • If you don't mind me asking, how did you form your opinion?

   • I hear what you are saying; can you elaborate a little more for me?

   • If you wouldn't mind sharing with me, what has led you to feel so strongly?

   • Did something happen recently or in the past that has led you to that conclusion?

3. **The SalesMaker communicates by igniting the customer's imagination.**
   SalesMakers use stories to communicate. There's a close called the Puppy Dog Close. The way the story goes is that a passerby of a pet shop notices a cute puppy in the window. The person stops to ooh and ah through the window. The astute shopkeeper sees the emotional reaction of the customer, grabs the puppy from the window, takes it outside and places it into the arms of the passerby. The passerby experiences ownership of the puppy. Is that passerby going to give that puppy back? Of course not. They want to keep feeling the way they now feel.

   In the same way, the SalesMaker can help the customer experience the emotional benefits of ownership using questions to ignite the customer's imagination. The most talented SalesMakers learn to create pictures in the customers' minds by the questions they ask. In automotive sales, they create the feeling of ownership by putting the customer in the driver seat or having them take a test drive. In the sales profession, we ignite a customer's imagination with the questions we ask.

Here are a few examples to help you create your own sales language that grant you access to your customers' imaginations:

- **RV Sales**: "Picture for a moment the open road, not needing a hotel, staying in places where there are not many others, and sleeping in the midst of scenic beauty every night. How would that experience change the way your kids see the world?" A SalesMaker might also show pictures from the ten most popular RV destinations and have the customer rank them from favorite to least favorite. This exercise will place the customer smack dab into the experience of RV'ing. How could you do the same exercise with your product or service?

- **Radio Sales**: "If you were handed a microphone in a radio studio and you had an audience of 20,000 people and could tell them anything about your business, what would be the three most important things you would want them to know?" Or "If you were in a sports arena with the attention of 40,000 people, how would you persuade them to use your product?" In the context of a conversation about advertising, questions like these paint pictures in the customer's mind about how many they will be reaching and what they might want to say to this large audience.

- **Home Remodeling**: "Imagine the perfect Superbowl Sunday with friends and family gathered together. What does the living room look like? Why does your house now become the destination place for everyone?" A SalesMaker could also show a magazine of fantasy football party set ups and have the customer identify the things in each picture they want to see incorporated into their new dream living room.

- **Life Insurance**: "How will knowing your family is protected add to you and your spouse's sense of security? Is there anything that you will do differently besides sleep better at night? Would your new confidence level cause you to risk more, do more, or just enjoy the feeling of security more often?"

- **Financial Planning**: "When you put money away in your younger years, how do you plan to use it in your golden years? What would you do today if money were not an issue? If your portfolio exploded upwards and you could live any life you wanted, what do you see yourself doing?" A SalesMaker could lead the customer to discover the top three things they would do in their retirement years after their nest egg has matured. In so doing, the customer's imagination is ignited.

- **Real Estate Sales**: "When you think of the ideal house for your kids to grow up in, what does that look like? Can you paint a picture for me of the perfect neighborhood for your family? Of all the homes you've lived in, what was your favorite feature? What is your one wish for the next house in which you'd want to live?"

- **General Sales**: "If you had a magic wand and could change anything about a purchase, what would it be? If money were not an object, what would you do? How do you plan to use this product a year from now? Who else will benefit long term from the purchase you are considering making?"

- **General Sales**: "Imagine with me for a moment what the ideal outcome looks like? How would you describe it?"

4. **The SalesMaker communicates in stories.**

Movie makers have a knack for getting to our hearts. Good story tellers know that a good story bypasses logic and goes straight to the emotional center of the brain. Storytelling opens the door to the heart while putting the mind at ease. Storytelling can evoke emotions that can cause a customer to connect, identify, emote, reach out, reconsider, and move forward. Tom Hopkins spoke of the dominant role emotions play in sales when he said, "People buy emotionally and then justify the purchase logically." In addition to the dominant role that emotions play when helping us to make a purchase, the value proposition and affordability must be present. There can be no doubt that the SalesMaker who learns to communicate in stories will have a better chance of closing the sale than those who don't. In what ways might you communicate in stories? Here are a few suggestions to get you thinking:

> "Storytelling opens the door to the heart while putting the mind at ease."

- **Similar Situation**: Articulating what a customer "just like them" went through and how they worked through it, and what the outcome was can often be the tipping point that creates comfort and removes conflict surrounding the purchase.

- **A Problem Solved**: "Mr. Jones, most of our customers come to us for the same reason you are here. You've come to the right place. Let me share with you what others who were in your shoes did..."

- **Helping Others**: Share how a purchase helped a family, a friend, or someone else.

5. **The SalesMaker communicates with technology.**

Years from now, they will still be telling business stories of why Facebook has been so successful. There can be no doubt that at the center of the social media giant's strength lies their ability to create "shared experience" with users. Sharing, interacting, connecting, and gathering around technology is considered to be one of the most engaging human behaviors created in the last hundred years.

SalesMakers can leverage the phenomenal opportunity technology creates by inviting customers into a shared experience with them. It may sound simple, but whether you are paid professionally in sales or simply interested in increasing your levels of persuasion, leveraging technology, social media, and Apps can create 'shared experience' and customer engagement very quickly. Thousands of Apps are available that can be used in the demonstration of your product and service that include pictures, video, calculators, measuring, demonstrating, scheduling, and communicating, and the list goes on. The more you can involve your customer in the process of experiencing your product or purchasing your product through technology, the better chance you'll have in building excitement for the purchase and advancing the sale.

6. **The SalesMaker communicates in cooperation with the mind.**

How do you capture a customer's attention? Are there technologies available today that create focus on demand? What if these technologies were techniques already embedded within us and all that was required to capture the customer's attention was to flip a switch? Let me ask a question: Is it easier to change the customer's mind or to come into agreement and cooperate with something they already believe, feel, or have experienced? The answer may be surprisingly simple. There are some things the mind cannot resist. If you speak to areas that are irresistible to the mind, you have the mind's attention. To do the opposite is to fight human nature. If you capture my attention, I am now focused on you and will give weight to your words. Next time you are conversing with someone, remember the following seven things the mind can't resist.

7 Things the Mind Can't Resist

1. **Fight or Flight**: The mind, when faced with fear, will get defensive and combative, or retreat. SalesMakers who are not aware of the words they use can unintentionally create an uncomfortable environment that causes a customer to disengage (flight) or become aggressive (fight). The next time you sense that your words are connecting, be aware of what you are saying and how you are communicating so you can reproduce it. Also, when you are creating an environment where the customer wants to flee your presence, make a note of how not to communicate and you will level up in your understanding of how communication can create fight or flight with a customer.

2. **Familiarity**: If you know what a customer has done, liked, or bought in the past, you will know what may bring comfort and familiarity to the present. The mind recognizes colors, sounds, smells, and feelings, from the past. When something is embedded within the subconscious, marketers call that branding. When it is brought back up, it is called recall. You have to know your customer to sell your customer. A memory, when triggered, will create a positive or negative association by carrying something from the past into the present. SalesMakers make it a point to create confidence and comfort on a sales call by bringing familiarity from the past into the present. They do this by probing the past so they know what to pitch in the present, and what areas to avoid.

3. **Obsession**: Every mind is obsessed with something. If you know what is playing in the background of the subconscious, then you can sometimes predict future behavior. This involves learning a person's triggers, actions, or preferences. Asking questions about what someone loves, hates, desires, or fears uncovers how an individual is wired and will give you a clue as to what

> "That's what great SalesMakers do. They are problem finders, problem solvers, and their customers love them for it."

is playing in the background. When you speak to what they are most often thinking about, you will capture their attention every time. In the Law of Connection, I outlined a number of past-, present-, and future-oriented questions you can ask your customer to better understand their motivations and world view.

4. **Pictures**: The mind thinks in pictures, and a wizard of words in the sales profession learns to create pictures in their customers' minds using analogies, adjectives, stories, and other communication tools. In the radio business there are no pictures, yet words cause the mind to create visions and pictures. Words have the ability to create pictures, and elicit emotions. The SalesMaker paints pictures onto the screen of the customer's mind to help them make meaningful connections between what they want and what the product can deliver. What adjectives can you use to paint a picture in your customer's mind about your product or service? Answering this question will also help you become a better story teller.

5. **Choice**: People love to express their opinions of what they like and dislike. When customers are given choices and asked to express themselves as to why they like one thing and not another, sharing an opinion is hard to resist. SalesMakers who learn to create choices throughout their communications will find that giving the customer options to choose from is the simplest, easiest, and best closing skill ever devised. If you never learn any other closing skill, learn to communicate with questions that present options versus "yes and no" answers and watch your sales soar. Further, asking a customer to explain or defend a preference of one thing over another will accelerate a sale toward the close. Nothing clinches our convictions more than needing to defend or explain them, especially when doing it with regards to something we want.

6. **Questions**: The mind's attention is easily captured by questions. Regardless of what is transpiring in a conversation, a question can change its focus and direction. One of the principles found in the Law of Discovery is that the person asking the question sets the direction of the conversation. If you have the ability to invoke specific desires and feelings with your questions, you not only have your customers' attention, you have their focus. Focus decides feelings! Inherent within

the nature of a question is its ability to direct focus. A SalesMaker who learns how to master the art of questioning has learned to set, direct, and influence the direction of a conversation.

7. **A Moving Moment**:

   After years of visiting Disney parks, my family was ready for something new. Going to Universal Studios for the first time created a sense of wonder and excitement we were unaccustomed to. We went from one astonishing moment to the next, and all we wanted to do was "remain in the moment" that had been so moving.

   When a SalesMaker creates an emotional experience for the customer that moves them, the customer is inclined to remain in that positive moment. When we experience something that moves us emotionally, everything around us slows down and our hearing, vision, and other senses become more acute. We are captured by the moment! When a SalesMaker sees their customers being swept away in a moment, there should be only one response. Remain in the moment until it is time to transition out of the moment. When the SalesMaker transitions, they ask the customer a "choice" question that will carry the moment forward into a buying decision.

   > If you speak to my focus and what I care about, you immediately have my attention. When you talk to me about what is on my mind, I then want to know what is on your mind."

Now that you are aware of the Seven Things the Mind Can't Resist, you will be able to identify them when they emerge in your communication with others. Consider asking yourself how these mental mechanisms already hard-wired into the human brain can help you capture a customer's attention and lead them to commitment. The longer you can hold a customer's attention, the better chance you will have at persuading them to make a purchase.

The SalesMaker Communicates using the Five W-Brothers:

Have you ever been in a conversation and didn't know what to say? Or, knew you shouldn't say what you wanted to say? A question is a SalesMaker's best friend for two reasons. One, a question can set the direction of a conversation or change the focus instantaneously. And two, because our focus decides our feelings, a question can displace the flow of energy in a conversation and redirect it towards a customer's primary focus, which is always a need. To ask someone about themselves, more often than not, will create a positive flow of emotion. We covered the five W-Brothers in The Law of Discovery. Starting a sentence with Who, What, When, Where, and Why are five conversation starters the SalesMaker can use to craft closing questions that advance the sale. Here are five examples of how starting your sentences with one of the five W-Brothers can correct the focus and flow of a conversation:

Asking **W**hat can uncover options that point to the purpose for the purchase.

Asking **W**hy is where passion for the purchase is revealed and hot buttons are discovered.

Asking **W**ho reveals if others will benefit or be positively impacted by the purchase.

Asking **W**hen tells you the timing, timeline, or urgency for the purchase.

Asking **W**here reveals the trade-offs being discussed and decided, usually involving the exchange of time and money for a product or service.

I encourage you to begin thinking through how you might customize some of the many strategies and examples for your industry. Putting the SalesMakers' communication strategies to work will make you instantly a better communicator, connector, and closer. Remember, the moment you begin to improve how you communicate, connect, and close, you'll see a change for the better in your level of influence, income, and relationships.

SalesMakers Convert Emotionally

Within every step of the sales process, the SalesMaker must close at an intersection of customer decision. Within each intersection of decision exists a positive or negative emotional charge given off by the customer. Skilled SalesMakers convert these

> "If there is a disheartening moment in the sales process, it is when the SalesMaker invests time and energy developing a customer relationship only to get stalled or put off entirely by an objection they can't overcome."

emotionally-charged moments into closing opportunities. One of the ways they do this is by converting customer concerns into closing currency.

Some of the intersections of decision can include: the appointment-setting stage; during presentation; while reviewing features and benefits; and during the final closing sequence. How well the SalesMaker can convert customer concerns into closing currency will dictate whether the sale ends in a close or a stall. The SalesMaker's ability to confront objections and resolve customer concerns in a way that makes them want to move forward with a purchase plays a major role in determining a SalesMaker's career potential—whether they become an average or master closer.

You are Not Just Handling a Problem—You are Handling a Person

A wise past candidate for governor of Utah, Carl W. Buehner once said, "People won't remember what you said, but they will remember how you made them feel." I couldn't agree more.

There are two critical elements a SalesMaker must be able to address when a customer voices a concern, objection, or any form of resistance. First, the SalesMaker must deal with the person on an emotional level in a way that makes them feel good through the sales process. Secondly, they must address the issues in a way that creates confidence and avoids conversations that could lead to conflict. Remember, when you are handling a customer's concern, you are not just handling a potential problem in the sale, you are handling a person and that persons feeling are valid, whether you agree with them or not.

> "Within every step of the sales process, the SalesMaker must close at each intersection of customer decision."

Know what You are Dealing With

There are three categories of issues that will emerge when a customer brings up a concern. They include: 1) objections that, when addressed, can lead to a sale; 2) negotiation ploys that, when handled properly, can lead to a close, and finally 3) there are people who are truly non-buyers that are just killing time. If you identify that you are dealing with a time waster and not a potential customer, end the sales process as professionally as possible and move on to someone who does have a need and an intention to resolve it. Customers who only like to visit but never buy are to be avoided.

For a car to get traction there must be friction between the tires and the surface of the pavement. Customer issues, when brought up, are the perfect vehicle for creating traction so the SalesMaker can convert a concern into momentum that carries the sale one step closer to the close. The opposite is also true. Like a car driving on black ice, the SalesMaker will struggle to create closing traction without some friction. If a customer doesn't ask a question, bring up a concern, or voice an objection, a sale is unlikely because interest level is low.

There are a few catalysts of closing that a customer's concern can create for the capable SalesMaker. They include:

1. Customer concerns tee up the SalesMaker to solve a problem. Without a problem to be solved, a sale is unlikely.

2. Customer concerns signal a turning point in the momentum of the sale. The customer has left the "looking" or "investigating" phase of the sale and has moved into the purchasing phase.

3. Customer concerns verbalize issues that could prevent a purchase. Bringing them from the shadows into the light is where they can be dealt with.

SalesMakers Convert Customer Concerns into Closing Currency

Here are six SalesMaker strategies for converting customer concerns into closing currency:

1. SalesMakers Confront Customer Concerns Confidently.

Confidence in life comes from the inside. Becoming internally confident is the result of preparation, practice, and life experience. There are a few easy steps the SalesMaker can take to ensure they confidently confront objections and overcome concerns in a way that makes the customer feel comfortable about moving forward.

> "Handling objections involves dealing with emotion; answering objections utilizes knowledge. You need to develop an answer before you get the objection."

- **P**reparation: Most objections the SalesMaker will hear have been said by another customer to another SalesMaker before. As King Solomon said, "There is nothing new under the sun." By reaching out to a seasoned SalesMaker within your industry or organization and learning the words to address a customer's objection, you will rarely be caught ill-equipped. In fact, you will eventually know how to competently handle more customer concerns and objections than any one customer would bring up.

> "When the SalesMaker is prepared, they know the objections in advance and their ability to successfully navigate them increases dramatically."

• **P**ractice: We never get good at anything without practice. The time to practice is before game time when the stakes aren't as high. John Wooden, former UCLA Basketball Coach once said, "When opportunity presents itself, it's too late to prepare." Those you might consider to be "naturals" have simply put more time and energy into practice than you have. Invest time learning the counter-arguments to each objection you already know. You will eventually become confident and competent in addressing customer concerns and overcoming objections. Practice can come through interaction with others or by interacting with ourselves by pre-playing out scenarios.

• **P**retend: The greatest performers in the world—whether in sports, theatre, or sales—have one thing in common. They are able to see it before they do it through mental role playing. In sales, success is often preceded by "hearing it," so you can then say it. The process of performing mental aerobics and role playing your answers to each objection is what will accelerate your growth in converting concerns into closing currency. The next time you are standing in line or waiting for something, you can use your down time to mentally roll play outcomes. Mental preparation will make you sharp when it's time to perform.

> "When opportunity presents itself, it's too late to prepare." John Wooden, former UCLA Basketball Coach

2. SalesMakers restore sales momentum with communication tactics.

To understand how to convert a concern into closing currency is to know that addressing objections is as much about process as it is outcome. The customer's issues are real to them and need to be handled properly, and sometimes delicately, for the sale to close. American writer Dale Carnegie said, "When dealing with people, remember you are not dealing with creatures of logic, but creatures of emotion." The following process for restoring sales momentum is another strategy for the tool belt of the SalesMaker when addressing customer concerns:

> "Learn from the stalls you encounter on every sales call. If you don't learn how to overcome them, you are guaranteed to repeat them. There is no excuse for being unprepared."

The Seven R's of Restoring Sales Momentum

Realize the momentum of the sale has just been stalled, and to restore it you must slow down to address the customer's concern. If it is important to the customer, it must become important to us. If we don't acknowledge its importance, the sale could stall further.

Resist the temptation to interrupt the objection or assume you know what the customer is going to say. Although you may be hearing the issue for the twentieth time, the customer may be experiencing it and vocalizing it for the first time.

Restate the customer's objection back to them in their own words to clarify what was said. This gives the SalesMaker a moment to pause and gather their thoughts while they get ready to help the customer think through their issue. A SalesMaker's goal isn't to just overcome an objection, but to help a customer resolve the issue within them so they have a positive feeling about the purchase.

Reconfirm that you understand the issue by asking for clarification where necessary. This may or may not be necessary, but when it is, it really is. If you are not clear on what is being communicated, probe deeper before you respond.

Relate to the customer's issue with empathy. When a customer knows that you understand and can relate to what they feel, they are more likely to buy because they buy into you.

Respond to the customer's question or issue with a rational answer to their concern. Your answer has to make sense. At the end of the day, if you are likeable but incompetent, the customer will lack confidence not just in you, but in the company and product you represent.

Re-engage the momentum of the sale by asking a question on the back end of your response that moves the customer toward the close. If you address the concern and don't ask a question to move past the issue, you risk another stall and possibly getting stuck in a quagmire of indecision.

3. SalesMakers navigate the emotional obstacle course that can stall a sale. Until a SalesMaker can identify the sabotaging sales emotion they are confronting, they are powerless to neutralize it. There is an internal tug of war that we all face when making purchases. The larger the purchase, the greater the inward wrestling can be. Think about the last purchase you made that was memorable, meaningful, or significant to you or your family. What emotions did you need to process during the purchasing cycle, both before you engaged a seller and after you completed the final buying sequence?

We, as SalesMakers, are also customers and we share a similar obstacle course of emotions and thought processes prior to making purchases. The SalesMaker who can identify the obstacles the customer is facing will have a better chance of communicating with the customer in a way that helps them to navigate, and eventually resolve, the obstacles stopping them from moving forward. Which of the following obstacles have you noticed your customers dealing with?

> "Until a SalesMaker can identify the sabotaging sales emotion they are confronted with, they are powerless to neutralize it."

The Emotional Obstacle Course of Decision Making
Buyer Barriers to Purchasing

Y/N		
✓	Price & Value.	Affordability, perceived value.
✓	Belief.	Connecting head & heart (gut feeling).
✓	Trust.	Confidence level in product or seller.
✓	Inward "tug-of-war."	Cost vs. benefits.
✓	I want to look around.	Too many options.
✓	The timing isn't right.	Fear of commitment.
✓	I want to think it over.	Uncertainty, self-doubt.
✓	I have to talk with my partner.	Needing approval of others.
✓	I can get it cheaper somewhere else.	Negotiation (better deal available).
✓	I am happy with what I currently have.	Comfortability, readiness for change.

4. SalesMakers can resolve confusion and disarm conflict by lending a listening ear as the customer processes out loud.

It's not uncommon for a customer to not really know how they are feeling about a purchase yet feel pressure. When this happens, they feel the need to leave and "think about it" on their own. If you have ever heard an objection and answered it to the customer's satisfaction yet the sale still got stuck in the quagmire of indecision, you have experienced a customer who was confused or lacked clarity about their concerns. The SalesMaker can head this off by encouraging a customer to express how they feel.

One of the ways a SalesMaker can convert a customer concern into closing currency is to simply hear the customer out. It is not uncommon for a customer to have unresolved concerns or objections and yet still decide in favor of the purchase. Simple phrases

> "You don't need closing or objection handling techniques for someone who really wants to make a change." Michael Oliver, Founder of Natural Selling

213

like, "I want to understand what you are thinking"; "Why do you feel the way that you do"; and "What other options should we be considering" can get them talking. Sometimes a customer just wants to be heard by a patient SalesMaker with an empathetic ear.

5. SalesMakers handle customers in a way that makes them feel good, even when walking through sticking points that have the potential to stall the sale.

The right words are not enough to close the sale! There is a finesse required by the SalesMaker that goes beyond words and tone if the sale is going to close. That finesse is referred to as "people skills."

If you've had the experience of satisfying a customer's concern with the perfect answer and they still would not buy, then you know that it takes more to close than just saying the right thing at the right time in the right way. The SalesMaker needs to know how to handle people. The following strategies for handling customers will significantly increase your level of people skills and closing ratios. You may not need every tactic on every sales call, but at some point you will encounter enough personality types where you will engage every strategy.

a. If your customer is right, tell them so.

b. If your customer is unhappy, ask questions.

c. If your customer is feeling down, encourage them.

d. If your customer makes demands, provide options.

e. If your customer reaches out, extend a helping hand.

f. If your customer is talking, listen, and then listen some more.

g. If your customer gives you an order, show them appreciation.

h. If your customer disagrees with you, seek to understand their point of view.

i. If your customer is frustrated with another vendor, find out why and avoid that behavior.

j. If your customer is upset, provide empathy as you work to smooth things over.

k. If your customer is opening up by being vulnerable, trade confidences to connect.

l. If your customer is emotionally closed, look for common ground on which you can agree.

m. If your customer looks puzzled while you are talking, slow down and ask to start over.

n. If your customer threatens you with a cancellation, apologize and ask where you went wrong.

o. If your customer opens the door for long term partnership, thank them for their trust in you.

> In a moment when a customer is reaching out to you, they will put a value on how you responded and how it made them feel, and decide whether to continue with the sale or close the door on the relationship."

6. SalesMakers convert customer concerns into closing currency by side-stepping them.

Sometimes the best strategy for handling a customer concern is to not handle it at all. This may seem contradictory to advice given earlier that required you to address a customer concern head on. However, the best way to deal with non-issues is often to side-step them. It is not uncommon to encounter a customer who likes to express concerns that are not priorities for them when deciding on the purchase. If the SalesMaker has addressed the priority issues and senses other issues emerging that may require a less-than-direct response, there are ways to neutralize those topics by side-stepping them.

Seven Ways to Disarm, Side Step, and Advance Past Objections

1. **Define the field of concern:** "Before we cover that, can you share with me what other issues are important to you before we move ahead?"

2. **The Switch Pitch**: "That's a good question! Another question our customers ask is…"

3. **Procrastinate:** "I don't know how to answer that, but I will find out for you."

4. **Determine Importance**: "On a scale of 1-10, how important to the final decision is the issue you just brought up?"

5. **Put it Off:** "I'd like to address some other issues that are important to us and circle back around to discuss that later."

6. **Feel & Found:** "That is a common question/issue that comes up. I have found that most clients feel that _____, and eventually found that _____."

7. **Confront & Challenge:** "I don't know how to answer what you just said. What is it that you are looking for?"

If emotions could only be categorized into two buckets on a sales call, they would be the positive and negative buckets of emotion. You might think that one is good and one is bad, but that would be incorrect. SalesMakers recognize that there is energy and emotion in both buckets, and it is that energy that can be converted into closing currency. A customer who voices objections and concerns is demonstrating that they are interested. The next time you get an objection, hear a concern, or are faced with a problem, get excited. You are one conversation away from converting a stall into a closed sale.

SalesMakers Close Conversationally

A few years back I took my son to a baseball showcase camp in Santa Barbara. Part of the three-day experience included having the parents attend a seminar with a college coach to hear about the process of attending a baseball school, scholarships, and so on. The head baseball coach from the University of California-Davis was there and with great candor, he doled out his wisdom.

> "There are consequences if you can't close. If you don't close, you don't eat."

Looking at the bleachers full of parents, he told us "You are not a coach. I am a coach." He was speaking to us dads who grew up coaching our sons in park district baseball programs. He pointed out that if our team lost a game, we still went out for pizza. In college sports, if the coach lost a game, he could be on the street looking for work.

In the same way, what differentiates a seller from a closer is that a seller may talk to customers with an interest in their product, but a SalesMaker convinces people to buy. They persuade to and through the sale until they consummate the sale with the close. I have known many sellers who are great sales people, competent in many areas of the sales process but they struggle to close. There are consequences for not closing. The SalesMaker who doesn't close, doesn't eat! How can you improve your chances of closing on every sales call? By shoring up what you know and infusing yourself with new closing tools, technologies, and communication skills designed to close the sale. Are you ready to start making more money? If so, keep reading.

Advanced Communication Skills And Closing Technologies Close More Sales

Let me ask you this: How many ways do you know to ask for the order? Embedded within the three sections of this chapter are dozens of techniques, insights, and closes to help you increase your influence and income. Not just this chapter, but this entire book is about moving people to decisions—closing. To close out this chapter on the Law of the Close, you will find actionable closes and more advanced communication strategies you can add to your tool belt as a SalesMaker.

Author Stephen Covey quoted from an ancient proverb that states, "If you give a man a fish you feed him for a day. If you teach a man to fish, you feed him for a lifetime." My goal is not to merely give you a fish today, but to teach you how to feed yourself for a lifetime using advanced communication skills and closing technologies. When you learn not just how to close, but why the closes work, you will be able to *craft custom closes* for every sales situation you encounter in your career.

The right use of words can create a magical sense of momentum in conversation. In sales, we make a living commensurate with our abilities to find needs and fill them, uncover concerns and resolve them, and finding problems and fixing them. With our words, we can stimulate, set, or influence the emotions of others. There is a great power the SalesMaker wields when they develop the ability to persuade others and move them from point A to point B in a conversation. These abilities of the SalesMaker include the ability to communicate strategically, converts emotionally, and close conversationally.

Furthermore, their powers don't remain at the office when the workday ends, they travel with them in every conversation, during every interaction with others, and are used in every relationship. Stewarding the powers of communication is a responsibility a SalesMaker embraces. They wield this power in service to others, not just themselves. Like all skill sets, sales skills can be misused to manipulate people instead of used to move and motivate them.

Here Comes the Pitch

In baseball, a new pitcher enters the game with a fresh arm in the final inning. He's called a "closer." Armed with a number of creative pitches, the closer in a baseball game throws every ball with a strategic purpose so they can bring the game to a close with a win. It's not realistic to think that a closer could strike out every batter every time. That would be naive. So, the pitcher develops a series of pitches for closing time. A closing pitcher may pitch the ball in such a way so that the batter grounds out, flies out, or strikes out. Pitchers with trained arms can even pitch to a batter in such a way that they can predict where the ball will be hit. Every pitcher has an arsenal of pitches to close out a game.

In the same way, a closer in the sales profession knows which closes to employ to create the response they need to close out the sale. Below you will find a number of "bread and butter" closes you can employ to take your closing ratios to the next level.

A Word of Warning! Don't Ever...

The assumption here is that before closing or asking for the order, the SalesMaker has already identified a need and the customer has displayed signs of interest. If a need has not been discovered, a path to solving a problem has not been uncovered, and interest is not obvious, DON'T ATTEMPT TO CLOSE. If you do, it will backfire. Asking for the order before the customer wants what you have never ends well. If needs and interest have not been established, the SalesMaker has more probing, presenting, and positioning to do. Here are a number of communication skills and closing technologies to help you close more sales more often for more money.

If the closes don't fit you perfectly, change them and adapt them to your industry or type of customer group. Personal customization, not memorization, is the key principle every Master Closer follows. To not customize a close so it works for you is just laziness.

1. **SalesMakers A.S.K. for the sale.** Some perceive closing a sale as forcing someone to do something they don't want to do. Nothing could be farther from the truth. What is a close after all? By definition, a close is a question, nothing more, nothing less. The most advanced SalesMakers close conversationally and intentionally by strategically posing the right question at the right time. A SalesMaker's ability to create a comfortable environment for saying "yes" in favor of the purchase is what separates the average from the great. How do they do it? SalesMakers close conversationally, with poise, patience, skill, and a *soft touch*. SalesMakers close by asking, not telling. A.S.K. is a three letter acronym that will help you to remember to serve up your close as a request.

   Ask the customer questions about their needs, wants, pains, problem, and why's.

   Seek areas of conversation that seem to strike a chord with your customer—these are hot buttons.

   Knock down fear, doubt, and insecurity surrounding the purchase by presenting the customer with options and the door to the sale will swing open for you.

   Consider a few ways in which the SalesMaker asks for the order.

2. **SalesMakers close by presenting alternate or triplicate of choice propositions.** We live in a consumer environment that has been democratized by the vast number of choices available to us as consumers. It is easy for a customer to say yes or no to a direct question. However, presenting options gives the mind something to say yes to and something to say no to. After a customer makes a choice, closing momentum can be accelerated by asking the customer, "I'm curious why you chose that option over another?" This can further anchor the customer's selection in their own mind. Closing becomes easier by posing alternate or triplicate choice questions. A simple alternate of choice question can include:

   • Which of the two options appeal to you most?

   • Which of the three options would you eliminate first, and why?

- Other than these two options, should we consider a third or keep what we have?

Insight: It is worth mentioning that when presenting multiple options, you will want to put more feature-benefit emphasis on the option you think best suits the customer's particular situation. By minimizing the less desirable option and emphasizing the most desirable option, the SalesMaker has the ability to influence the sale in a specific direction while leaving the door open to selling the customer what they want to buy.

3. **SalesMakers close by asking about customer preferences.** It can often feel impolite to ask a BIG buying question of a customer without knowing where they are in the buying process. Asking a closing question can backfire if it is asked too soon, like asking for her hand in marriage on the first date. Minor issue or trial closing questions are less threatening and let the SalesMaker test the waters to know if the customer is ready to move forward. Asking a customer about their preferences with secondary issues helps them to process their emotions and make preferred selections before they make the big buying decision. Without asking the major buying decision, the SalesMaker can pose a series of secondary issue and alternate choice questions that allow the customer to make a simpler, non-threatening, preference decisions. When the SalesMaker asks enough secondary issue questions, the collective answers often make asking the major buying decision unnecessary. Closing on a customer's selection preferences using an alternate choice question may sound like this:

   "Suzie, when you think about the colors of the kitchen, which cabinets seem to fit better, the oak or the cherry?" "Do you prefer your cabinets in a glossy or flat finish?" "Are you in a rush for them this month or could you wait until the first week of next month?" "Do you have an installer in mind or would you want us to have one of our professionals take care of it."

4. **SalesMakers close when the customer begins to ask questions.** The best time to close is when the customer is asking a question. Customers going from a passive position of "just looking" to intentional investigating is a clue that they are ready to be advanced toward the close. Closing on a customer's queries is the best way to build closing momentum. When the customer is asking questions, they are reaching

out to the SalesMaker and their questions can be converted into closing momentum. You may only get two or three questions from a customer so you need to be ready to convert on them when they appear. Be patient and wait for the customer's questions to come your way and then advance the sale.

Insight: The best way to prepare for these golden closing moments is to write down all the questions a customer could possibly ask and then craft answers that advance the sale. By way of example, consider these to get you started:

- Sally SalesMaker, how long does delivery take? "John, we have multiple options for delivery, when do you need the item?" This is an answer with an indirect ask for the order. When John answers the question, he has said yes to the purchase.)

- Sally SalesMaker, how much is this going to cost me? "John, that depends on which options you want. The base model starts around $30K at $400/month and an upgraded model is around $35K at $425/month; which model most appeals to you?"

- Sally SalesMaker, can you throw in the delivery for free? "John, our drivers won't deliver unless they are getting paid, but I may be able to add a third-year bonus to the warranty program if you can purchase the two-year warranty today?"

- Sally SalesMaker, what is the monthly payment if we finance this home? "John, that depends on your priorities. Do you want to pay the home off faster such as in 15 years, or is a lower monthly payment more important to you?"

Insight: The best time to close is when the customer is asking questions about the product, delivery, pricing options, and querying about other preferences they are signaling are important to them. Smart SalesMakers create a closing environment where it's comfortable for the customer to ask these queries and when they do, convert them into closed sales.

5. **SalesMakers close using five quick-connect questions.** In many sales industries, the sales process often takes two to three meetings with the customer before a closing opportunity emerges. The first call is for needs analysis where probing and presenting of features and benefits take place. I could often tell if a customer would buy or not on the

first call, long before I presented a proposal, by asking my five quick-connect closing questions. If I had done a good job in my probing and pitching on the first call, the customer would give me the answers to the five do-or-die questions at the end of the meeting. Do you know what your five quick-connect closing questions are for your industry? In media sales (and before I leave the meeting), here are the questions I ask that let me know if I have a good prospect ready to advance to proposal stage:

#1 Decision - BUDGET: "John, we have three types of clients we work with. We have the large national clients of the world who spend $15K or more per month. Then there are the medium level advertisers who usually spend $10-15K per month. But the heart and soul of our customer base are those on a pre-set budget who can afford $5-10K per month. Where do you see yourself fitting in?" Painting pictures with associations helps customers to feel their way to decision. In determining your customers comfort level on spend, you can customize the above question to fit your industry, customer, and investment levels.

#2 Decision - LENGTH OF CAMPAIGN: "John, most of our new clients will start off with a 3 or 6 month campaign and then renew long term after they see it working for them. Where is your comfort level?" Customers almost always like to hedge their bets and commit to the least amount when given a choice so frame your questions wisely. If you don't like the goal posts of this question, change them and make them adaptable to your industry and customer.

#3 Decision - START DATE: "John, if we were able to put something together that you like, I wouldn't be able to get you on the radio until the first of next month due to our inventory demand. Is the first okay or would you prefer to wait until the 15th?" Posing a question that delays satisfaction even when a "yes" is on the table can create a powerful pulling effect.

#4 Decision - CREATIVE: "John, I have a handful of copy points from your website and from what we've been discussing, but there is one last question I need to ask you. If you were in a stadium and speaking to 50,000 of your potential customers, what would be the most important three things you would want them to remember about your business?" A question that takes a customer from their intellect into their imagination creates a pleasant experience as mentioned earlier in this chapter.

#5 Decision - NEXT APPOINTMENT DATE: "John, I usually schedule my appointments a week out, does this same time next week work for you?" In a two call sales process, if the customer will not give you the next appointment that often means they are putting you off.

6. **SalesMakers close by navigating around customer Put-offs.**

    Not wanting to be rude, or in an attempt to avoid confrontation, a customer will often make up a reason for not being able to say "yes" today. The customer, not sure how to exit, will often manufacture different ways to save face so they can gracefully exit the conversation. This is their way of avoiding confrontation or making the SalesMaker feel uncomfortable. The SalesMaker who can unearth the hidden emotions and bring to the surface unseen motives and concerns has a good chance of turning a stall into a sale. Pulling this off in a comfortable and non-confrontational manner is more challenging than it sounds.

    Our goal as SalesMakers is to remove resistance, not create friction. Yet we must learn to navigate these barriers to the sale. There are also customers that require a more direct approach. These customers are the types that need to be challenged in an appropriate way to make a decision. Knowing your audience and what will work is crucial to understanding which close to use in order to advance the sale. Here are a few ways the SalesMaker can navigate a stalling, undecided, or deal-seeking customer and bring them to a point of decision. If you are new to sales, you may not be able to envision situations that might require these, or have developed the confidence yet to use all of them. For now, employ the closes you are comfortable with.

    A. **The Scale Close:** The 1-to-10 Scale is a question that when posed properly, at the right time and in the right way, can have a powerful effect in helping the customer discover internal machinations they may not even be aware of. Bringing hidden concerns to the surface is where the SalesMaker can help the customer. Also, for customers who are uncertain and want to "think about it," the 1-10 Scale question can also reveal a true hidden objection. Here is how you may word the 1-10 Scale Close: "John, if you had to pick a number on a scale of 1-10, 1 meaning you absolutely hate it and would not buy it or 10 meaning you absolutely love it, what number would best represent how you feel?" After John gives the SalesMaker say 7, they would follow up with "What is keeping you from a 10?" and handle the issue from there.

B. **The Partner Put-Off:** Used for the customer who says, "I'll get back with you after I talk with my partner/spouse." "That's fine John. Knowing your partner as you do, what do you sense will be the favorite and least favorite elements of the program?" The SalesMaker then has an opportunity to re-engage the customer and hear not just what a partner might think, but more likely what John himself is thinking.

C. **Disarm The Decision:** "John, what is the best and worst case scenario if you don't go home with the product today. What other options do you have?"

D. **Take It Off The Table:** "John, maybe this isn't right for you. I'm not comfortable moving forward unless you are certain about what you want. Can you please refresh my memory on what you are trying to accomplish? What pain point are you trying to remove?"

E. **Prioritize The Decision:** "John, most people I deal with who were in your shoes had three priorities they had settled on that helped them make the decision. What are your top three priorities?"

F. **Divide And Diminish The Dollars:** "John, if it's the money that is holding you up, where did you want to land financially-speaking compared to what we are looking at here? What is going to be comfortable for you?" The SalesMaker can then counter the money objection with a summary of features and benefits. Or they can take the dollar amount that John is concerned about and diminish the difference that the customer doesn't want to pay by dividing it over days, weeks, or months to put the amount into perspective.

G. **Tie Down The Negotiating Customer:** "John, we can't keep going back to the well, continue to nibble away and ask for one thing after another. If we can make this final concession work, are there any other issues we need to discuss before we move forward?"

H. **Value Costs More:** "John, the best things in life always cost more than we think they will and deliver more value that we hoped they would. The flip side is true too. The wrong choice at any price is still the wrong choice. Is it more important to save a few bucks or get what you really want?"

I. **Last Call For Commitment:** "John, we've been talking for some time now and I feel I need to ask you, what do I have to do in order to earn your business today?"

J. **The Tipping Point:** "John, if you had to decide today, what is the tipping point for you that would cause you to say yes or no? You must have an idea of what is going to make or break the deal for you."

K. **The Combination Close:** You will often use 3-4 combinations of closes in order to take a customer from "thinking about it" to deciding. The most impactful closes will always be the closes you craft yourself to fit the need in the moment.

> "Knowing your audience and what will work is crucial to knowing which close to use in order to advance the sale."

Conversational closing is meant to feel informal and allow the SalesMaker to effortlessly guide an interested customer toward commitment. New skills may feel mechanical at first, but once adapted to your style, industry, and customer group, they will flow naturally.

Developing the closer within you starts with new words, new skills, and embracing new ideas of how to ask for the order. What feels foreign to you now, will feel comfortable in time if you put it to work in your day to day sales practices. Leveling up in your influence, income, and sales volume, and growing in your ability to close the sale is non-negotiable. You have now learned over two dozen new ways to communicate strategically, convert emotionally, and close conversationally. Which ways of closing the sale will you employ first? Where do you start in developing the closing language of the SalesMaker?

> "You are never more than one decision, one action, one person, or one new skill away from improving your financial positon today."

On the following page, you will discover a few closing gems that a fellow SalesMaker captured while reading the

Law of the Close. I want to encourage you to read what they wrote, add your take-aways to theirs, and prioritize which closing tactics you can adapt quickest and incorporate starting this week. As you live the Law of the Close, you will soon be communicating strategically, converting on customers' emotions, and closing conversationally. Armed with a vast repertoire of closing skills, your sales career can now be unleashed to soar. As you begin to close like a SalesMaker, you will discover why the Law of the Close is actually the law of the land in selling. That law says, "'Everybody sells, but it takes a SalesMaker to close the sale." That's the Law of the Close.

C.I.A. CONTRIBUTORS

The LAW OF THE CLOSE

Chris Mills, iHeart Media

Nick Malievsky, Zillow

Brian Slepetz, Clear Channel Airports

My name is **Chris Mills** and I've been in sales and marketing for 11 years. I work at **iHeart Media**. I attribute my success to building relationships. People are why I get up in the morning. Helping companies create revenue is how I close sales. I love selling because it gives me a different obstacle every day and I like working with companies that want to grow. I consider myself someone who pushes hard and works with conviction. Here are some of the sales nuggets I picked up in the Law of the Close:

1. Customers can't be pushed into buying, they must be invited. I've never been a pushy salesperson, so this resonates with me. I close all the time following this philosophy—ask them, don't tell them. Invite them, don't push them.

2. Customer's concerns tee up the sales maker to solve a problem. This relates to me because all I do is solve problems; just like a lawyer or doctor. In fact, when I hear a customer concern, I know the conversation is teeing up for me to close. An objection is an invitation to close.

3. "You are not just handling a problem—you are handling a person." Even though I have dealt with the same objections and obstacles

hundreds of times, I need to remember that the person I am selling is walking through the buying process with me for the first time, and close with care for the person, not just the commission.

4. I was a walk-on pitcher at Arizona State University, so I appreciate the baseball reference. Every pitcher has a different pitch to close out the batter. We train for this moment, a closing moment. It's not that different in sales. I will make sure I have a closing strategy for every closing call I go on to close out the deal. I am asking myself now, "What are my best shut down pitches?"

5. Anchoring questions is an awesome technique. I don't always let the customer anchor his belief in my product in a positive manner. Most of the time I just agree. From now on, I will pause when a customer says something positive about my company and ask them why they feel that way; and in so doing will further solidify their belief.

6. I love the Law of the Close because it refines my tools and makes me think about approaching sales & closing techniques differently.

My name is **Nick Malievsky** and I've been in sales for ten years. I work at **Zillow** and my role is to sell listings on Zillow and help others on my team to do the same. I attribute my success to consistent self-development and a strong mindset. I love selling because I love to be challenged and I love to close. No two days are alike. Here are some of the insights I gathered from the Law of the Close.

1. Switching from yes and no questions to open-ended questions will help me to advance customers toward the close. Closed-ended questions will get me a short conversation with little to no results. But, if I recraft my closing language to start with questions like Who, What, Where, When, and Why, I can keep asking my way to the close.

   My job is to sell the ownership experience—to sell the dream! If I can communicate the WII-FM ("What's in it for me?"), I can close the sale. A successful sales person paints the wonderful picture that the product or service delivers and the customer is motivated to buy. This is a great way to close the sale.

   There is a language of closing I am always improving on. I stay away from words that create fear, but instead focus on words that create hope, expectancy, and belief in my product. Power words transfer confidence and push the sale into existence. Part of my closing language includes Power Words like dominate, investment, essentially, absolutely, and success.

Ask, Seek, and Knock. A sale can typically take up to five asks. Every ask may bring a new objection but it also brings me closer to the close. Being prepared to know objections before they come up helps me to close in almost any scenario.

2. If I am confident in the moment to close I may ask, "We can get you started today. Sound good?" If I am less sure, I will present the customer with options they can pick from. Either answer confirms they are moving ahead.

Convert emotionally and be excited. If I don't get excited about my product, I won't have excitement to transfer to the customer.

3. The closing skills in the Law of the Close are practical and easy to reproduce. I will convert and adapt some of them to my industry for myself and my sellers.

4. Communicate with technology. I can't imagine not selling with technology and matching everything to technology. We live in a world where I can order groceries, pay my bills, and watch any movie I want without having human interaction. Selling with technology is the new normal.

My name is **Brian Slepetz** and I have been in sales and marketing for 15 years. I am a Senior Regional Marketing Consultant at **Clear Channel Airports**. I attribute my success to learning from my grandfather, who started at the bottom with a newspaper company and worked his way up to being the president and publisher. His ambitions to be successful and develop his wisdom helped him get to the top. I believe that there is not an option for taking no in sales. You present your case in a different way and never give up. I love selling because I get to interact with many types of people and I am constantly learning new methods of business practices. The freedom sales gives me over my time and the ability to determine my own income level is amazing. Here is a summary of my observations, ideas, insights, or sales nuggets that connected with me as I read the Law of the Close.

1. There are many ways in which I can ask for the order. I need to always be closing. Whether it is a trial close or presumptive close, I am going to continue to try and advance the process of the sale toward the close more often.

2. Connection: With 15 years of experience in selling, I have come across many types of people, seen many creative ads, and different types of displays as they evolved with time. I pledge to use more examples during my meetings to put visions in the prospects' minds so they can imagine what they would create. Painting a picture in their minds only helps draw the prospect closer to the sale.

3. I like the power of words section. I will be open to learning more words, reading more relevant material to be able to expand my dictionary of words in communication.

4. I will work harder to know the objections in advance so I am ready when they come up in conversation.

5. Asking more opened questions will help me close more sales. One question I love that engages the customer's imagination is: "If I put you in a stadium in front of 40,000 people, what are three key things would you tell them about your business?"

6. I vow to mix up my closes more regularly versus having the same approach. Growing my closing skill set will ensure I close more sales.

7. Listening encourages the prospect to talk. This is a challenge for me because I love to interject during discussion and close the sale. Instead of interjecting an opinion, I will ask a question that advances the sale.

Put the 7 Empowering Laws of the SalesMaker to Work And Convert your Insights into Income

Now that you've completed the Law of the Close, it is time to convert learning into earning. The first step is to return to the sections of this chapter that you highlighted, underlined, or made notes from. Of the key points that you connected with, pick three that resonate the most with you. Following the simple formula for transformation found in the C.I.A. process in the introduction (Connection, Insight, Action), identify and write down that which resonated with you. Then, identify the insights you gathered, and finally, decide how you might put them into action. Reading, doing, believing in, and incorporating three sales insights into your daily routine will create a transformative impact on your sales volume and sales commissions.

Here is how I will convert my insights into income:

C = Connection: As I read, the following content, principle, or idea that connected with me was:

_____

_____

I = Insight: As I reflect, the idea or insight I received is:

_____

_____

A = Action: The action I will take to convert my insight into income will be to:

_____

_____

CHAPTER 7

LAW OF THE PROSPECTOR

The SalesMaker develops potential *within* them, they discover opportunities *around* them.

I want to take you to a day of discovery in my life. It wasn't as much a single day, but a series of days that brought me to realize what I was meant to do. "Find what you love, and then spend the rest of your life doing it!" That is the advice of those who are lucky enough to find their vocational callings, callings that become like a first love. That sense of calling comes to them more like a discovery, not a decision. For those lucky enough to find it, they are romantic about their stations in life because they love, and if they are really lucky, are *in love* with what they do. When you have discovered what you are meant to do, you have found your calling in life.

The only other time I experienced this sense of destiny was when I was dating my wife. Again, it wasn't as much a single day of discovery but a series of days that led to the revelation that "she's the one." On that day, I realized, I don't ever want to be without her. That was the day I knew I would spend the rest of my life with her, if she would say "yes."

You may be wondering why a story analogous to romance is making an appearance in a sales book. It's because when destiny shows up on your doorstep, you either recognize and embrace it or reject it and retreat from it. The sales profession is NOT for everyone. Just as there is a right "someone" for everyone, there is a calling for everyone. For those who feel a sense of calling to this line of work, it can feel like a love affair. Love affairs are not perfect, but they carry within them an energy that keeps us coming back for more.

If you haven't experienced this and you are more than a few years into your career, you may want to rethink whether or not you belong in sales. You may want to consider another line of work within sales. Whether you find yourself in outside sales, inside sales, business-to-business sales, business-to-consumer sales, enterprise sales, or retail sales, when you've found the place where you belong, you know it. When you are where you belong with your vocational calling, there is no mistaking it. Also, when you are not where you belong, there is no mistaking it. You feel it in your gut. It resonates within your bones, and you can't wait to begin developing your potential.

Potential Requires a Seed of Faith in Oneself and in the Future

I'll never forget the day I realized I was free. Free to explore limitless possibilities. Free to pioneer what had the potential to be a limitless career. Excited to embrace the unknown, knowing that where I was going was greater than where I had been. I remember the day the revelation hit me. I would never be the same. Limitations no longer governed my day but the ideas of what could be. The sense of unlimited potential was birthed in me and the idea that my success would not be capped by limitation but governed by developed potential was thrilling to me. I was in my second year of selling.

Potential Has No Value Unless it is Developed

The realization of potential in itself is not enough to create success. You must develop the seeds of potential within you—no one can do that for you. I learned that listening to the greatest motivational speaker of the 20th century, Zig Ziglar. There was a day I decided to commit to developing the potential within me and the opportunities around me. On that day, I also realized that there was a success track I could run on and that track would lead me toward reaching my potential. That was the day I realized success was a journey, not a destination. I knew I had a long way to go, but was willing to get going, and I wasn't looking back. During the year following that day, there were a few other important insights I discovered when I realized sales was my career calling.

- On the journey to success, the road is uphill. To develop the potential within myself, I would need to grow myself. This would mean learning from mentors to whom I had access.

- As I grew in skill, influence, and relationships, so would my opportunities. The higher I climbed the growth ladder, the more I could see. As you change, your perspective changes and your sight expands.

- Seeing opportunity comes before seizing it.

- Developing strong sales skills would not be enough. I would need to develop strong inward character traits if I was to reach my potential. I had a long way to go, but was willing to make the climb toward success.

Success doesn't come without a cost. What is the price of entry into this life of limitless possibilities? The price is a willingness, nothing more, nothing less. It's a willingness to become more than you are. It's a humble acceptance that you are not yet who you are meant to be, but are heading in the right direction. You are willing to trade your comfort zone for character growth.

Potential is like a hidden gem in the human heart. It requires discovery and development if it is to be realized. As SalesMakers develop the potential within them, they increasingly see opportunities around them. This is the Law of the Prospector. Who they are decides what they see.

Analogous to the trajectory of upward growth of a SalesMaker, a prospector in their first year of sales is able to see some of the opportunities around them, but may not notice all of the opportunity within reach. As they grow and mature in sales, their sight expands to see more. As they see more, they are able to seize more.

Have You Fallen in Love Yet with What You Do?

I would like to dedicate the Law of Prospector to those who have discovered that sales is more than a career, but a vocational calling. How do you know that you've found what you were meant to do? There seems to be a fit with the people in the place where you are. You experience moments of bliss, almost timelessness, and you can hear or feel a tug at the heart and a faint echo whispering, "I was made for this."

Have you felt that tug before, or heard the whisper of destiny calling to you? Maybe you're remembering now what it felt like or sounded like. Like a marathon runner who gets a second wind, your calling exists in the second wind you get when you truly understand that sales work is what you were meant to do. When you work, you feel the wind at your back and a degree of ease in doing tasks that others may struggle with. What others have to work overtime to accomplish, you achieve in no time. It's as if you've found the slip stream of life. The wind isn't just pushing you to go faster, but the purpose ahead of you is pulling you up to take you to higher ground. That is what a SalesMaker experiences when they've discovered that sales is their calling, and not just a career. The motive that brought you into sales or the circumstances that keep you in sales are now secondary to the unlimited potential that this profession affords.

Understanding the Law of the Prospector

The Law of the Prospector is an acronym with a dual meaning. Each letter in the acronym represents a skill or character quality the SalesMaker needs to be successful. Why is it not enough to learn sales and focus on becoming a skilled sales tactician? Because a superior skill set will only take you so far. It is character that will sustain you where sales skills fail you. Sales skills will get you to success, but it is character that will keep you growing after you have experienced success. Where skill level will take you to one level in your career, it is character that will help you discover unseen levels.

Why the reason for the dual meaning in prospector? Because prospecting is entirely about character. The challenges in the marketplace will create headwinds the prospector must face daily. Some of those headwinds will be the result of outside circumstance, but many of them are due to internal wiring. Unless a SalesMaker learns how to manage, direct, and grow their character, they will be limited in what they can achieve. The biggest challenge I have ever had to manage has always been myself. I have found that the better I get at managing me, the more control I have in creating success around me.

Have you had this revelation, or are you still looking to outside circumstances that are out of your control to bring the world within your control? Have you taken responsibility for your success, or do you think it's someone else's job? Every SalesMaker at some point must choose to change their thinking if they are to change who they are. For transformation to take place, we must confront our mindsets and internal tendencies and learn to channel them into high producing activities. With the Law of Prospecting as a canvas, I want to paint you a picture of skills and character traits that will help you level up as a SalesMaker.

Prospecting will Grow your Character, Income, and Survival Instincts

There is a special place of honor in my mind for those who are responsible for prospecting, lead generation, customer development, and those who know what it means to hunt, dig, sow, and seed for new prospects. For those responsible for their own lead generation, it is not enough for them to be good at Sales, they must become prospectors. If you are responsible for finding customers to sell, you are a prospector.

Prospectors Create Prosperity

The combination of work ethic, skill set, and mindset works in aiding the prospector to become a successful SalesMaker who makes an income higher than those only waiting to be fed leads by others. Those willing to plow the ground of the marketplace, sow the seeds of opportunity, and develop prospects into partners quickly find themselves growing to five, six, even seven figure incomes depending on their industries.

Prospecting is the Cure for the Comfort Zone

To survive, a company must be fed with a consistent infusion of customers. For most companies, new business is the life blood that makes their success possible. Regardless of whether a company has an inside or outside sales force, a marketing department, advertising agency, or a public relations department, someone somewhere at some point must sell something for the company to stay in business and prosper. That is where the prospector comes in. Of all sales skills, prospecting is the most difficult. It requires SalesMakers to consistently and intentionally drive themselves out of their comfort zones and engage in business activities that require them to face rejection and failure, and then repeat the process over and over again. All successful SalesMakers who are responsible for generating their own leads are prospectors of opportunity.

Of the core competencies in sales (connecting, prospecting, presenting, positioning, probing, negotiating, closing, and servicing), prospecting is the activity most often underdeveloped. I've met many sellers who are highly competent at leading with questions, writing presentations, and even closing. However, a SalesMaker can be a master in every other core competency, but still be limited in their success if they fail to develop the skill of prospecting to find and cultivate new customers.

My friend Lance, a business owner tells me of his days when he ran a mortgage office. He tells of many mortgage officers making six figure incomes and more until home sales dipped and the economy slowed. Those waiting for customers to walk in off the street or to be fed leads eventually washed out and left the business. They had not developed the skillset of the prospector. But those who had developed their ability dig for, find, and develop prospects into customers continued to thrive.

What separates one SalesMaker from the next? Skillset and character are what sustain a SalesMaker regardless of the economic environment. A seasoned SalesMaker has learned to prospect and develop the opportunities around them, and character within them. Regardless of the outside environment, their financial environment is stable or growing. There is a difference between high income earners and highly-competent SalesMakers who have mastered ALL the core competencies of a SalesMaker, not just the skills that feel comfortable. What's the difference? It starts with being a PROSPECTOR, not just a seller.

Prospecting is Hard Work

It is difficult, not because it is complicated, but because it requires more self-management than any other sales activity. Prospecting requires management of time, attitude, emotions, processes, people, pipelines, opportunities, obstacles, and other issues that require active engagement with no promise of a payoff. Although every prospect doesn't turn into a customer, every prospecting call requires the SalesMaker to invest in the prospect as if they would.

Prospecting Separates Pretenders from Performers

There is a clear distinction between those who prospect for leads and those who don't. Prospectors plant and seed the marketplace in order to produce customer leads. Although every SalesMaker sells, not every SalesMaker prospects. Some sellers are not responsible for their own lead generation. Their company supplies leads for them. SalesMakers responsible for finding prospects and developing them into customers on their own require a higher level of motivation, character, and skill set to be successful. Prospecting is what separates performers from pretenders. If a prospector isn't planting the seeds of opportunity regularly, they will not reap the financial rewards. It is also the act of prospecting that puts destiny in the hands of the SalesMaker. The SalesMaker is able to raise their income in proportion to their ability to prospect. Prospectors reap a harvest from seeding the soil of the marketplace while average income earners settle for living on low hanging fruit. While one seller might just wait for business to fall in their lap, the prospector plants the seeds of opportunity, and nourishes them. Then, as their seeds of opportunity grow, they harvest the rewards from what they've planted.

The Prospectors Creed

The successful SalesMaker is driven by their belief system. What they believe energizes them and propels them forward. Consider developing your own personal Prospector's Creed that represents your passionate belief with regard to the pursuit and purpose of your career.

Here's an example to consider: "My success in sales will be in direct proportion to my commitment to prospect and develop customers. I must get through gatekeepers, find creative ways to communicate, connect, and then close decision-makers I meet. I will take responsibility for generating my own leads and training myself, while I accept that the outcome is the result of the decisions I have made. No one is responsible for my growth or success but me."

I'd like to share with you modern proverb that has been credited to Dan Montano who was a securities analyst.

"Every morning in Africa, a gazelle wakes up. It knows it must outrun the fastest lion or it will be killed. Every morning in Africa, a lion wakes up. It knows it must run faster than the slowest gazelle, or it will starve. It doesn't matter whether you're a lion or a gazelle, when the sun comes up, you'd better be running."

That proverb may come across as being like the phrase "survival of the fittest." That is because it is. SalesMakers sink or swim based on their abilities to create opportunities. They and they alone must take responsibility for their success, overcome internal and external obstacles, and persevere through the challenges the marketplace will present to them. No one is going to find and sell the customers for you. No one is going to overcome your weaknesses for you. No one is going to make you do what you know you must do! YOU and you alone are responsible for your success. YOU and you alone have the ability to create the future you want. You must take hold of the potential within you, grab the reigns of destiny and drive your way toward success. No one will ever do that for you or be as vested in your success as you will. Today is the day you decide you move from the backseat as a passenger and take the wheel and start plotting your trajectory.

The Prospector's Story

Russell Conwell, famous for his essay titled "Acres of Diamonds," delivered his inspiring story to over 6000 audiences in his day. To summarize his famous essay as it applies to sales, one might conclude that those willing to put in the work to explore opportunities within and around them will discover what they seek.

Acres of Diamonds

"Acres of Diamonds" is a story of a farmer living on the African continent who heard tales of other farmers who made millions discovering diamond mines on their properties. The tales so excited the farmer that he sold his farm to go prospecting himself. After searching the African continent unsuccessfully in hopes of discovering his own field of wealth, he gave up. Realizing he had wasted all of his resources, he threw himself into a river and drowned.

Meanwhile, the man who bought his farm was walking his property one day and noticed a sparkle of light gleaming up at him from the bed of the stream that resided on the property. He bent down and picked up the sparkling stone. It was a good-sized one, and admiring it, he brought it home and put it on the mantle of his fireplace. A friend, while visiting him one day, noticed the stone and picked it up for a closer look and almost fainted from the weight and look of the stone. The friend asked the farmer if he knew what he'd found. When the farmer said he thought it was a piece of crystal, the visitor told him he had found what was later proven to be one of the largest diamonds ever discovered. The farmer stood in disbelief and told his friend that the bottom of his stream was full of similar looking stones.

The first farmer sold everything and set out to prospect for opportunity in another place. The second farmer discovered an acre of diamonds already within his reach. His newly discovered acre of diamonds already belonged to him; he just had to notice the riches that were already his. That particular discovery turned out to be one of the most productive diamond mines on the African continent.

The writer Earl Nightingale, in his version of "Acres of Diamonds," observed that "The first farmer had owned free and clear, acres of diamonds. But he had sold them for practically nothing, in order to look elsewhere. The moral is clear: If the first farmer had only taken the time to study and learn what diamonds looked like in their rough state, and to thoroughly explore the property he had before looking elsewhere, all of his wildest dreams would have come true."

This has always been one of my favorite stories because it symbolizes a dual meaning, like the dual meaning found in the Law of the prospector. Opportunities abound within and around the SalesMaker. If the SalesMaker can learn how to identify opportunities in their undeveloped state, they can discover, develop, and realize their potential. Most of the time, opportunity is within reach, waiting to be discovered and developed. Where and what is this opportunity? It is the potential within you that needs to be realized and it is the opportunities around you that need to be cultivated. Both require discovery and development if they are to become cornerstone of the SalesMaker's success.

The Prospectors Pursuit is Noble

What makes the sales profession the noblest of professions? It is serving the needs of others. It is putting the needs and welfare of others above your own. It is employing high moral principles while pursuing business. It is developing a high level of character and stamina that is required to embrace the daunting challenges a SalesMaker must face and overcome on the street every day if they are to be successful.

Prospecting is a necessary task. Many prospectors begin every month with empty pipelines knowing if they don't find and sell new prospects, they won't receive income. This places them in an ongoing position of sink or swim. The successful SalesMaker succeeds at prospecting by developing a winning plan so they are thriving and not merely surviving month-to-month. This plan includes following a practical system for growing their sales and themselves.

Foundation for Success

The Law of the Prospector will guide you in understanding ten essential qualities of a successful SalesMaker. These qualities are embodied in successful SalesMakers who are tasked with finding and developing customers as part of their regular sales routine. The Law of the Prospector is outlined as an acronym with each letter in the word "prospector" representing a skill, character quality, or mindset that contributes to success. Here are the ten characteristics of the SalesMaker outlined as the acronym P-R-O-S-P-E-C-T-O-R:

Purpose Driven Mindset: The SalesMaker lives life in pursuit and on purpose.

Relationally Discerning: The SalesMaker invests in high-producing relationships while bypassing low-producing prospects in order to maximize their efforts.

Overcomer at Heart: The SalesMaker has the strength of heart to conquer roadblocks, obstacles, and challenges.

Systems Minded: To acquire new customers, the SalesMaker develops and then follows a plan that creates success.

Planter's Passion: The SalesMaker creates new leads by sowing many sales seeds. Planting plenty, they produce a prosperous harvest.

Emotionally Self-Controlled: The seasoned SalesMaker has learned to direct their thoughts so they are able to navigate the obstacle course of emotions they will encounter daily.

Cold Calling Mogul: The SalesMaker creates an empowering belief system that drives them to consistently pursue new customers.

Tactical with Time: A SalesMaker's calendar is protected, focusing on priorities, passions, and high-producing actions.

Opportunity-Oriented: The SalesMaker recognizes opportunities and seizes them.

Restorative: SalesMakers regularly replenish mental, emotional, physical, and spiritual energy stores which allow them to remain at the top of their games.

The 10 letter acronym of P-R-O-S-P-E-C-T-O-R is not meant to be an exhaustive list of character qualities that will build a foundation of success for a SalesMaker, rather just a beginning. It's been said that we don't need to be told what to do, only reminded of what we already know. Adding skill set training whether for sales or attitude is the first step but the challenging part is living it out and practicing what we have learned. It is my hope that the Law of the Prospector will equip and strengthen you to do more and achieve more as you reach to raise the ceiling on your sales, income, and earnings potential.

May I suggest you don't read through this chapter like you have the others? Instead, tackle each of the 10 sections at different sittings and work out your C.I.A. action plans for each one separately. You may want to read one a day and consider how to incorporate something you read that day into your daily routine. Or you may want to consider tackling one a week starting with the section that resonated with you the most. Skill sets are easier to develop than character qualities, but they all have one thing in common: the day you make the decision to change what you know, and who you are, is the day you begin to grow. The following 10 qualities of the SalesMaker do not need to be read in order, so start with the one that has the biggest attraction to you first. The P-R-O-S-P-E-C-T-O-R acronym is almost a book within a book designed to give you quick nuggets to help you level up fast. Grab the section that resonates most and invest yourself there.

Purpose Driven Mindset

The SalesMaker lives life in pursuit and on-purpose.

The first characteristic of the SalesMaker is that they are in pursuit of something or someone, and always going somewhere. They are purpose-driven, goal-oriented, and in pursuit. Developed over time, the internal drive

"You can hope, you can wish, and you can pray. But when you pray, your feet better be moving." African Proverb

of the SalesMaker thrives on the day-to-day challenge of the hunt, the thrill of the chase, the freedom to control and direct their destinies, and the unlimited

"If you don't crave new relationships in your life, you will find ways to avoid prospecting and creating new connections."

potential of the marketplace. They are energized by the unknown and the idea of creating new relationships at will. The ability to make a sales call and immediately impact their financial trajectory is exhilarating. Sales for the SalesMaker is more than the ultimate profession, it provides a daily adrenaline rush! If this doesn't describe you, quit sales, there will are easier careers to pursue.

> "Purpose is the source of motivation for a SalesMaker. It is with Purpose that the SalesMaker is empowered to prospect and produce a harvest of plenty."

The SalesMaker thrives on the act of pursuit. They guard against complacency in order to pursue their purpose with passion and focus. The mindset of a successful SalesMaker is one of a victor, not a victim, making intentional choices instead of reacting to accidental circumstances. Whether they are on the hunt for a dream, a goal, or the fulfillment of a desire, sales (and its income potential) is the vehicle they have chosen. Sales isn't just a job for a successful SalesMaker; it's a calling. They are driven in their pursuit.

The SalesMaker lives with purpose. The SalesMaker is a conqueror who is always expanding territory by taking ground one decision maker at a time. They know that the biggest challenge often lies within them. It is the battle between living life with purpose versus in passivity. Intentional action, not accidental events, drives their decisions with direction, leading them to their destiny. Consider the contrast!

> "I'm a great believer in luck. I find the harder I work, the more I have of it." Thomas Jefferson

SalesMakers are Driven to Live with Purpose	Average Sellers Live in Passivity
If it's meant to be, it's up to me.	Everything that happens was meant to be.
My decisions create my destiny.	Chance is the 'fate' of all.
I create my own destiny by the seeds I sow.	What will be will be—Que Sera, Sera.
Good things come to those who work for them.	Good things come to those who wait.
Focus on what's controllable and push forward.	Focus on uncontrollable things and get stuck in worry.

> "Hard work spotlights the character of people: some turn up their sleeves, some turn up their noses, and some don't turn up at all." Sam Ewing

Relationally Discerning

The SalesMaker invests in high-producing relationships while bypassing low-producing prospects in order to maximize their efforts.

Some prospects turn into customers and produce plenty while others only produce pain. The SalesMaker must discern the difference between the right types of relationships that are worth investing in versus the wrong types of relationships that should be jettisoned. Every SalesMaker has a responsibility to themselves and their companies to invest in relationships that can be converted into revenue while avoiding those that cannot.

> "The SalesMaker must identify with whom they fit and with whom they don't. They aren't right for everyone, and everyone isn't right for them."

Who a SalesMaker accepts into their world of selling and servicing is as important as those they reject. For a SalesMaker to maximize their time and energy, they must eliminate customers that waste time and drain energy. There are right types and wrong types of prospects and the SalesMaker must have a clear picture of both. Here is an example of what right versus wrong relationships might look like for the SalesMaker.

The Right Relationships Will:	The Wrong Relationships Will:
Energize you.	Drain you.
Perceive you can meet their need.	Tell you they have no need.
Welcome and receive you.	Reject you, and then forget you.
Put you off only temporarily.	Put you off indefinitely.
Signal a connection with you.	Show contempt toward you.

Be accepting of your presence.	Resent your presence.
See value in your product & proposal.	Devalue or disrespect what you value.
View you as a solution to a problem.	Perceive your presence as a problem.

Every SalesMaker is not right for every customer. Get over the idea that you can sell everyone. You can't. Some people may not fit with you. If it's not a fit, get out of there.

Relationship Rehabilitation

Let's face it, letting go is hard to do, especially for a skilled SalesMaker trained to open doors, set appointments, and make sales. We believe we can do just about anything. It's hard to admit as a SalesMaker that we won't connect well with everyone. While a successful SalesMaker should overcome obstacles, misapplied perseverance can be detrimental. If you are going the wrong direction, going faster will only get you to the wrong place quicker. Sometimes, a SalesMaker needs to cut their losses, change direction, and find a new relationship worth investing in.

Instinctively, we all know there are customers with whom we don't jive. There are even customers that suck the life out of us. Regardless of the level of effort a SalesMaker invests in developing a prospect, some prospects won't convert into customers. Others may turn into high maintenance, yet low-producing customers. Whoever said that the customer was always right was not dealing with prospects with bad behavior as a SalesMaker may. It takes a degree of self-confidence and courage to admit that one cannot win over every customer.

Identify Relationship Strengths

Some relationships are better left undeveloped and uncultivated, while others are to be identified for their worth and the value they bring to a SalesMaker's pipeline. In the book titled, "Strength Based Selling," Tony Rutigliano and Brian Brim advise that "Having a solid, specific selling process that filters out the wrong customers is extremely important to success." If the SalesMaker doesn't filter out the good prospects from the bad during the cold calling or discovery process, they will find themselves spinning their wheels and going nowhere. To be able to discern and discriminate between high-producing customer relationships and low-producing ones is a strength of every successful SalesMaker. Revenue follows relationships, but the relationship fit has to come first.

Be Adaptive, Not a Door Mat

Skilled SalesMakers have learned to adjust and adapt to appeal to the largest number of potential prospects. This willingness to adapt allows them to fit with many types of customers. Relationships can be broken into two types: Those that strengthen you, and those that weaken you.

Cut the Poor Customer Relationship Cord

We are constantly adding or reducing the value we bring to people and they do the same in return. Just as we add to or subtract from our relationships, customers become pluses or minuses in our lives. If there is a customer who consistently drains you, consider cutting the relationship cord.

I have had to fire a few customers in my career. They were not easy decisions, but I felt lighter, freer and I never regretted cutting the cord. In fact, each time I had to do this, I wished I had done it sooner.

The SalesMaker must decide which relationships strengthen them and which weaken them, and then make adjustments. Who the SalesMaker accepts as a prospect is as important as who they reject. Making the wrong decision on a relationship choice can create misery.

Invest in High-Return Relationships

It takes courage to say that someone is a drain on resources and not worth an investment. It takes courage to admit that we may have missed an opportunity and reinvest ourselves in a relationship we may have been neglecting. Every minute invested in a wrong relationship is a minute taken from developing a relationship that has potential to turn into revenue. SalesMakers value everyone, but shouldn't put the same value on every sales opportunity. Their focus needs to be on relationships that deliver a return. They have a production responsibility to their company and themselves. Every relationship does not produce the same outcome.

> "SalesMakers value everyone, but shouldn't put the same value on every sales opportunity."

An Overcomer at Heart

The SalesMaker has the strength of heart to conquer roadblocks, obstacles, and challenges.

An "Overcomer at Heart" is a resourceful specialist. Like the great escape artist Houdini, they are breakout artists. The chains that they escape and the challenges they overcome are now just part of a day in the life of a SalesMaker. Overcomers at Heart have developed mindsets that enable them to overcome obstacles. They are confident in themselves. SalesMakers are not unaffected by setbacks, but are accustomed to facing and fighting through them. SalesMakers are Overcomers at Heart, not because they are always victorious, but because they embrace challenges, face fears and work through them. They develop a habit of winning.

Everyone is overcome by something at some time. No one is exempt from struggle, bad habits, bad luck, or bad choices. However, successful SalesMakers are able to identify sabotaging thoughts and behaviors and correct them before they are allowed to interfere with their pursuit. Some changes come easier and more quickly than others. It is important to identify obstacles to success and work to remove them. When a change is made for the better, the SalesMaker heads in a direction that is positive and prosperous for themselves, their companies, and their customers.

The SalesMaker's Biggest Challenge to Overcome

The biggest challenges for a SalesMaker are the attrition of accounts and acquisition of them. SalesMakers responsible for new account acquisition place themselves in environments where they face rejection, hostility, disinterest, indifference, and many other negative behaviors. Dealing with constant rejection and rude behavior can cause the SalesMaker to develop an apprehension for calling on new customers. This apprehension may be identified as call reluctance—an invisible wall of emotional resistance that prevents a seller from calling on a customer. For some SalesMakers, it can feel like a physical force preventing them from doing their jobs.

Stephen Walsh in a Southern Business Review article says that call reluctance is an "elevated level of apprehension, sometimes seemingly overwhelming, that may inhibit the number of calls a person will make, and perhaps, rendering the individual incapable of working at all."

Hedge fund consultant, Richard Wilson says, "There are some days where I am just 'on' and can make 50 calls and initiate some great relationships, and then there are days where I make a decent amount of calls but find myself drifting toward less productive activities like cleaning out emails or organizing past prospect research."

When apprehension raises its ugly head or you're just not feeling "on" is when call reluctance begins to grow. It's critical that you recognize the attributes of call reluctance as quickly as possible. Take the quiz below to determine if you ever have or are currently experiencing it.

Call Reluctance Quiz

(Y/N)	Symptoms of Call Reluctance
	I get uncomfortable when meeting new people.
	I dread using the telephone to make appointments.
	I spend more time planning and organizing than prospecting.
	I tend to fill my day with all sorts of activities other than prospecting.
	I have to psych myself up in order to set new business appointments.
	I experience anxiety whenever I start to prospect or set appointments.

All career SalesMakers experience call reluctance at some point. This invisible wall of emotional resistance can torpedo a sales career if it is not confronted and overcome. Whether or not a SalesMaker gets call reluctance is not the issue. It is how well they manage it once encountered that matters.

At the heart of reluctance or apprehension is fear. Early in my speaking career I would experience fear and apprehension during the preparation stage of my speech, but not while presenting on stage. This perplexed me because preparation has always been a strength of mine and speaking is enjoyable for me. Yet I was troubled because I could not identify the source of the fear.

During that time, I had the opportunity to sit next to Dave Blanchard, CEO & Founder of the Og Group at another speaker's presentation. I asked him what he thought and this is what he said to me, "Scott, the source of fear is self-focus." That one statement made me realize that if I kept my focus on helping others and using my gifts to serve others, my focus would always be in the right place and I would overcome fear. I never forgot what Dave shared with me that day. Whenever I start to feel uncomfortable, I check to see if my focus is on myself or others.

SalesMakers can overcome call reluctance by switching their focus from themselves to the customer. Instead of thinking about how they might feel during the next sales call or what they may experience, refocusing their attention on the how they can create connection and a good experience for the customer will lead to a productive outcome.

Here are the memorable acronyms for F.E.A.R. that help me to always overcome:

Face Everything And Run

OR

Face Everything And Rise!

SalesMakers who choose to face everything and rise are Overcomers at Heart.

A SalesMaker's Strategy for Overcoming

The act of making ourselves do something we don't want to do is not new, but it can mean the difference between surviving and sinking for a SalesMaker. Have you recently had a bout of call reluctance? Who won the battle, you or call reluctance? Consider the following simple steps to making yourself do what you know you must do when you know you must do it.

1. **STOP the mental negotiation.** If you have a weakness in this area, you may be no match for talking yourself into doing what you don't want to do with your current mindset. When we are overcome emotionally, a rational intellectual argument doesn't always work. If you find yourself losing more internal battles than you are winning, refuse to fight. Once you catch yourself starting to talk yourself out of what you know you must do, end the internal conversation.

    An athlete I was mentoring once asked me, "How do I make myself not want to play video games and instead go to the gym every day?" I explained to him that it's not easy to make yourself *not* want something, but if you want to be successful and have victory over self, you are better off to avoid self-defeating activities all together. This is how one becomes an Overcomer at Heart. Refuse to negotiate with yourself.

2. **STEER your attention in a new direction.** What captures your attention eventually captures *you*. Whatever you keep in front of you will eventually grow inside you. This is because the human spirit is an incubator; whatever you put in it and consistently feed grows. From the book of Proverbs, it says, "What you think about you bring about."

Stopping the mental negotiation is one step, but it is not enough. Redirecting your focus and setting your attention on something new will empower you to overcome that which might be trying to overcome you. If you are constantly thinking about what you don't want to do, that's what grows. If on the other hand you shift your mental focus and steer it toward a positive outcome or payoff, the unbearable becomes bearable.

James Allen, author of "As a Man Thinketh" said, "You are today where your thoughts have brought you. You will be tomorrow where your thoughts take you." For the SalesMaker, the importance of leveraging this universal truth cannot be overstated. At the heart of becoming an Overcomer at Heart is the willingness to change the subject in your head and intentionally steer the internal conversation toward the outcome you want long term.

3. **STAND UP to yourself.** Every now and then, we need to tell ourselves to shut up and sit down. That may seem a little extreme but Joel Osteen, one of the most watched television pastors on the planet says, "If you don't talk to yourself the right way, your self will talk to you." If your internal conversation is causing you to be overcome by what you feel versus what you know is right, it's time take the reins, and regain control. Every now and then, we all must take the reins and bridle our hearts from doing what they want. Being an Overcomer at Heart sometimes means using our better judgement, and volition to bring our emotions back under the control of our will. That

> "Self-discipline is the result of doing what you know must be done regardless of how you feel about it."

requires standing up for what you know is right, not necessarily defending what feels right in the moment. The SalesMaker is always focused on thinking and doing what is right, regardless of what feels good in the moment.

4. **STICK it out.** Sometimes it is just not enough to stop thinking one way or to steer yourself in the right direction. Leadership guru John C. Maxwell says this about creating change, "What we do is make the decision and then manage that decision." For a SalesMaker to become a successful Overcomer at Heart, they must overcome consistently. Through patience, practice, and perseverance, the SalesMaker gains new knowledge as they pursue the process of overcoming, building new habits, and creating new and better results. These include:

- **Making the right choice.** This may not be a one-time event. Based on the difficulty of the internal tug-of-war, it may be necessary to make a good and right decision more than once before a new habit is formed. Consistently doing what *is* right over what *feels* right will make you an Overcomer at Heart. Everyone must climb this hill and conquer this challenge. You are not alone, so stick with the struggle and you will eventually overcome.

> "Nothing happens until someone meets someone else, and asks them to buy something. A seller's level of success is determined by their ability to find and then convert prospects into customers."

- **Successfully overcoming something the first time doesn't guarantee results the next time.** The SalesMaker must be on the alert for areas of mental weakness for which that they may have to mount a mental challenge multiple times before change sets in. What you consistently stand up to will eventually stand down. Don't let your emotions bully you. Stand up to them like you would a bully you are tired of cowering to.

Being System Minded

To acquire new customers, the SalesMaker develops and then follows a plan that creates success.

All functioning, producing, successful SalesMakers use systems. They will tell you that they have systems and thought processes governing how they work each day. Those systems are part of their formula for creating success, making decisions, processing options, resolving conflict, and finding new customers.

High volume, sales careers demand that SalesMakers develop systems that allow them to streamline repeatable steps while eliminating drains on productivity. A successful system has a purposeful structure that organizes routines into manageable processes. Some systems are based on activity, others on productivity.

Systems Must Serve the SalesMaker

For a system to be successful, it must serve the end user. By design, systems seem rigid and structured; yet they should be flexible enough to help the SalesMaker maximize productivity. With that in mind, consider the following to be fluid and flexible as the system manager. Apply these tips and techniques. Modify them, bend them, and figure out which elements you want to add in creating your own prospecting system as you pull from the following 15 guidelines.

> "Every sustainable success had a system or success formula. Find out the system and way of thinking that produced the success, and you are well on your way to customizing your own success formula."

15 Guidelines of Which You Should Be Mindful when Developing a Prospecting System

1. **Be Protective.**
   Prospecting must be a scheduled event. Scheduling daily and weekly prospecting appointments with yourself will ensure you are investing time in the single most important activity in the sales profession, that of business building. When you set an appointment with yourself to prospect, don't break it. Be protective of this time.

2. **Be Productive.**
   Set activity goals, but hold yourself to daily productivity benchmarks. It may take ten calls or emails to get one face-to-face appointment one

day, but fifteen calls to set one appointment on another. When dialing for dollars and pounding the keyboard, stay in pursuit until you hit your productivity benchmark, not the activity goal. Sales are made through direct contact. Efforts are not rewarded based on how many customers you called, only by how many you can meet, advance in the sales process, and close.

3. **Be Flexible.**

If what you are doing is not working, change it up. If the decision-maker you are trying to reach is unreachable at first, call at a different time. Changing your routine will create a different result.

4. **Be Available.**

The SalesMaker calls based on their schedule, but the customer responds at their convenience. With all the time and energy invested to reach a decision maker or the M.A.N. (the person with Money, Authority, and Need), you must be available when they reach out to you. The greatest annoyance is chasing down people or playing telephone tag. In sales, the seller is paid to hunt for the customer, but the customer doesn't have to hunt for sellers. If you miss an opportunity to respond when the customer needs what you have, another seller may fill the need.

5. **Be Concise.**

Have a relevant reason to call the prospect. Having "relevant business reason" (or RBR) can mean the difference between gaining and losing the prospect's attention. Most customers won't say it, but within the first 30 seconds they are thinking "Do I like you?", "Why are you here?" "Can you help me?" "Am I interested?" "Does this person have anything to say I want to hear or are they just talking and taking up my time?" Within the first 30 seconds of your encounter with a new prospect, state who you are, why you are calling, give your credentials, and tell them what's in it for them (a major benefit). If you don't, you will lose them.

6. **Be Cautious on Social Media.**

When using social media sites to contact and connect with prospective customers, be aware of the fine line between professional selling and personal boundaries. Social media can be a great tool for reaching out to the seemingly unreachable. Be aware that social media environments—although open to the public—are not always welcoming to salespeople.

7. **Be Smart.**

   Leaving one or two messages is the maximum in voicemail, email, or on social media. If you reach out to a prospect too often, you can go from professional seller to professional stalker very quickly in the eyes of the customer. If you find yourself being avoided consistently, return at a later date or move on to other prospects.

8. **Be Option-Oriented.**

   When setting appointments for telephone, video, or face-to-face meetings, always give the prospect options for meeting times. Examples include: 10am or 3pm; morning or afternoon; early in the week or later in the week; this week or next week; today or tomorrow. Prospects like choices.

9. **Be a Prospector, Not a Busy Body.**

   Planning and preparation have their place, but be sure not to spend all your time preparing to prospect but not actually prospecting. If you find yourself doing busy work during key prospecting time, you may be dealing with a case of call reluctance. There will always be something easier to do, more fun, less emotionally tasking, and less difficult than prospecting for new customers. The easiest person for a seller to sell is themselves when it comes to talking ourselves out of doing what we know we must do. Don't prioritize busy work over prospecting work.

   > The more you sow, the more you grow. Sales is a numbers game. As goes your sowing, so goes your sales. The more you plant, the more you produce."

10. **Be Good to Yourself.**

    When you achieve your prospecting productivity goals, reward yourself. What gets rewarded gets done, so make the payoff worth it!

11. **Be Growing.**

    When you fail, fail forward by learning from every prospecting call. With every customer contact, comes an opportunity to learn and better predict human behavior the next time. With every rejection comes an experience or insight that can help you overcome the next objection. Mastering the skill of failing forward is a hallmark of every great achiever.

12. **Be Interesting.**

Say something worth hearing, whether it's a reference to a current event, a statistic about something the prospect may be interested in, or a personal story. Strive to create warmth, interest, and connection. Before making contact with someone, have something to say that will capture their attention. Consider creating a story of the day, or mentally stockpiling a few talking points as conversation starters. Whatever you do, don't show up unprepared for a conversation, because nobody wants to be bored.

13. **Be Focused.**

Focus is the ability to pay attention to what matters most in the moment. Multi-tasking is another word for mental fracturing. A divided mind is NOT a focused mind. The moment you allow interruptions, you lose ground. Refuse to take phone calls, answer emails, or open the door to the idea that there is something more important than seeding the soil for your next sale.

> "My success is due more to my ability to work continuously on one thing without stopping than to any other single quality." Thomas Edison

14. **Be Seeding, Always.**

Consistently planting is the one term that most describes the behavior of the SalesMaker who has developed a winning prospecting system. Planting precedes growing and the ground can only grow what is planted. Consistently seeding is the lifestyle of the Prospector.

15. **Believe in Yourself.**

If you don't believe in yourself, no one else will.

> "If you believe you can, you are right. If you believe you can't, you are right." Henry Ford

Planter's Passion

The SalesMaker creates new leads by sowing many sales seeds.
Planting plenty, they produce a prosperous harvest.

Just as a farmer likes the feel of the dirt between his fingers while working in the field, a SalesMaker enjoys the process of sowing seeds in the marketplace that lead to a sale. Seeding the ground, nurturing a sale so it grows, and then reaping a harvest is the daily delight of the SalesMaker. But Prospecting is likened to plowing the ground. For many it is the hardest part of sales. As a SalesMaker becomes more skilled, they are able to labor less or develop shortcuts for streamlining their processes, but plowing is still plowing. Regardless of how skilled or seasoned a SalesMaker becomes, cultivating new customers takes time and is considered heavy lifting in sales. Prospecting, planting the seeds of interest within a prospect and then giving them time to grow into a closing opportunity can take a lot of time and effort.

> "Planters plant while procrastinators pretend to plant. One produces plenty, while the other poverty."

The Size of the Financial Harvest is Determined by the Number of Sales Seeds Sown

The universal law of sowing and reaping says that "we reap what we sow." In every walk of life, the principle of sowing and reaping is alive and active. We get a return or reward based on our labors—a return on investment (ROI). Seeding is part of selling, and how much a SalesMaker prospects and plants will determine how much they reap. If you are responsible for generating your own leads, then you know that money doesn't magically appear out of thin air, it is earned one seed and one sale at a time.

The Law of the Harvest = The Ground Can Only Grow what the Seller Seeds

For the sower of sales seeds, some grow into small sales, some big sales, some no sales at all. Plowing and planting always precede harvesting in selling. If a SalesMaker doesn't seed the ground of the marketplace, it is impossible to reap a harvest of customers. That is why daily production is the SalesMakers focus. A SalesMaker who refuses to sacrifice their comfort zone today will find their barns empty tomorrow.

Procrastination is a Planter's Worst Enemy

If you are like me, you can talk yourself into or out of anything. Human nature causes us to naturally gravitate toward the easy activities and naturally shy away from the things we don't like. If SalesMakers aren't careful, they can talk themselves into a cycle of procrastination. Procrastination is putting off until tomorrow what should be done today, and it can sneak up on anyone. The modern-day philosopher Jim Rohn said, "If you really want to do something, you'll find a way. If you don't, you'll find an excuse."

Here are a few favorite quotes I've collected on procrastination. The authors are unknown.

"I like work. It fascinates me. I can sit and look at it for hours."

"One of these days I'm going to get help for my procrastination problem."

"Last year I joined a support group for procrastinators. We haven't met yet."

"The best part about procrastination is that you are never bored, because you always have something to look forward to."

"Tomorrow is often the busiest day of the week."

Nobody wants to admit to procrastination. Yet, at some point, everyone has done it. SalesMakers hold themselves accountable, planting regularly so they can produce consistently.

> "I bought a book on procrastination but never got around to reading it."
> Jovi Santiago, General Sales Manager, iHeart Media

Consider the following contrast between a SalesMaker who hunts for new accounts and a procrastinator who pretends to plant.

The SalesMaker Who Seeks Opportunities	The Procrastinator Who Retreats
Earns without income limits.	Earns under an income ceiling.
Is motivated by potential.	Is handicapped by fear.
Leaves their comfort zone.	Hides in their comfort zone.
Chooses to hunt, then feels good.	Waits to feel good before they hunt.
Plans their days around priorities.	Fills their days with busy work.
Raises expectations for themselves.	Settles for the expectations of others.
Embraces the benefits of discipline today.	Accepts the pain of regret from yesterday.

> "Every SalesMaker has both a hider and hunter within them. Recognizing this is the first step to managing it."

> "SalesMakers who refuse to get uncomfortable today in order to prospect will find their bank accounts empty tomorrow."

Emotionally Self-Controlled

The seasoned SalesMaker has learned to direct their thoughts so they are able to navigate the obstacle course of emotions they will encounter daily.

SalesMakers become self-controlled through practice, channeling their emotional energy into productive outcomes. Whether the events encountered throughout the day create a negative or positive emotional charge, the goal is always to change or channel the emotion so the outcome serves the SalesMakers higher purpose.

> "Like a city that is broken into and without walls is a man who has no control over his spirit." Proverbs 25:28

A person's thoughts will determine the emotions they feel. Brian Tracy said that "95% of our emotions come from self-talk." When thoughts enter our minds, we have to make choices. We can accept them; dwell on them; reject them; or change them. When we dwell on thoughts, we feed them. A SalesMaker who refuses to dwell on rejection and instead change the inward conversation will starve negative thoughts thus allowing positive thoughts to grow. You must make many conscious choices throughout the day as to which emotions you will allow to increase and which you will fight to decrease. You will do this based on the thoughts you allow to linger in your neural net. Intentionally making decisions is what it means to be emotionally self-controlled. No one can control your emotional state but you.

SalesMakers take responsibility as the Chief Emotional Officers of their internal lives. No one can manage your mind and emotional state but you. You and you alone are responsible

> "The mind is a wonderful servant, but a terrible master." Robin S. Sharma

for your success. You and you alone are responsible for what you allow yourself to feel. We cannot always control what happens to us because of outside circumstances, but we can decide what happens inside us. If you don't take your time to self-discipline, self-correct, and self-direct your internal world, you will have less success influencing the factors that impact your external world.

> "I am convinced that life is 10% what happens to me and 90% how I react to it." Chuck Swindoll

In sales, rejection is unavoidable. Whether prospecting, presenting, or closing, a SalesMaker must develop tools to overcome and conquer the inevitable unpleasant experiences and rejections they will face. Learning how to compartmentalize, categorize, or redirect unwanted emotions is a skill every successful SalesMaker must master. Learning to change or channel emotions is a basic coping skill of all successful people. Emotions can invigorate us or immobilize us. If we don't control our emotions, they will control us. That which a SalesMaker sets their attention to directs their actions. Following are four self-engaging ways with which you can strengthen your ability to self-direct, regardless of how you feel.

> "When you are able to bridle your emotions, you'll be in control of your most formidable foe."

1. **Emotional Intelligence.** One hallmark of successful SalesMaker is that they are emotionally intelligent. According to Daniel Goleman, Best Selling Author of Emotional Intelligence, an emotionally intelligent person is one who is aware of their emotions, the emotions of others, and has the ability to use this emotional information to direct themselves and others toward positive outcomes. You must master your own moods if you are to be able to effectively navigate and influence the emotional responses inherent in the sale cycle. Engaging your emotional controls allows you to manage your mind,

> "The greatest discovery of my generation is that human beings can alter their lives by changing their thoughts." William James, American Psychologist

set and direct thoughts that dictate emotions, enjoy emotional peace, resist negative thoughts, and enforce emotional mastery.

2. **Spiritual Intelligence.** It would be disingenuous to talk about controlling ones thoughts, emotions, and behaviors without mentioning my own relied upon personal source of strength. My faith and belief in God greatly influence my interior thought life, and it is from this relationship with the Divine that I derive much of my strength. Whether you consider a relationship with God, a belief system, or religion as a source of your strength, every SalesMaker needs a little help from on high. Pierre Teilhard de Chardin, a French theologian and philosopher, said "We are not human beings having a spiritual experience, but spiritual beings having a human experience." We are pre-wired to reach out and up. Discover a source of strength outside of yourself to add to your inner strength.

3. **Experiential Intelligence.** The best teacher is not necessarily experience itself, but evaluated experience. Experience won't make one wiser, but applying what one learns from experience, is what gives birth to wisdom. Just as a SalesMaker becomes aware of conditioned or repeated responses by customers, they can also become aware of their own pre-programmed emotional responses to certain stimuli. Take time to reflect on your emotional reactions and trigger points and you'll be more capable of handling your own moods as they surface. Sometimes, just being aware of your internal habitual emotional responses can be enough to neutralize them.

> "Reflection turns experience into insight." John C. Maxwell

4. **An Emotional Bounce-Back Strategy:** If a SalesMaker can learn to save a sinking sale by navigating the emotional obstacle course of others, then they can save their own sinking attitude by managing their emotional responses to stress and rejection with a pre-planned strategy. Your ability to change and channel emotions is critical because unhappy or negative sales people are less likely to prospect or sell. At some point, you are going to have a bad call, a bad experience, a poor relationship, or a bad day. Disappointments in sales are inevitable. If you are going to get through it, you will need to learn how to walk through it. Consider how an emotionally-controlled SalesMaker chooses the right response over the wrong when faced with rejection.

Healthy Response	Unhealthy Response
Erase the last call by making another call.	Emotionally sink & avoid the next call.
Mentally revisit & replay successful memories.	Mentally replay negative experiences.
Treat every failure as a learning experience.	Dwell on the pain of rejection & retreat to lick your wounds.
Compartmentalize professionally.	Internalize emotionally & take it personally.
Redefine and repurpose difficult experiences.	Remember & replay painful experiences.
Resist & reject counter-productive self-talk.	Come into agreement with negative self-talk.
Challenge the source of self-defeating thoughts.	Allow internal negativity to go unchecked.

> "Emotional pain can be a mentor or a tormentor. It is our choice whether we use the energy that comes from sales rejection to redirect ourselves toward success or sink into a state of discouragement."

Cold Calling Mogul

> The SalesMaker creates an empowering belief system that drives them to consistently pursue new customers.

The most appreciable asset of a SalesMaker is their thought life. Their attitudes, the way they think, believe, and navigate the ups, downs, victories and valleys of a sales day all play a part in their sense of well-being. When cold calling, your mental toughness, and determination need to be strong. With training, you can develop a mindset that embraces the rigors of cold calling. That mindset can make the difference between your inclinations to make many calls, few calls, or no calls at all.

If you are 100% responsible for new customer acquisition, your ability to cold call and build a customer base is at the heart of your job. Your mindset or approach to cold calling matters most, as it dictates whether your call volume for the day will be high or low. With the right mindset, you are unstoppable. With the wrong mindset, you will be underpowered mentally and emotionally. A mindset is a mental approach toward people and situations. Successful SalesMakers develop and protect their mindsets above all else.

> "If you knew you could create connection and convert every cold call to a warm experience, nothing could stop you from making the next call."

Here are a few prospecting mindsets to consider developing:

1. **There's No Such Thing as a Cold Call.** Whether a sales call feels cold or warm has nothing to do with whether or not you know the prospect.

    SalesMaker's win others over during first time calls through the warmth they bring to the conversation. It is the SalesMaker's ability to thaw the atmosphere of a cold call and transfer warmth to the prospect that creates the connection. The better you are at creating warmth on a sales call, the quicker you will be able to develop rapport and common ground. Strategies that make a first time call a warm and pleasant experience may include:

    - Starting a conversation using a story about someone they know.

    - Expressing appreciation for something you value in the prospect.

    - Asking questions about something the prospect might care about.

    - Smiling when greeting new prospects.

    - Being vulnerable, transparent, and professionally authentic.

    - Saying something nice about the prospect or their business in the first sixty seconds.

    - Having something relevant to say or show to the prospect that adds value to them or piques their curiosity.

2. **Prospect for Friends, Not Customers.** My father was in the auto business early in his life. His advice to me when shopping for a vehicle

was to first decide what I wanted to buy, and then to shop for the right salesperson. Most people want to have relationships in business. When prospecting, approach the process as if you are searching for a friendship to ensure that a relational connection is made before a financial transaction takes place. This way, you will be focused on the fit of the relationship before focusing on the financial value.

Put yourself in the customer's shoes for a moment and ask yourself, are you more prone to do business with a friend with whom you can relate or a salesperson you don't know? If a customer doesn't like you, your chances of doing business with them decrease significantly. When you prospect, find a friend and a financial relationship can follow. It's amazing how much more easily dollars flow when doing business with friends.

3. **Everybody is a Customer.** The mindset that served me well while prospecting in the advertising business was the realization that all retailers will eventually advertise. It's just a question of when and with whom. I knew that at some point, every prospect I met would eventually need what I was selling. I believed that it was just a question of who they would buy from and when. This belief empowered me to focus on developing relationships with prospects. Then, when their need arose, I was already in position to reap the rewards. It is a sales truism that people buy from people they like and trust. With this in mind, you can get into position to make sales by focusing on ways you can add value to your prospects. If you are top of mind when their needs arise, you will be their first call.

4. **If you don't have access or interest, get out of there.** SalesMakers instinctively know when they are welcome and when they are not. They know if there is warmth or coolness toward them in conversations. They can feel it the air and know if they should remain or make their way to an exit.

A SalesMaker's instincts distinguish who is right for the sales funnel and who should not be pursued. If you believe you are right for every customer, you will only frustrate yourself. If there is an openness and access, prospects will share information and insights into their needs, and display a

> "Salespeople instinctively know where they are welcome and where they are not. Go where you are celebrated, not tolerated."

level of interest and energy when talking with you. Recognize when doors of access and opportunity are open. Where there is no access, there is no interest and it's time to get out of there. Once a SalesMaker has made contact, connection, and found common ground, if they don't find there is a personality fit, a financial fit, a problem they can solve, or a path to the sale, they should end the discussion and find a new opportunity. Go where you are greeted warmly, needed, and heeded. Retreat from those who reject you. Remain with those who celebrate you.

5. **Look for people with whom you can connect.** SalesMakers must decide what type of seller they will be when meeting customers for the first time. Will they set out to close or connect with a prospect on a first-time call? The subtleties between the two may seem slight, but they are distinguishable. Prospects can easily discern genuineness and authenticity.

  Here are some differences in mindset between a cold caller in pursuit of a sale versus a connector in pursuit of common ground.

Cold Callers with Call Quotas	Connectors
Are self-focused.	Are other-focused.
Are in search of a quick close.	Are in search of common ground.
Are on the hunt for an account.	Are hunting for a need to fill.
Count the commission before they close.	Connect emotionally before closing financially.

When the SalesMaker's motives are to build relationships instead of achieving closing quotas, they are at ease. They are able to create comfort, confidence, and trust with customers on the first sales call. Without comfort, confidence, and trust, sales are not possible.

"Successful SalesMakers are able to bring customers to a place where they feel the relationship is the reason for the transaction versus the transaction being the reason for the relationship."

Tactical with Time

> A SalesMaker's calendar is protected, focusing on
> priorities, passions, and high-producing actions.

Everyone has 24 hours or 1440 minutes per day to use as they wish. These minutes can be invested or wasted, but not carried over to the next day. Some see time as something to be used up, while others see time as an asset to be invested. When the SalesMaker invests time, they use it to plant where they can reap the highest return. Return on time is a metric the SalesMaker is always thinking about. They ask themselves the question, "What is the most productive activity I can do right now to help me achieve my goals?"

What Value do You Place on Your Time Each Day?

Time is more valuable to some than others. What value would you place on yours? In the "Value of Time" poem below, time cannot always be measured in dollars. At times, it is measured in other meaningful forms.

The Value of Time
(Author Unknown)

To realize the value of one year: Ask a student who has failed a final exam.

To realize the value of one month: Ask a mother who has given birth to a premature baby.

To realize the value of one week: Ask an editor of a weekly newspaper.

To realize the value of one hour: Ask lovers who are waiting to meet.

To realize the value of one minute: Ask the traveler who has missed a connection.

To realize the value of one second: Ask a person who has survived an accident.

To realize the value of one millisecond: Ask the person who has won a Silver Medal in the Olympics.

For the SalesMaker, time represents productivity and money. For this reason, a SalesMaker's calendar is carefully set, controlled, and protected from less important, low-producing activities. Time cannot be managed, stopped, or created. Time can only be invested and purposed. Your time can be used to plant relationships that yield high returns.

If a farmer plants corn, he will grow corn. If he plants apple seeds, the seeds will eventually grow into an apple tree. What gets planted determines what grows. In the same way, your time is like a seed that gets planted. Whatever you plant determines what grows. If you invest your time into servicing, you will produce loyal customers. If you invest your time into business-building activities, you will reap new business. If you invest time in meeting new people, you will produce new relationships. Whatever you plant with seeds of time you will grow.

Here are ways in which SalesMakers employ their time for maximum return.

Six Strategies for the SalesMaker to Maximize Return on Time

Reevaluate. SalesMaker's consistently audit their calendars to identify high- and low-producing activities. Their calendars are portfolios of time that require occasional rebalancing in order to produce high returns.

Reassign. Time can't be managed, but it can be given an assignment. It can be repurposed. Consider giving each working hour an assignment, whether it is business-building, follow-up, cold calling, servicing, working with digital media, or downtime. Giving your time an assignment ensures it is working for you and producing the result you want.

Refuse. Refuse access during business hours to relationships and activities that do not contribute to a high return on time. Time wasters and energy drainers will derail production.

"Without a redistribution of your time portfolio, you will continue to produce the same sales results."

Recommit. SalesMakers schedule business-building hours on their calendars during peak prospecting hours. Peak prospecting hours are when prospects are most likely to be reached or to respond. Prospecting and cold calling early in the day allows the SalesMaker to get it done before energy stores start to run low!

Redeem. SalesMakers learn to maximize the time between events and appointments. If you arrive early for an appointment or are waiting in line somewhere, use the otherwise wasted minutes for cold calling, prospecting or other business-building activities. Use those moments to redeem unused minutes every day.

> "Give every hour an assignment. Success is a scheduling event."

Reinvest. Channel the emotional highs of the day by parlaying them into new business appointments. Nothing creates success like success. When you are coming off a big win, leverage that emotional high and build on that momentum by converting it into prospecting time.

> "The difference between highly-paid, successful sales people and average-earners is how they invest their time each day. Some convert time into treasure while others trade time for pleasure."

Opportunity-oriented

The SalesMaker recognizes opportunities and seizes them.

What makes a SalesMaker opportunity-oriented is the lens of possibility through which they see life. Being opportunity-oriented is a mindset. Positioning and programming your mind to identify opportunities is the first step. What a SalesMaker looks for, they eventually find. This is because of the way in which the reticular activating system works in the human brain.

The reticular activating system is the attention center of the brain. Once set, positioned, or fixed in a direction, it becomes a neural net that seeks and collects information that links it to what it seeks. If a SalesMaker's attention is on finding new business opportunities, everywhere they look they will discover green shoots of opportunity that lead to new business. On the other hand, if a seller does not fix their attention on developing new prospects, the opposite will happen. Their degree of success will be average at best. There are three mindsets that can be used to position the neural net in order to create prospecting success.

> "A Prospector believes that golden opportunities are already within their reach, merely awaiting their recognition."

Optics of a Prospector

1. **Opportunity is a matter of perspective.** An opportunity-oriented SalesMaker sees things differently than other sellers. They think differently about their surroundings and potential. They see opportunity that the casual observer may miss. Where others see dead ends, SalesMaker's see potential. They cultivate territory and develop ground that others may ignore. They are diligent in developing the hidden riches under their feet. They are convinced that they are at any time, one person, one cold call, and one conversation away from financial growth. This is their mindset. Success is always within reach.

   In every sales organization, sellers can be divided up into two groups. One group sees potential around every corner and the other group sees obstacles.

   Here's an example from the broadcast sales business: Two groups of SalesMakers at a radio station were tasked with developing a new category. The category was automotive. After monitoring various radio station ads, it became apparent that auto dealers didn't use radio in that town. One group of SalesMakers saw no potential because car dealers didn't use radio to advertise. The other group of SalesMakers saw uncultivated opportunity and developed the opportunity into a portfolio worth over $2 Million in annual automotive advertising billing. What was the difference? The opportunity-oriented SalesMakers saw potential, while the others only saw obstacles.

2. **Opportunity is discovered, but only after digging for it.** Many people have what is called "destination disease." Wherever they are, opportunity is always in another place, in another person's hands, or out of their reach. The grass is greener on the other side in their minds, so they are always peering over the fence at another person's plot of opportunity wishing it was theirs. They wonder if they too could stumble upon luck as their neighbors had. Successful SalesMaker's do not think this way. They believe that opportunity is all around them waiting to be discovered and developed. They are the creators and cultivators of opportunity because they are willing to look for it and then work for it. Another story found in Russell Conwell's famous "Acres of Diamonds" speech, mentioned earlier in this chapter, is about a gold mine in California.

During the 1800's gold rush, a young couple set out to discover their treasure. Caught up in the hype and the dream of finding gold and staking their claim, they sold the family farm and left home with the hope of discovering their fortune. Years later, they found themselves in another country, destitute and broke. Not having discovered any riches, they decided it was time to start over and went back to see their old farm before beginning their new lives.

As they approached the old farm, there were fences surrounding the property and they couldn't get in. It turned out that the farm they gave up to buy picks, shovels, and gold panning gear to prospect elsewhere was found to be one of the largest gold mining reserves ever

> Before you go looking across the street, always identify the potential under your feet and develop the opportunity within your reach."

discovered. The moral of the story is to always identify the potential under your feet and develop the opportunity within your reach.

> Prospectors extract potential from the opportunities that exist around them. They believe that everything they need is within reach, often right under their feet."

Success isn't easy—it requires hard work, digging in the ground beneath you, and developing the SalesMaker within you. Money doesn't grow on trees; it grows out of hard work. If your golden opportunity isn't visible on the top of the ground, start digging for it. It's likely closer than you think; it may be under your feet.

3. **Opportunity is created through problem-solving.** John W. Gardner, former Secretary of Health, Education, and Welfare said, "We are all faced with a series of great opportunities brilliantly disguised as insolvable problems." Unless a SalesMaker can discover a problem and provide a solution, closing a sale will be more than challenging. Where there is a problem, there may be energy, resources, and a willingness by customers to pay for a solution. The bigger the problem, the higher motivation a customer will have to resolve their issue. SalesMaker's see problems as golden opportunities to present solutions and make sales.

Customers are always in pursuit of something that goes beyond the obvious. They are trying to solve a problem. Every customer has visible and invisible needs. The visible need is why they are meeting with you. The invisible need is why they will buy from you. When you get good at asking questions that uncover problems, you become a solution-provider, better positioned to close sales. Zig Ziglar said, "You can have everything in life you want, if you will just help enough other people get what they want." Sales are closed then problems are resolved, not before.

> SalesMakers see a problem as a golden opportunity to make a sale, not an obstacle to closing the sale."

Here are a few questions that can help you uncover golden opportunities hidden within problems.

- What other options do you have?
- What problem are you trying to solve?
- What does the perfect purchase look like?
- What is the biggest challenge you are facing?
- What made you want to meet with me today?
- If I could solve any problem for you, what would it be?
- If you could change anything in your life, what would it be?
- Of all your priorities and pain points, what is at the top of the list?
- What will be the outcome if you are not able to get what you need?
- If you could change anything about the purchase, what would it be?
- Did something recently happen that caused you to consider buying now?
- If you could change anything about what you currently have, what would it be?
- Was there anything that disappointed you last time you made a purchase like this?

To solve problems is to sell. Below the surface of every customer's budget challenge is a problem fueling the motivation to adjust it in order to make the purchase. A solution unlocks the dollars associated with problems. More sales are made by problem-solving than by offering features and benefits. The more time a SalesMaker invests in talking about what a customer cares about, the more likely a sale will be made. All successful SalesMakers have one thing in common; they are problem solvers.

> "A good question is like a shovel that uncovers what can't be seen on the surface."

> "A concern shared outwardly is an unspoken assignment for the SalesMaker. If the SalesMaker can solve the customer's problem, remove their pain point, or address their concern, the reward is financial. A customer's concern is an open door to a financial opportunity."

Restorative

> SalesMakers regularly replenish mental, emotional, physical, and spiritual energy stores which allow them to remain at the top of their games.

A SalesMaker's daily emotional and intellectual output requires an enormous amount of energy. They are required to perform on a moment's notice with customers, when prospecting, and whenever opportunity presents itself. It can be a challenge to maintain a high energy level throughout the day and into the evening hours. A day in sales can feel like a marathon because customer needs never end. It could also be equated to a sprint because you need to be running at full speed to keep up with the demands of the job, meeting expectations, and exceeding performance metrics.

If there is one characteristic consistent in successful high performing people, it is that they possess high energy levels. You will never meet one who is low on energy unless it's at the end of the day. People who cannot maintain high energy are unable to push through barriers, overcome obstacles, and make themselves do what is necessary to deliver consistently.

Discover your Refueling Stations and Visit them Often

Every tank runs dry. Sales people are in constant "giving mode," investing and pouring themselves into others. The question is not if your tank will run dry, but when. Do you have a routine for recharging? Have you set up boundaries in order to maintain margins and white space, or are you constantly running on empty? Establishing non-negotiable blocks of time in your routine will keep you out of the empty zone and protect your bandwidth.

Are you aware of the warning signs that tell you when your fuel gauge is starting to flash red? The warning signs could be tiredness, anxiety, becoming short with others, or still feeling drained after resting. When that happens, you may need more than a rest. You may need to be recharged from multiple sources. Symptoms of *selling on empty* can show up in a SalesMaker's ability to communicate, connect, and continue to cultivate new business relationships. An empty tank does not lead to high performance.

Where do you Turn when you find Yourself Selling on Empty?

How do you refill your tank? Developing an awareness of what and who fills your tank will allow you to visit the filling stations in your life with regularity, keeping your batteries charged, and your engines running at full strength. What are your refueling stations?

"You and only you are responsible for motivating yourself, energizing yourself, and keeping yourself on track. If you don't do this for yourself, nobody else will."

Refueling Stations are Your Streams of Strength

When I think of renewal, I don't think of resting or engaging in down time activity. For me, a change of scenery is usually what I need when my batteries are running low. Rest and recovery are important, but sometimes renewal is what a SalesMaker needs more than rest. Rest is for the body and mind, but renewal can feed the soul and spirit. If you are full of physical energy but drained emotionally, knowing how to refill your emotional stores can be critical to your ability to return to peak performance. When you have a full tank of emotional, mental, physical, and spiritual energy, you are able to cold call, overcome challenges, win others over, and navigate the stress, demands, and everyday challenges you face. However, if you are unaware that you are traveling through the day on an empty tank and not at your best, this leads to diminished performance and potential. When SalesMakers feel at their best, they perform at their best.

Develop strategies to refill your energy stores and reignite your passion for selling. Refueling requires a balance of mental, physical, emotional, and spiritual infusions. Well-being comes in many forms. I've listed below a few questions that have helped identify refueling stations in my life. These are activities that restore strength and health to me. They positively impact my mental, physical, emotional, and spiritual sense of well-being. As you read through them, consider which strategies might help you.

> "When SalesMakers feel at their best, they perform at their best."

Pleasure: What activities bring you joy, bliss, or a sense of renewal? I enjoy exercising, writing, speaking, reading, taking a road trip with a great audiobook, prayer and meditation. Each of these activities are not just a source of enjoyment for me; they are forms of escape and renewal. Some refueling routines I can do for an hour in the morning, during the lunch hour, or at a quiet time in the evening. They are simple, easily-implemented and reproducible. Whenever I am feeling a little drained, finding a few minutes to an hour to do something pleasurable doesn't just lift my spirits, it refreshes me and renews my resolve to continue on. With a fresh infusion of energy, I am able to pick myself up and re-enter my race. As my strength returns, so does my confidence, creativity, and the will power to tackle tasks I might otherwise avoid. What activities refill you mentally, emotionally, physically, and spiritually?

Positive People: Which relationships lift you up and strengthen you? SalesMakers need to surround themselves with positive people who bring energy to them, and avoid emotional vampires who drain the selling life out of them. Every relationship can be categorized as one that drains or energizes you. Some people give off a positive emotional charge while others emit a negative one. SalesMakers need circles of people they can plug into from time to time for an infusion of positive energy. Develop a network of regenerators. Avoid people who only want to weep and wail about their troubles. Instead, pursue people who are passionate about success. Who are the people that you can turn to for refueling?

Purposeful Pursuit: What passions can you engage in? What subjects, topics, and interest invigorate you? Pursue these through books, audio programs, videos, seminars, retreats, group classes, experiences, or themed events. For every problem that weighs you down, there is an expert with a solution. Pursue your passion and remove the weights that drain your passions. The more time you spend in what ignites your passion, the higher your energy stores will rise.

Practice Strengths: What natural talents can you develop into strengths? Your energy level is directly tied to how you are leveraging your strengths and managing your weaknesses. If you are focusing on working your strengths throughout your day, your chances of operating at full power are high. On the other hand, if you are working from a position of weakness, you will struggle to maintain high energy stores. Successful SalesMakers know there are zones of strength and zone of weakness. The more time you spend in a strength zone, the more robust your attitude, energy level, and performance will be. Have you identified your strengths and weaknesses?

Priorities Realigned: On which items should you focus and which should you discard? I have found it liberating to discard unnecessary or unwanted information, papers, or objects. Whether it's a mental spring cleaning or a complete clearing of the decks, identifying what I want to keep and what I want to eliminate is empowering and energizing. Whether you are discarding a file cabinet of information in your mind, or a physical one in your office, eliminating the unnecessary will allow you to maintain high energy stores. What priorities do you need to realign?

Places of Inspiration: Where can you go to feel energized? Places that inspire me and bring me to renewal are places I want to revisit often. Every environment has an atmosphere and ambiance. A place of inspiration I return to each morning and evening is a red leather reading chair in the corner of my home office. It is in this place that I think, consider, write, pray, and make decisions about the day ahead. Sometimes I just sit there in quiet meditation, listening and reflecting on the day behind. A place of inspiration can include your own neighborhood. Take a stroll at night with a loved one, a jog around the block with a dog, a midnight walk on the beach, or a dip in the ocean. Watch a late-night movie, or go on a date to a romantic restaurant. What places carry an ambiance that refreshes and renews you? My wife likes the feeling that a spa or a movie theatre gives her. Scheduling visit to a place that inspires you can create a rebirthing effect. Whether you are inspired by a sunset, fine art, gardening, or walking a golf course, knowing where you can retreat to for a lift will keep you soaring the skies of the successful SalesMaker. Where do you go when you want to feel inspired?

As you have discovered, the word P-R-O-S-P-E-C-T-O-R has a dual meaning in the Law of the Prospector. Prospecting business is critical for all SalesMakers responsible for lead generation. But for a SalesMaker to reach their potential in a sales career, they must also develop within them characteristics of success. The ten qualities of a successful SalesMaker is a starting point. Qualities that include living life on purpose, becoming an overcomer, developing "doing-and-thinking" systems for success, becoming aware of opportunities around you, and much more. Developing sustainable success in sales throughout the course of a career requires diligent practice and time, investment, and a commitment to ongoing growth. The steps to set your feet on a trajectory toward reaching your potential and growing your business can be found in the Law of the Prospector which says, "The SalesMaker develops the potential within them, they discover opportunities around them."

C.I.A. CONTRIBUTORS

The LAW OF THE PROSPECTOR

Steve K. Sombrero, NAI Chaney Brooks Realty
Gary Goslin, Karat Bars Gold International

My name is **Steve Sombrero** and I am the president and principal broker for **Chaney Brooks & Company**, Hawaii's leading commercial real estate brokerage and management company since 1958. I absolutely enjoy my job as it entails strategic marketing and sales of our services to clients from diverse markets and industries. As the head of the organization, it is my job to identify and develop both land and human potential to achieve their highest and best values. I take great pride and satisfaction in coaching and encouraging our property managers and brokers to achieve their sales and personal financial goals. The points and principles in the Law of the Prospector are absolute gems. Here is a short list of some of the gems and takeaways I received from this chapter:

1. "On the journey to success, the road is uphill… the higher I climbed the growth ladder, the more I could see." This is so true. Starting out in sales is always the toughest because you have yet to be known by your customers. But, as you put in your time and hard work developing your reputation and experience in the business, you will create an entire community of deal facilitators that refer business leads to you. In fact, you no longer have to chase deals because the deals will now come looking for you.

2. "The SalesMaker invests in high-producing relationships, and must identify with whom they fit and with whom they don't. They aren't right for everyone, and everyone isn't right for them." One of the biggest mistakes sales people make is that they become willing to catch every single ball that

is thrown at them. They simply don't know how to say "No." I train my team to choose their clients and their projects very carefully and be willing to turn down jobs. Otherwise, they become too busy juggling balls in a circus with other clowns and bozos—and fail to close their deals.

3. "There's No Such Thing as a Cold Call." One of my favorite Hawaiian phrases is "If You No Ask, You No Get." Too many people are simply too ashamed or too afraid to ask. I have probably brokered more "landmark" deals in the business than most brokers in Hawaii because I am not ashamed to ask. We now live in a world where people are more accessible than ever before through mobile phones and social media. There is no more excuse not to make that call. Seek, ask, and knock it out of the park!

4. "Opportunity is created through problem-solving." This is the primary reason why most commercial real estate brokers do better in a down-market. Real estate owners don't need realtors in a good market or unwilling to pay their keep. Interesting though, even in a good market, property owners are struggling with problems they create in their own minds, anticipating the next market crash.

5. "You and only you are responsible for motivating yourself, energizing yourself, and keeping yourself on track. If you don't do this for yourself, nobody else will." I have found that high performance SalesMakers all have a robust life outside of work. They enjoy some kind of sports (golf, surfing, hiking, or fishing) or are involved in some type of community organization, church or nonprofit organization. They look forward to their weekends, but always come back to the office recharged and ready to solve problems and not be the problem. At our office, we have a Deal Bell that is rung by brokers who close transactions. I was told that the sound of that bell means different things to different people. For the broker ringing the bell, it is a nice commission check. For the broker not ringing the bell, it is wake-up call to get going on their deals. For our back-office staff, it means that there is a company lunch coming up that will be paid for by the bell ringer. For me, it is the sweet sound of assurance and acknowledgement that the company is on the right path towards continued success.

My name is **Gary Goslin** and I have worked as an **International Sales Executive for Fortune 500 Companies** as well as in the Direct Marketing Industry with record-breaking companies for over four decades. I was also one of the pioneers who helped Anthony Robbins launch his *Personal Growth and Success* seminar business in the 1980's! I attribute my success to the love I have for my industry, the people we serve, and helping both to grow. The Law of the Prospector is a roadmap to success. Here are a few golden nuggets I received.

1. Purpose Driven Mindset: The SalesMaker lives life in pursuit and on purpose. Developing a purpose-driven mindset is important to achieving my goals. Having an end in sight motivates me to press on past the discomfort of the day. The Purpose Driven Mindset precepts are so rich in wisdom and inspiration that I am compelled to begin to pursue even greater goals of sales growth and income, fine tune my plan, and commit to the discipline.

2. Relationally Discerning: The SalesMaker invests in high-producing relationships while bypassing low-producing prospects in order to maximize their efforts. "Who a SalesMaker accepts into their world of selling and servicing is as important as those they reject." This is such an important truth. It reminded me of the times when I invested in both high- and low-producing prospects, and enjoyed the fruits of the high and suffered the pain and loss of the low. I will focus on profiling and prioritizing my prospects. The relationship list is a good guide for evaluating the value of a prospect.

3. Restorative: SalesMakers regularly replenish mental, emotional, physical, and spiritual energy stores which allow them to remain at the top of their games. The high-producing people I work with I refer to this as "Lightning Bolts." To be a premier SalesMaker with excellence requires high energy, and Scott's model for refueling and recharging is a great strategy for staying charged at the highest performance levels.

4. Overcomer at Heart: The SalesMaker has the strength of heart to conquer roadblocks, obstacles, and challenges. The wisdom Scott shares here is profound, and is coming straight from his own courageous heart and experiences! Since I am so privileged have a very deep, rich personal friendship with Scott, he has shared with me, heart-to-heart, many of the extreme challenges he has faced in his life and how he overcame them. So these wise distinctions are coming from a man who has traveled the road of the overcomer!

5. "The source of fear is self-focus." This is the statement made me realize that if I kept my focus on helping others and using my gifts to serve others, my focus would always be in the right place and I would overcome fear.

Put the 7 Empowering Laws of the SalesMaker to Work And Convert your Insights into Income!

Now that you've completed the Law of the Prospector, it is time to convert learning into earning. The first step is to return to the sections of this chapter that you highlighted, underlined, or made notes from. Of the key points that you connected with, pick three that resonate the most with you. Following the simple formula for transformation found in the C.I.A. process in the introduction (Connection, Insight, Action), identify and write down that which resonated with you. Then, identify the insights you gathered, and finally, decide how you might put them into action. Reading, doing, believing in, and incorporating three sales insights into your daily routine will create a transformative impact on your sales volume and sales commissions.

Here is how I will convert my insights into income:

C = Connection: As I read, the following content, principle, or idea that connected with me was:

_____

_____

I = Insight: As I reflect, the idea or insight I received is:

_____

_____

A = Action: The action I will take to convert my insight into income will be to:

_____

_____

SALES SUCKS UNTIL YOU LEARN HOW TO SELL!

The sales profession can be incredibly difficult and demoralizing if you do not know how to sell. As with any profession, getting good at it, not just becoming competent, takes a higher-than-average level of commitment. There are no shortcuts to success. If there were, all SalesMakers would reach their potentials and enjoy the high incomes that go along with being top performers.

What often separates the successful from the average is not skill, but the willingness to do just a little bit more—in a consistent manner. In sales, you are responsible for developing yourself. It is not the job of managers, mentors, teachers, or trainers to develop you. Only you can give the gift of learning to yourself. Only you can convert learning into earning.

Sellers sell so they can persuade buyers to buy. Singers sing to sway an audience into returning for another performance or buying a recording. Preachers preach to persuade people to believe certain things and behave certain ways. Athletes sport their athletic prowess to win over coaches, fans, and get endorsement deals. Regardless of your chosen field or profession, wherever you find success that involves communicating, connecting, and persuading, you will see the 7 Empowering Laws of the SalesMaker in operation. They affect everything!

Some of the most important sales in life don't involve money. Most sales are emotional in nature, not financial. It's important to realize that whether or not you have chosen sales as a vocation, you are selling during every human encounter. That's why these skills are so critical.

We all have a degree of untrained, inbred instincts that are in operation, either consciously or unconsciously, that impact the emotional environment around us. These instincts have been developed since birth. Emotionally, we all crave moving someone closer to us, winning someone over, or persuading someone to look on our idea or course of action with favor. Some are naturally better than others when persuading simply because of how they chose to communicate in their personal environments. The lessons they learned may have been accidental, but not intentional. It is my hope that you can now *intentionally* leverage the 7 Empowering Laws of the SalesMaker to improve your ability to persuade in all types of situations. Whether the sale you make is emotional, financial, or of another sort, living the Laws will help you level up your powers of persuasion.

> "Advanced learners are those who can import and improve from everything around them, not just the experiences that make them feel good. In fact, painful experiences, when processed properly, can become our best tutors."

SalesMakers win others over and strengthen their relationships by adding value to them. Whether you add value personally, professionally, financially, emotionally, or spiritually, when people receive value from you and feel valued when they are with you, your influence grows—and so will the likelihood of getting them to follow you financially.

The exchange of positive emotions is important for every relationship. Wielding the powers inherent within the Laws of the SalesMaker will help you create closeness in personal relationships, not just to close financial relationships. All great SalesMakers learn to leverage their knowledge in the service of others while accomplishing the goals for the organizations they serve.

Don't Believe the Lie

Today's fast food, drive-thru, get-it-now culture would have you believe that success is only one purchase, one day, one something away, but success requires more than a glancing look and a passive attitude. Reading one book, attending one seminar, or joining one more sales webinar alone will not make you successful. The idea that success comes overnight is not true. Transformation takes time as new skills need to be worked into a daily routine, tested, customized, and proven. As a dedicated student in the sales profession, learn to distinguish between what is helpful and what is not. This requires commitment, dedication, and a willingness to try and to fail.

There are a lot of people in the marketplace promising overnight results. Don't you believe it! Getting lucky on a sales call, taking orders, or riding an economic wave is not the same as being a true SalesMaker. Success may not come overnight, but it does come to those who study and pursue it.

If you don't have a daily routine for studying sales and success, set aside 15 minutes to one hour at the beginning or end of each day to invest in yourself. Investing in "you" will be the greatest decision you ever make, because it will return to you dividends that pay for a lifetime. Employing and following the simple steps of C.I.A. you read at the beginning of this book is a good way to start your growth journey with *Persuade, The 7 Empowering Laws of the SalesMaker*.

Start Now, Start Today

Nike's famous brand slogan "JUST DO IT" has resonated with people ever since it was first introduced. The desire to improve and the willingness to take the steps to bring that desire into destiny is what separates the achievers from the dreamers. Starting on your journey today will ensure that you are farther along tomorrow.

If you have the same goals this year as last year, or the same struggles this year as last year, you are standing still. It's time for a SalesMaker makeover. Choose some of the strategies from these pages that you will implement starting today and get into action.

A good friend of mine, Rob Welsh, tells me that some salespeople with ten years of experience actually only have one year of experience repeated ten times. His point is that they never improve. On the other hand, there are those who have only been in the sales profession for a few years but exhibit a skill level higher than many seasoned veterans. What is the difference? That second group is learning not only from every experience they have, but from the experience of others. They have made a commitment to trying new ideas and then staying the course.

You are Only One Idea, One Person, One Decision from the Next Level in Your Life

One idea can change your life! I hope this book has provided way more than one idea for you to work with. You are capable of MORE than you can possibly imagine. Finishing this book is evidence that you want MORE, believe there is MORE, and are reaching for MORE.

- MORE (and better) relationships.

- MORE income and influence.

- MORE communication prowess.

- And MORE ability to connect with others emotionally and financially.

With MORE, you can do MORE, serve MORE, and live MORE abundantly. Life is about so much MORE than making a living and accumulating wealth, but it is hard to focus energy and time on higher purposes if we are only focused on making a living or resolving debt. The skilled SalesMaker develops the ability to create MORE results exponentially, in every area of their life. One area of personal growth will bleed into others, strengthening you in multiple ways. My hope for you is that you find financial freedom by growing your skills and earnings so that as you sell MORE, you are able to contribute MORE to the people and pursuits that drive the higher purposes in your life.

> "Practices are many, principles few. When you live the Laws of the SalesMaker, dollars will follow you."

May you grow up into the full measure of your potential as you learn, live, and level up utilizing the 7 Empowering Laws of the SalesMaker.

For more information on *Persuade, The 7 Empowering Laws of the SalesMaker*, visit www.ScottHogle.com.

BIBLIOGRAPHY

The 21 Irrefutable Laws of Leadership, John C. Maxwell, Thomas Nelson, 1998 & 2007, Nashville, TN

Everyone Communicates, Few Connect, John C. Maxwell, Thomas Nelson, 2010, Nashville, TN

How Full Is Your Bucket, Tom Rath & Donald O. Clifton, Gallup Press, 2004, New York

NOW, Discover Your Strengths, Marcus Buckingham and Donald O Clifton, 2001, The Free Press, United States

The Matrix Movie, 1999

How to Communicate with Confidence, Mike Bechtle, 2008, Revell, United States

The 15 Invaluable Laws of Growth, John C. Maxwell, Hachette Book Group, 2012, United States

Customer Love, Mac Anderson, 2008, Simple Truths

How to Master the Art of Selling Anything , Tom Hopkins, 2015, Made for Success Publishing

"Advertising in America, What works, what doesn't, and Why," Roy Williams, 2003, Wizard Academy Press

Monday Morning Memos, Roy Williams

Blink, Malcolm Gladwell, 2005, Little, Brown Company, New York

Trust Your Intuition, Sylvia Clare, 2002, How To Books

Dilbert cartoon on intuition... I applied for a license

ASPIRE Discovering Your Purpose Through the Power of Words, Kevin Hall, 2009. Bookwise Publishing

"Wizard of Ads", Roy Williams, 1998, Bard Press

The Science of Getting Rich, Acres of Diamonds, As a Man Thinketh - The most famous works of Wallace D. Wattles, Russell H. Conwell, and James Allen all in one volume! 2011, Limitless Press LLC

Lead the Field, By Earl Nightingale - Lesson 1: The Magic Word & Acres of Diamonds, BN Publishing 2006

"Strengths Based Selling," Tony Rutigliano and Brian Brim, 2010, Gallup Press, New York

Get Smart!: How to Think and Act Like the Most Successful and Highest-Paid People in Every Field, Brian Tracy, TarcherPerigee; Reprint edition (March 14, 2017)

The Purpose Driven Life, Rick Warren, 2002, 2011, 2012, Zondervan